Running Great Meetings & Workshops For Dummies

A Wiley Brand

Running Great Meetings & Workshops FOR DUMMIES®

A Wiley Brand

by Jessica Pryce-Jones
&
Julia Lindsay

Running Great Meetings & Workshops For Dummies®

Published by:
John Wiley & Sons, Ltd.,
The Atrium, Southern Gate,
Chichester,
www.wiley.com

This edition first published 2014

Registered office

John Wiley & Sons Ltd, The Atrium, Southern Gate, Chichester, West Sussex, PO19 8SQ, United Kingdom

For details of our global editorial offices, for customer services and for information about how to apply for permission to reuse the copyright material in this book please see our website at www.wiley.com.

For general information on our other products and services, please contact our Customer Care Department within the U.S. at 877-762-2974, outside the U.S. at (001) 317-572-3993, or fax 317-572-4002. For technical support, please visit www.wiley.com/techsupport.

A catalogue record for this book is available from the British Library.

ISBN 978-1-118-77046-7 (hardback/paperback) ISBN 978-1-118-77044-3 (ePDF)
ISBN 978-1-118-77043-6 (ePub)

Printed in Great Britain by TJ International, Padstow, Cornwall

10 9 8 7 6 5 4 3 2 1

Contents at a Glance

Introduction *1*

Part I:Getting Started with Meetings and Workshops *7*

Chapter 1: The Business Case for Better Meetings and Workshops 9
Chapter 2: Planning Your Meeting 21
Chapter 3: Planning Your Workshop 47
Chapter 4: Getting Ready for the Big Day 77

Part II: Running Great Group Sessions *105*

Chapter 5: Handling the Start of Your Session 107
Chapter 6: Continuing Your Meeting or Workshop 135
Chapter 7: Dealing with the Tough Stuff: Troubleshooting 161
Chapter 8: Handling What Happens Next 189

Part III: Building Your Skills *207*

Chapter 9: Building Participants' Knowledge and Practise 209
Chapter 10: Running Focus Groups 233
Chapter 11: Taking It to the Next Level 253
Chapter 12: Running Remote or Virtual Meetings and Workshops 285

Part IV: The Part of Tens *307*

Chapter 13: Ten Common Mistakes on the Day 309
Chapter 14: Ten Things You Have to Do When the Pressure Is On 317

Index *325*

Table of Contents

Introduction *1*

About This Book 1
Foolish Assumptions 2
Icons Used in This Book 3
Beyond the Book 4
Where to Go from Here 5

Part I: Getting Started with Meetings and Workshops *7*

Chapter 1: The Business Case for Better Meetings and Workshops 9

Reviewing Why People Hate Meetings 10
Being clear about what everyone dislikes 10
Recognising how many meetings are unproductive 13
Working out the incredible costs of poor meetings 14
Understanding the ripple effect 15
Knowing what everyone wants from their meetings 15
Recognising When People Get a Lot from Their Workshops 16
Developing a great design 17
Delivering brilliantly 17
Understanding Meetings and Workshops 18
Recognising the similarities 18
Understanding the differences 19
One more thing 20

Chapter 2: Planning Your Meeting 21

Deciding Whether You Really Need a Meeting 22
Reflecting on Your Objective 23
Content-free versus content rich meetings 24
Getting to a one-sentence objective 26

Understanding the Function of an Agenda 29
Writing a great agenda 29
Getting your agenda items for a meeting 30
Managing your sponsors and stakeholders 31
Planning agenda items 32
Recognising a poor agenda 37
Structuring a Great Agenda 38
Reviewing a good agenda 38
Writing really simple agendas 42
Planning For and Managing Personal Energy 43
Double-Checking Your Preparation 45

Chapter 3: Planning Your Workshop 47

Understanding What Workshops Are All About 48
Recognising when you might want to run a workshop 49
Following your decision: Making a project plan 50
Identifying Your Stakeholders 50
Finding your key players 51
Meeting your sponsor and any key players 53
Defining Your Outcomes 53
Checking your outcomes 55
Reviewing some good and some bad outcomes 55
Understanding why you spend so much time on outcomes 57
Establishing the return on investment (ROI) 57
Getting Ready to Do the Design 60
Thinking it through 61
Considering whether to stay on-site or go off-site 63
Checking out the workshop room 63
Doing Your Design 64
Getting in the right frame of mind 64
Working on and with your personal style 64
Recognising all the different activities available 68
Getting a rough design together 69
Writing up your one-page design 70
Breaking the ice 72
Writing your detailed running order 73
Getting sponsor sign-off 74
Supporting materials 75
Joining instructions 75
Building your skills and getting good at group work: Next steps 76

Chapter 4: Getting Ready for the Big Day 77

Developing Your Essential Skills 78
Asking good questions 78
Listening to others and the overall conversation in play 84
Recognising the levels of listening 86
Observing others 89
Understanding Groups 96
Understanding group norms 97
Communicating in a group 98
Decision-making 98
Surfacing issues and concerns 99
Doing real work 100
Assessing the gel factor 101
Building self-awareness 101
Practising What You'll Say 102
Rehearsing 103
Visualising your session 104

Part II: Running Great Group Sessions 105

Chapter 5: Handling the Start of Your Session 107

Managing Yourself 108
Wearing the right clothes 108
Checking your materials 110
Eating the right food and drinking the right drink 110
Getting there early 111
Imagining yourself doing well 112
Meeting and greeting everyone 112
Kicking Off the Session 113
Creating the atmosphere you want 114
Outlining the agenda 115
Housekeeping 116
Clarifying expectations 116
Allocating roles and responsibilities 118
Setting up ground rules or a code of conduct 119
Decision-Making 120
Understanding the decision-making process 121
Understanding your decision-making options 122
Working with weighted decision-making 123
Recognising Personalities in the Room 125
Working with Bolton & Bolton's Social Styles 126
Working with Honey & Mumford's Learning Styles 130

Chapter 6: Continuing Your Meeting or Workshop . . . 135

Managing Process 136
Checking in 136
Signposting 138
Summarising 139
Linking 139
Stating what's been said: Paraphrasing 141
Writing up key information on a flip chart 142
Giving clear instructions 143
Facilitating Group Discussions 145
Introducing a discussion topic 146
Getting input to a topic 146
Allowing a conversation to move sideways 147
Shutting up 148
Dealing with an elephant in the room 148
Dealing with comments skillfully 149
Managing Process Problems 151
Managing time 151
Dealing with rabbit holes 152
Using parking lots 153
Opening old issues up, closing current ones down 154
Managing energy 155
Managing guests 155
Dealing with unexpected situations 157
Revisiting and reviewing expectations 158
Reviewing Your Meetings and Workshops 158
Reviewing a meeting 159
Using online tools 159
Reviewing a workshop 160

Chapter 7: Dealing with the Tough Stuff: Troubleshooting . . . 161

Managing Typical Barriers to Success 161
Knowing What to Do When It's Not Working 162
At the start of your session – when the group helps you 163
At the start of your session – the group doesn't help you 164
During your session 166
Dealing with Run-of-the-Mill Difficulties 167
Handling Interruptions 169
Phones 169
Laptops and tablets 169
To-ings and fro-ings 170

Dealing with Difficult Behaviour 170
Managing distorted thinking 170
Dealing with difficult individuals 171
Tactical seating 177
Recognising Personal and Hidden Agendas 178
Tuning in to personal agendas 178
Tuning in to hidden agendas 179
Dealing with personal and hidden agendas 179
Dealing with recommendations 180
Managing Conflict 180
Recognising unhealthy and healthy conflict 181
Getting the group to understand what's happening 182
Dealing with conflict: A process for a group 183
Dealing with conflict: A process for individuals or factions 184
The main take-away 187

Chapter 8: Handling What Happens Next 189

Reflecting On Your Meeting or Workshop 190
How did it go at a big-picture level? 190
What specifically should I keep doing? 190
What specifically should I start doing? 191
Writing Up Meeting Minutes 191
Writing up simple minutes 192
Writing up more formal minutes 193
Using meeting software 195
Calculating Your Return on Investment 196
Evaluating your work 197
Expressing ROI 198
Reporting On and Closing Your Project 199
Reports 200
Review meetings 200
Understanding project closure 201
Reviewing your entire project 201
Writing up your report 205

Part III: Building Your Skills 207

Chapter 9: Building Participants' Knowledge and Practise 209

Working with Case Studies 210
Understanding what they are all about 210
Knowing when to use the case study method 211

Thinking through your purpose ... 212
Using great cases ... 212
Managing everyone's preparation ... 214
Working with the group ... 215
Working with Role Play ... 217
Believing that it's the right thing to do ... 218
Calling it what you will ... 219
Developing realistic and appropriate role plays ... 219
Setting the role play up for success ... 221
Managing and explaining the process ... 221
Understanding your role play options ... 227
Reinforcing the standard ... 228
Using Video ... 229
Reflecting on personal performance ... 229
Observing personal performance ... 230
Reviewing footage ... 230
Getting the right technology ... 231
Having the right software ... 232

Chapter 10: Running Focus Groups ... 233

Knowing When to Use a Focus Group ... 233
Thinking About What You Want to Achieve ... 234
Side effects of a focus group ... 235
Characteristics of a focus group ... 235
Preparing for Your Focus Groups ... 236
Defining a clear purpose statement ... 236
Building your timeline ... 237
Getting the right people in the room ... 238
Generating the right questions ... 239
Developing a script ... 241
Recording information ... 244
Preparing your kit ... 244
Running a Focus Group ... 245
Working with observers ... 245
Pausing ... 246
Checking your technology ... 246
Writing It All Up ... 247
Transcribing your material or writing up your notes ... 247
Sorting and then analysing your data ... 248
Interpreting your data ... 249
Writing up your report ... 250
Putting it all into action ... 251
Recognising the disadvantages of focus groups ... 252

Chapter 11: Taking It to the Next Level 253

Brainstorming: Best Practise 253
Recognising problems with brainstorming 254
Brainstorming effectively 255
Managing large group brainstorming 264
Managing small group brainstorming 265
Brainstorming alone 266
Working with Some Common Group Tools 267
3Ws 267
SWOT Analysis 269
RACI analysis 272
Force field analysis 273
Ishikawa or fishbone diagram 275
Decision trees 278
Using Appreciative Inquiry 280
Understanding Parallel Process 283

Chapter 12: Running Remote or Virtual Meetings and Workshops 285

Managing Remote Meetings 286
Recognising when to have a remote meeting 286
Inviting the right people 287
Limiting the agenda 287
Finding a good time 287
Sending invitations and call details 288
Sharing materials 288
Managing your kit 289
Getting going on time 289
Reaffirming the ground rules 289
Stating your goal 290
Using a wingman when working remotely 290
Keeping it relevant 291
Handling PowerPoint 291
Taking control when you can 291
Being respectful of time 292
Signposting 292
Using 'let's' to drive direction 292
Thinking about your voice 293
Asking questions for active participation 294
Recording your meeting 295
Saving all the information 295
Reviewing your meetings 295

Managing Hybrid Meetings 296
Working with ten top best practises 296
Reviewing Available Technology 298
Understanding Remote and Virtual Workshops 301
Embracing yet more technology 302
Recognising the challenges 303
Thinking about virtual learning 303
Building your next steps 306

Part IV: The Part of Tens 307

Chapter 13: Ten Common Mistakes on the Day 309

Failing to Set Up Group Work Properly 309
Talking Too Much 310
Ignoring Emotion 311
Failing to Join the Dots 311
Failing to Deal with a Difficult Person 312
Failing to Recognise an Expert in the Room 312
Failing to Change What You're Doing 313
Thinking about the Detail Rather Than the Big Picture 313
Failing to Push a Group 314
Being Too Dogmatic 314

Chapter 14: Ten Things You Have to Do When the Pressure Is On 317

Preparing Brilliantly 317
Having a Plan to Move Away from It 318
Creating Rapport 318
Building Trust with the Group 319
Taking Breaks 320
Being Fair to Everyone 320
Dealing with the Unacceptable 321
Using Humour 321
Noticing When the Group Is Going Off Track 322
Holding It Together 322

Index 325

Introduction

Welcome to *Running Great Meetings & Workshops For Dummies,* a book that will help you get the most out of the time you invest with your colleagues, coworkers, clients or customers.

If you're reading this book, it's probably not because you regularly attend lots of fantastically efficient, effective and energising meetings or workshops. But this book is for you if you are keen to make running brilliant meetings and workshops a core skill, and you want people to walk away from events you lead saying, 'That was fantastic. I can't believe the time passed so quickly. When are we next getting together?'

Every chapter is designed to help you understand a different aspect of workshops or meetings, from the planning and preparation through to the delivery and follow-up.

The information we present has been honed by years of leading successful meetings and workshops and by making many mistakes along the way. We've written about all of it, so you can fast-track your journey to excellence.

About This Book

Reading this book will give you a really solid blueprint for running great meetings and workshops. But reading is a tiny part of the process. Your challenge will be to go away and do some hard work to put it all into practise. That way, you'll make the fastest progress and get the quickest results while building community, commitment and contribution – for everyone you work with.

This book is written from the point of view of a practitioner – which means it's professional and practical.

We've written this book in a rough order to help you plan, prepare and deliver a session; then we've added on information about how you can develop your practise. That means more complex ideas and techniques come later in the book. But you can read the chapters in any order you like or just turn to what happens to matter to you.

To make it even easier, there is some material you don't need to read at all:

- **Sidebars:** In most chapters, there are sidebars of grey shaded text. They contain case studies that illustrate points we make or additional information. Read them if you like; skip them if you prefer.
- **Thanks:** This is interesting to friends, colleagues and family, but maybe not to you.

To help you navigate this book, we used a few conventions:

- *Italics* are used to introduce new terms.
- **Bold text** highlights important actions or insights.
- Case studies in grey boxes (the sidebars) are real situations we have experienced.
- *Session* is the word that we use to cover both meetings and workshops.
- *Participants* is the word we use to cover anyone who attends either meetings or workshops.

Foolish Assumptions

In writing this book, we assumed some things about you. These are that you

- Are up for learning and would love to lead great meetings or workshops
- Are not a total novice so you know something of the world of work, meetings and workshops

You might be reading this because you

- Got a promotion or a new job and want to make a great first impression with your team.
- Have been asked to run your first workshop and want to feel really confident in what you are doing.
- Have heard negative comments about the group sessions you run.
- Find that you are bored with what you do and want some new ideas to make your sessions positively different.
- Like practical information without too much theory attached.
- Want to know what works in a pragmatic and easy-to-read style.
- Don't have a whole lot of time.
- Are really focused on what to do and how to do it.

Icons Used in This Book

Throughout the margin of this book are small pictures, or *icons.* Here's what each one means:

This icon highlights shortcuts or information that will make easy work of running great meetings and workshops. You won't want to miss any of these fabulous tips.

Remember this information, and your meeting or workshop will be a success.

Heed our warnings, and you'll save yourself time and trouble in the long run.

Beyond the Book

To help you, we also provide some downloadable tools and bonus articles. Here's what you can find at www.dummies.com:

- **Cheat Sheets:** You'll find help with remembering what you need to do to prepare for any workshop as well as a reminder of the key skills you need to put into practise as you lead any meeting or workshop. You'll find them at www.dummies.com/cheatsheet/rungreatmeetingsworkshops.
- **Dummies.com online articles:** You also have access to three online articles. One article explains the pros and cons of different room setups. Another article helps you understand the basics of learning by doing and getting direct experience. The final article gives you ten practises that can help you lead excellent meetings and workshops. You can find these articles at www.dummies.com/extras/rungreatmeetingsworkshops.
- **Companion files:** In addition to the material in the print or e-book you're reading right now, this product also comes with some access-anywhere goodies on the web (www.dummies.com/go/rungreatmeetingsworkshops). These include
  - A worksheet with questions to help you build a great project plan
  - A worksheet to help you articulate your workshop outcomes
  - A sample running order
  - Sample joining instructions
  - Answers to the closed-open question exercise
  - Two breathing exercises
  - Tips for working well with different behavioural styles in meetings or workshops
  - Self-reflection documents for after your workshop
  - Sample worksheet for observers watching a role play

Where to Go from Here

Of course, we'd like you to give this book to anyone who has to run a meeting or at least recommend it so that meetings everywhere get better. And workshops achieve a real return on investment.

Failing that, we recommend that you just turn to whatever chapter piques your interest or helps you with an upcoming need and go from there. Alternatively, when you are in full crisis and it's the night before a big day, just open up the section you need. That's what the book is for – to be used in any way that works for you.

If you want to get really good, there's another option: Come and learn from us. We teach people the craft of leading meetings, leading workshops and facilitating groups with an emphasis on 'learning by doing.'

Finally, we'd love to meet you, just to say 'hi' and to thank you for buying this book. Please do connect on LinkedIn if you want to get in touch.

Part I

Getting Started with Meetings and Workshops

getting started with

meetings and workshops

For Dummies can help you get started with lots of subjects. Visit `www.dummies.com` to learn more and do more with *For Dummies*.

In this part . . .

- Understand why it's critical that you run great workshops and meetings.
- Plan a meeting that maximises your time.
- Run a workshop that keeps people coming back for more.
- Mind all the details, from guest list to room setup, to prepare for your workshop or meeting.

Chapter 1

The Business Case for Better Meetings and Workshops

In This Chapter

- Reviewing why people hate meetings
- Recognising when people get a lot from their workshops
- Understanding meetings and workshops: similarities and differences

Everything important that you'll ever do at work involves other people. Even if a large chunk of your working day is solitary, at some point, colleagues, contacts, critics or clients come into the equation. They check in with you or you with them because everyone wants to be clear about who's on track, who needs help, or who's made fantastic progress. But doing this one person at a time is inefficient.

So you have a meeting.

In most of our organisations and certainly those where interesting knowledge-work is being done, complexity is the order of the day. What we all do has become more specialised, more process-oriented and more project-driven. This means lots of complex problem-solving and continuous learning as everyone pulls together to meet deadlines, respond to changing environments and maximise both performance and productivity. You simply cannot do this one person at a time.

So you get together for a workshop.

When you leave a meeting or a workshop having done really great work in a group, you'll feel buzzed and motivated. But the problem is that many meetings achieve just the opposite: Participants walk out deflated, de-energised and sometimes desperate. This chapter outlines the reasons for those negative feelings and then points you in the right direction for fixing them.

Reviewing Why People Hate Meetings

If you don't enjoy your meetings, you're part of a very large worldwide club. Many people feel the same as you. But here's the strange thing: Even when you hate your meetings, when you emerge feeling frustrated and furious, you still brace yourself and trudge off to attend the next one. Then you schedule yet more.

Too many of us are on meeting treadmills believing that poor meetings are a necessary evil of business life. We go to them because we feel we have to; we go to them to be seen. But we don't enjoy them because they suck. They're poorly planned, badly run and add zero value.

And we all sit quietly back colluding while colleagues make it much worse when they fail on the preparation front. The result is that because nothing much gets done, more and more participants behave badly, but no one ever puts it right.

So what needs changing?

Being clear about what everyone dislikes

To clarify what people dislike most about their meetings, we decided to run a small research project. We asked a class of 80 executive MBA students doing a part-time degree what their top reasons for disliking meetings were. Then we collated the most repeated themes and put them into a questionnaire.

We ran that questionnaire online and face-to-face in Kenya, Singapore, South Africa, The Netherlands and the UK. In the end, we had 675 answers from 28 different nationalities, all of whom were running teams. Some were supervisors, and others were senior managers. Table 1-1 lists the top seven reasons they gave for disliking their meetings.

Table 1-1 Top Seven Reasons People Hate Their Meetings

I Dislike Meetings Because . . .	*Percentage of Answers*
They are poorly structured	21
They go off-topic	18
They are too long	17
There isn't an agenda	16
Others don't prepare	16
The presentations are boring	6
We don't do feedback	6

Poorly structured

This item is a travesty. It takes about five to ten minutes tops to create a decent structure to a meeting; it's not a lot of hard work. All it involves is knowing the items you want to deal with and putting them into some kind of sensible order without leaving the toughest subject to last.

That this appears at the top of the list shows you that meeting leaders aren't bothering to do even a tiny amount of thinking before getting into a room. If they don't, why should anyone else? (See Chapter 2 for how to design a great agenda.)

Go off-topic

What this implies is that meeting management skills are poor and that people running meetings can't steer productive participation. What we see in practice is that the chair or manager of a meeting often gets caught up in the conversation. So they are talking rather than thinking about what's happening and how to keep it all on track. (Read Chapter 4 for the skills it takes to keep a meeting on track.)

Too long

We all work with people we love and sometimes with those we love to hate because my, how they talk. Many meeting leaders and participants don't bother to think before they speak and develop their thoughts out loud. Listening to a windbag isn't fun, and Occam's razor needs to shave everything every time. (Occam was a 14-century monk who said, 'Entities should not be unnecessarily multiplied,' meaning 'keep it short and simple'.)

In other words, running last week's meeting and dragging in any new subject isn't helpful. And if you fail to close down irrelevant conversations, you simply prolong the agony. (Chapters 5 and 6 help you get this right.)

No agenda

Every meeting you walk into should have an agenda that considers the best use of time, energy and attention. If you don't have an agenda, any subject's on the table and that approach is absolutely off the menu.

Of course, sometimes it's hard to be that planned, but you can still take the first five minutes of a meeting to make and agree on an agenda and good outcomes. (Chapter 7 helps you manage a lot of the things that can derail a meeting, so you can stick to your agenda.)

Others don't prepare

We're sure that you spend a lot of time getting ready (we're optimistic here) while others don't. They haven't read their documents, have failed to investigate the information they said they would and have not completed their part of the bargain.

If that's a regular occurrence, what norms have been set up? What have you all agreed to? This suggests that there's some meeting governance that needs readjusting and the simplest way to tackle this is with ground rules. Chapter 7 deals with troubleshooting, while Chapter 8 helps you reflect on the meetings you run, what works and what could be better.

Presentations are boring

Yup, we're with you there. Participants who prepare slide-decks in font size 10 and then read every single thing to you in a monotone are the end. At best, you check email or drift off; at worst, you plan idle revenge. Any way you look at it, you're not participating.

The solution? Video them and make them watch it and working through. (Chapter 9 helps you manage that.)

No feedback

Once you've sat through a dull and dreary meeting, lots of you gather up your belongings and leave without addressing the elephant in the room. But without feedback, you are condemned to repeating the cycle over and over. Just knowing that you're doing nothing to tackle the situation is morale-crushing and doesn't make you feel good about returning to the next meeting with the same participants. (You can get insights about reviewing face-to-face and remote meetings in Chapters 6 and 12 respectively.)

Recognising how many meetings are unproductive

It's clear that meetings the world over waste time and reduce productivity. Because we strongly suspected that, when we designed our survey we asked people what percentage of their meetings were productive, neither productive nor unproductive or just unproductive.

Table 1-2 shows you what we found.

Table 1-2 Percentage of Time in Productive and Unproductive Meetings

Perception	*Percentage of Time*
Productive meetings	39
Neither productive nor unproductive	31
Unproductive meetings	30

At least most people are going to meetings that are more productive than unproductive, which is good news.

But these numbers get more interesting when you start asking everyone what percentage of their week everyone spends in meetings.

When we averaged out the amount of time these 675 respondents spent in meetings, it came to 34 per cent of their working weeks. By the way, that ranged from a tiny 10 per cent up to a stonking 90 per cent.

Let's make an assumption about the data. Assume that most people average a 40-hour working week (and there's bags of evidence including lots we've got that this is the case). That means your average professional is spending about 13.5 hours in meetings every week. Of those meetings, 30 per cent of them are unproductive. That means four hours a week, or 10 per cent of their regular working life, is wasted. Over a year, that adds up to a horrendous five weeks, if you assume a 48-week working year.

Now factor in meetings, which are a bit 'meh' because they are neither productive nor unproductive. They give you *another* five weeks: so all in all, we've got ten weeks a year, or 2.5 months of work. Per professional.

Think what an incredible difference that would make in your organisation if you could just make the majority of your meetings efficient and effective. The cost of all this lost productivity is ferocious.

Working out the incredible costs of poor meetings

The cost obviously varies depending on what you earn and where you're based. But Table 1-3 lists the cost of wasted time based on a national average salary in the UK and United States.

Table 1-3 Cost of Wasted Time

Country	*Salary**	*5 weeks*	*10 weeks*
UK average employee	£26,500	£2,548	£5,096
UK frontline manager	£35,300	£3,394	£6,788
USA average employee	$40,500	$3,894	$7,788
USA frontline manager	$49,300	$4,740	$9,480

** Based on data from the ONS, National Management Survey, Chartered Management Institute, US Census Bureau and Bureau of Labor Statistics 2013*

If this is the cost for one person, imagine what the totals are for a group of six senior people sitting together, even if they only waste ten minutes.

If you want to start tracking your meetings precisely – and we recommend you do that – there are plenty of meeting apps to help you. All you need to do is enter your salary and start your meeting.

But it's not just the cash that matters. There are consequences in plenty of other areas, too.

Understanding the ripple effect

When meetings are suboptimal, then it's not just the financial cost of time lost in that meeting. There are other effects that ripple out from there, causing yet more damage:

- **Relationship costs:** When people get together in a room and their expectations aren't met, they feel incredulous, cheated, frustrated, angry or lethargic – in any combination. And when someone experiences these negative emotions about someone else, trust decreases. In a working relationship that suffers from low trust, there's less effort and input. After all, if I can't make something happen for you, why should you go over and beyond for me?
- **Reputational costs:** You know what it's like. You come out of a poor meeting, and someone who knows the meeting leader asks you how it was, and you roll your eyes or sigh. That person then commiserates with you before finding the next person to gossip with. Bad meetings with ineffectual leaders are the grist of others' gossip mills. After all, you own my reputation, even if I manufactured it.

Knowing what everyone wants from their meetings

We asked everyone who completed the questionnaire what they wanted from their meetings. Figure 1-1 shows a word cloud of what they said. The larger the word, the more people said it.

Figure 1-1: What people want from their meetings.

Pretty obvious, isn't it? But the great news is that all of this isn't rocket science. You're not born good or bad at running meetings; it's something you learn by recognising what works, testing what you like, tweaking what you do and trying again. Everything you need to succeed is outlined in this book.

But what about workshops?

Recognising When People Get a Lot from Their Workshops

Workshops are less problematic than meetings because most people recognise the investment they involve and therefore work harder to get them right. Plus, an executive sponsor means scrutiny, and no one wants to explain to someone senior how they just wasted $50,000. It's not a comfortable conversation to have.

Having mined our in-house data from the 1,300 workshops that we ran in 2013, it's clear that they involve two fundamental dimensions:

- Doing a great design
- Delivering brilliantly

Developing a great design

Getting the development right includes four massive must-haves:

- **Building appropriate content:** Participants want to know that what they are doing is relevant and will help them achieve the outcomes that meet their individual and group expectations. They want to get results.
- **Creating a tightly structured, logical process:** Items need to make sense to everyone, and they need to flow from and build on each other.
- **Planning realistic timings:** No one likes feeling rushed in what they do or that they haven't had long enough to do something properly. Nor do they like it when the pace feels slow.
- **Ensuring active participation:** You want two- or three-way conversation between the workshop leader, group and group members.

You can get all of this and more in Chapters 3, 4 and 5.

Delivering brilliantly

Participants want a workshop that's led by someone who

- **Is an expert in the process or content:** That way, participants feel they are in good hands and secure in what they are doing.
- **Stays calm under pressure:** This workshop leader can deal with any hiccups and can adapt when necessary.
- **Recognises what's happening in the room:** This workshop leader is attuned to energy and engagement.
- **Enjoys the process:** If the workshop leader enjoys it, so will everyone else.

Chapters 6, 7, 9 and 11 can help you with these, while Chapter 12 gives you great hints and tips for working with remote groups.

Understanding Meetings and Workshops

On face value, who cares whether you're having a meeting or attending a workshop? It's just a group of people talking in a room. But actually it does matter.

If you should have had a meeting but you planned for a workshop, you'll have done a lot of redundant work. And if you are having a meeting that should have been a workshop, you'll get a lot of complaints from participants because you won't use their time well. So it's worth looking at the similarities and differences between them both.

Recognising the similarities

Workshops and meetings have these attributes in common:

- **An agreed purpose,** so you all know why you are there.
- **Outcomes,** so you know what you want to achieve.
- **Input,** so you have shared information that builds alignment and understanding.
- **A process,** so you know how you are getting from A to B.
- **A leader** who is there to help make all of these things happen.
- **Enough preparation,** so everyone can make a valid contribution.
- **Ground rules,** so everyone knows the rules of engagement.
- **Interactive activities** that take advantage of everyone's skills, knowledge and expertise.

But meetings and workshops have some differences, too.

Checklist questions for running a workshop

You should run a workshop if you can answer yes to three or more questions from this list:

- Do we have sponsors or stakeholders with an interest in the problem we are trying to solve or issue we want to fix?
- Is this the kick-off of an important strategic initiative?
- Do we need budget sign-off to get together?
- Would this be best run by an expert?
- Will our session last more than half a day?
- Will the discussions get heated or result in conflict?
- Will the cost of doing nothing be worse and more expensive pain in the future?

Understanding the differences

There are important differences between meetings and workshops, and you need to recognise them so you plan and prepare the right event.

You have a meeting when you

- Want to do business as usual
- Need to get everyone around a table to solve a one-off situation
- Ensure that glitches are solved by everyone involved
- Need to discuss and decide things as a group
- Want to re-clarify or ensure agreement and alignment around existing issues or ongoing projects

You have a workshop when you

- Have a sponsor with a vested interest in the outcome of this particular session
- Have to initiate a new project or process

- Have complex problems or issues to solve that you want everyone to buy-into and work on in some detail
- Want to learn something new or update your skills
- Recognise that you need an expert in process or content to lead the session

In short, meetings involve the daily doo-doo; workshops don't.

Meetings are more run-of-the-mill, and workshops require much more effort. It's impossible to wing a workshop without courting absolute catastrophe; it's entirely possible to breeze unprepared into a meeting – which is a huge part of the problem.

One more thing

There's one special get-together we haven't yet mentioned – we're referring to focus groups. We've added a special chapter for you on focus groups because they are becoming more and more common and require some special attention.

You run a focus group when you want to

- Find out what certain groups of people think
- Get feedback on new ideas or products
- Gather in-depth qualitative information quickly
- Benefit repeatedly from group-work

Well-structured and well-run focus groups are always more than the sum of their parts, and Chapter 10 helps you achieve that from the get-go.

Chapter 2

Planning Your Meeting

In This Chapter

- Reflecting on your meeting objective
- Writing agendas
- Planning for and managing personal energy

If you're going to hold a meeting, you have to have a plan. It's as simple as that. And the more complicated your meeting or workshop, the more complicated your plan will necessarily be. Sounds like common sense, but common sense is pretty uncommon when it comes to meetings and organisations! So this chapter helps you think through all the things you need to plan to make sure everything runs as smoothly as possible on the day. Your approach has to be that you have a plan in order to deviate from it at best or abandon it at worst. But you never ever make anything up as you go.

That means you have to think through everything you need to do, create a robust agenda and worry about all the possible contingencies. Because meetings are the living proof of the old 80:20 rule working at its best. Eighty per cent of your meeting and workshop success lies in the preparation. Only 20 per cent rests with what actually happens on the day.

So the old Boy Scouts adage, 'Fail to prepare, prepare to fail' couldn't be more true for when it comes to getting people to work together in a room. In fact, if everything looks really easy to a participant's eyes, you've planned and managed your process really well.

This chapter guides you through what you need to bear in mind at your planning stage once you've decided that yes, you really do need to get everyone together to have that meeting.

Deciding Whether You Really Need a Meeting

So you're wondering if you need to organise a meeting and wavering about whether or not you should. And you're right. The last thing you should do is get people together unless they are going to get a lot out of it. And by a lot, we don't mean a lot of information. The last thing that any meeting should do is tell participants what they could better and faster absorb if they read it. But that's what many meetings do: Tell everyone what they already know in a 'death-by-PowerPoint' process.

In fact, you can always tell if meeting participants are getting value from a meeting or workshop. If they lean forward looking at the speaker, then they are likely to be engaged in the process. When they are engaged, they write things down. If they're disengaged, they don't write but they do surreptitiously sneak a peek at their iPads or smart phones and then as noiselessly as possible answer the most important mails.

So when don't you need a meeting?

If all you want to do is tell people that everything is running tickety-boo, you can stop reading this book right now. Try an email, a quick conference call, a blog, vlog or, best of all, use social media: They are much better platforms for spreading those messages and cost much less than a meeting.

If, on the other hand, you have important news or key information to share with a business critical group, then perhaps you need a meeting – especially if the content is likely to be emotional or complex, and you need everyone to be there to ensure that they have all understood the same thing. If those key people are going to take responsibility for what you're telling them and be accountable for making it happen and deal with issues along the way, well, you've got no choice. You have to have a meeting.

And just so you're sure, you can use Table 2-1 as a checklist for when to have a meeting.

Table 2-1 Shall We Meet?

Do Hold a Meeting to . .	*Don't Hold a Meeting If . .*
Reach a group decision.	There's a better alternative.
Identify an issue.	It's always in your diary.
Solve a problem.	It makes no difference to processes or people.
Brainstorm new ideas.	The costs outweigh the benefits.
Demo a product or system.	Key people can't be there.
Manage conflict.	No group discussion or decision is needed.
Sort out misunderstandings.	You could send an email.
Communicate complex or sensitive issues.	You haven't got a clear objective.

But most importantly, if you are going to have a meeting, you need a clear objective.

Reflecting on Your Objective

To get a clear objective, simply ask yourself 'Why are we all getting together to have this particular meeting?' This question helps you re-evaluate what you want to achieve from bringing everyone into the same room. And lots of people in a room cost time and money. So this simple question helps you stop getting together just because that's what you've always done.

When you analyse meetings, it's clear we meet regularly for three main reasons:

- To keep each other mutually informed about what's happening.
- To discuss options about what we should do.
- To decide on a way forward.

We also get together more irregularly to

- Take a deep dive into a problem, its causes and solutions.
- Learn something that improves our performance so that we can serve stakeholders better.

Each of these reasons requires planning in greater or lesser amounts. But the further down the list you go, the more you'll need to plan. That's because the first three kinds of gatherings are meetings that are generally best supported by a content-free approach, which takes less time, while the fourth and fifth are best supported by a content-rich facilitation that needs intensive planning. That's why we've put workshop planning into Chapter 3.

Content-free versus content rich meetings

Content-free meetings are all about having a clear framework for a meeting process. Everyone is aware of what that framework is, and the job of the person leading or chairing the meeting is just to guide all the participants through it. So it's suited to your every-day run-of-the-mill kind of meetings – for example, the Monday morning meeting when everyone updates everyone else about their week's priorities or any potential hitches and glitches. That's a content-free meeting in its simplest form.

A more complicated content-free approach explores what a problem is, why it takes places and how to address it. This is, of course, a more difficult type of meeting to design, but it's essentially knowledge sharing to get to a decision. When you're designing or delivering this kind of session, you don't need to be a subject matter expert if your process is really robust.

The aim of a content-free meeting is that participants get information that helps everyone collectively do things differently.

Content-rich meetings and facilitated sessions are harder to implement, and they are frequently what trainings, seminars, leadership and team development sessions aim to do. When you design or attend one, the purpose is to give you some insights or information that you then explore or possibly practice. The overall aim is to arrive at a change for the better in your approach, attitude, skills or behaviour.

As a result, this kind of meeting needs a lot more information and preparation by the person who is running it. That's because you either need to be a workshop process expert or content expert to lead or manage the event. In other words, you need to be credible if you're going to stand at the front of the room, and you need to be able to model what you are proposing or teaching yourself.

The aim of a content-rich meeting is that participants leave with personal insights prepared individually to do something differently or contribute something extra.

Understanding the similarities

Ideally, both content-free and content-rich meetings are

- Designed in consultation with the participants and other stakeholders
- Have clear inputs from the meeting leader and participants
- Are designed around a logical process and output
- Lead to clearly defined follow-up actions

Understanding the differences

Table 2-2 describes some differences between content-free and content-rich meetings.

Table 2-2 Differences Between Meeting Types

Content-Free	*Content-Rich*
Can be led by anyone comfortable with the process	Must be led by an expert
Less preparation involved in the design	More preparation involved in the design
Interest mainly comes from participants	Interest tends to come from a wider group of stakeholders
Fewer stakeholders to manage and consult with	Greater number of stakeholders to manage and consult with
Less cost	More cost
Easy to scale and repeat	Less scalable as more specialised
Conclusions and actions agreed on by the group	Conclusions and actions owned by individuals
Follow-up done at group and individual level	Follow-up done at individual level

For the rest of this chapter, we assume you're interested in a content-free meeting process and that you aren't planning a workshop. But if you are, simply turn to Chapter 3.

Getting to a one-sentence objective

Once you've decided whether you're having a meeting to inform, discuss or decide, you can then start to think about what your one-sentence objective is for this particular meeting. Getting to a one-sentence objective means that you have an anchor for everything you do in your meeting. That means you'll get more work done and waste less time. And the result of that will be that participants will feel a sense of action and direction, and they'll love your meetings.

So, as Stephen Covey said, 'Start with the end in mind' and develop a great meeting objective. The immediate benefit is that it makes agenda writing so much easier because everything on your agenda should relate to and support your one-sentence objective.

The attributes of a one-sentence objective

A good one-sentence objective is

- **Clear.** Anyone attending will know what your meeting is going to do as you have squeezed out any ambiguity. To do this, try to use verbs like discuss, review, evaluate, agree on, contract, develop, determine, generate, identify, prioritise, solve, focus, explore, learn, understand, investigate or review. Of course, this list isn't exhaustive; it's just to give you some ideas for getting clarity.
- **Contextualised.** All meetings and workshops happen within a context, and you need to articulate what that context is. Otherwise, you have an open invitation to go off-track. If people can misinterpret you, they will – not because they are malicious, but simply because they want to explore and test boundaries.

- **Specific.** That means your meeting simply can't be hijacked by a participant who wants to hold a different but related meeting on the same topic. You have ensured that you frame your objective in a way that not only suits your context but also narrows the focus so you get done what you need to do without over-running.
- **Actionable by the people in the room.** That means the people who attend are accountable and responsible for further actions outside the meeting. They therefore have a vested interest in attending the meeting and contributing to it. There is simply no point having a meeting full of people who are neither accountable nor responsible; they've got better things to do.

The really disappointing meeting

We recently decided we wanted a new PR company to work with us. So we wrote a tender specification and a document about who we were and what we wanted from working with a PR agency. Having done some research, we developed a short-list of five organisations and invited three to pitch to us.

To get it right, we told them all they could have any access they liked to anything they wanted: accounts, clients, materials and employees. And there was a clear front-runner. This company asked all the right questions, talked to all the right people and came back to us on a couple of occasions to check they were on the right lines. So we were really excited about meeting them and hearing their pitch.

When we got there, we were kept waiting, which is always a bad sign when you're the client. Then we walked into one of the most disappointing meetings we have ever attended. There was no agenda, we weren't asked what our expectations were and we were presented with 30 minutes of monologue about who we were.

We left after 40 minutes feeling really unsatisfied; what had started so well ended so badly. The problem was that the agency simply hadn't thought through what we wanted to get out of the meeting. If they'd stuck to the objective that we had defined and then tied it to an agenda, the agency might have won the business. They would have been forced to think through what they were doing and why. But they didn't – on either front.

Great questions for a great one-sentence objective

Here are four really useful questions that will help you get to a great one-sentence meeting objective:

- **What do we want to get done in this particular meeting?** This helps you generate clarity.
- **Why is it important to get that done right now by this group?** This helps you tie what you're doing to the context.
- **What specific outcomes must we have arrived at by the end?** This helps you narrow your focus.
- **Who in the room will be accountable and responsible for implementation afterwards?** This helps you get the right bums on the right seats because everyone cares about the topic.

Reviewing some good and some bad one-sentence objectives

Just so you're really clear, Table 2-3 shows three good and bad one-sentence meeting objectives. What do you notice about the good ones?

Table 2-3 Good and Bad Meeting Objectives

Bad Meeting Objectives	*Good Meeting Objectives*
Review the Simpson project prior to quote.	To review the Simpson project, plan timings, reality-check those timings in light of the updated risk analysis, discuss options and decide next steps before submitting our quote on Tuesday.
Management update.	To review last week's scorecard priorities and to plan this week's; discuss and decide next steps for three on-going concerns: staffing (lab capacity); sales pipeline (previous two weeks); and quality assurance supplier issues (insights and actions).

Bad Meeting Objectives	Good Meeting Objectives
New proposition development.	To brainstorm key ideas and phrases, draft our new proposition and plan its roll-out.

Understanding the Function of an Agenda

An *agenda* is a plan of what is going to happen at your meeting, and it sets out the order in which you'll discuss or deal with different topics. A good quality agenda makes all the difference between an efficient and productive meeting and a shambolic disorganised one. Writing a good agenda looks easy, but like all well-written documents, this can be tough to do. In essence, a good agenda is the backbone of your meeting, and so unless you spend time thinking about it, your meeting is much more likely to feel spineless and flabby.

Writing a great agenda

Writing a well-crafted agenda is a must if you're going to have a well-structured meeting. It doesn't need to be complicated, but it does need to reflect your one-sentence outcome. As you write it, you need to take into account potential late comers and early leavers. That means not tackling issues that are critical just when people are coming or going or when you're getting close to a break.

Here are some other things you need to think about as you plan your agenda:

- How you get agenda ideas
- How you manage sponsors or stakeholders
- How you structure an agenda
- How you manage timings

- How you plan so that different people lead on different subjects
- Who takes what role in your meeting

Getting your agenda items for a meeting

In order to structure an agenda, you need topics or items. If you're convening a meeting for the first time, you'll need to consult with participants and ask them to submit the items they think most relevant. Remember that the responsibility for the agenda isn't just yours! It belongs to everyone who's attending your meeting. So if they want it to be successful, they need to participate from the outset.

Don't be surprised if people don't reply when you first contact them to get agenda items; they are busy, too. Just send another email to remind them, making sure you sound excited and upbeat, and then call them all up if you're still drawing a blank. That way, they know you mean business now and in the future. And if they are invested enough to want to attend your meeting, then they should contribute ideas.

The easiest and most collaborative way of getting agenda items isn't necessarily by email: Using email can simply spawn tons of extra traffic when everyone copies everyone else. Using a Google document or SharePoint instead will minimise traffic. And by setting a clear deadline, people can submit on time and in one place, meaning that all you have to do is shape rather than collate the content.

Once you've got ideas, then you need to thank everyone who's submitted something or made a suggestion and start work on the agenda itself. You may also need to whittle topics down to make them relevant and manageable. If you're doing this to an idea that originated from someone with a tender ego, then you'd be well advised to pick up the phone and call them. They won't appreciate an email telling them you don't like what they submitted or want to alter their timings, however nicely you phrase it. This takes us into thinking more about your sponsors and stakeholders.

Managing your sponsors and stakeholders

If you're kicking off an important initiative, you're bound to have a sponsor or two and stakeholders whose needs you'll need to take into account and whose backing could make or break what you do. So here are all the actions you'll need to plan to ensure your success:

1. **Meet them early to find out**
   - What their one-sentence objective is
   - What outcomes they want or expectations they have
   - What agenda items they feel strongly about
   - What success looks like
   - What they want from you before, during or after your meeting
2. **Confirm all of these items in an email back to them.**
3. **Work out who or what could support or derail the process.**
4. **Get any other key influencers on-side.**
5. **Confirm what level of input and communication everyone needs.**
6. **Contract clearly about who needs to know what by when.**
7. **Make a clear project plan if it's complex so you know what to do and when.**
8. **Stick to what you've said you'll do and do it.**
9. **Debrief at the end and report back on this.**
10. **Get feedback from sponsors and stakeholders on how to improve.**

The golden rule for sponsors and stakeholders is 'no surprises'. So if you hit a time, cost or quality issue, or you can't meet a key deliverable for any reason, for goodness sake, don't bury your head in the sand. We've never ever seen a problem go away – but we have seen people forced to go away. And that shouldn't be you.

Once you've got your sponsors in the loop, your stakeholders connected and ideas for your agenda items, you can get down to the nuts and bolts of planning the agenda because you can incorporate everyone's ideas and input.

Planning agenda items

One of the easiest ways to plan agenda items is with a mind-map, which presents all the information you need on a page. There's plenty of great software around to help you. Check out Wikipedia for the latest paid or free versions, many of which have collaborative tools and some of which are also integrated with Microsoft Office or Mac. The beauty of this is once your ideas are sorted and clustered, you can export your mind-map into an instant structured and organised document which you can then just tweak and edit.

Figure 2-1 shows an example of a mind-map used to structure an agenda.

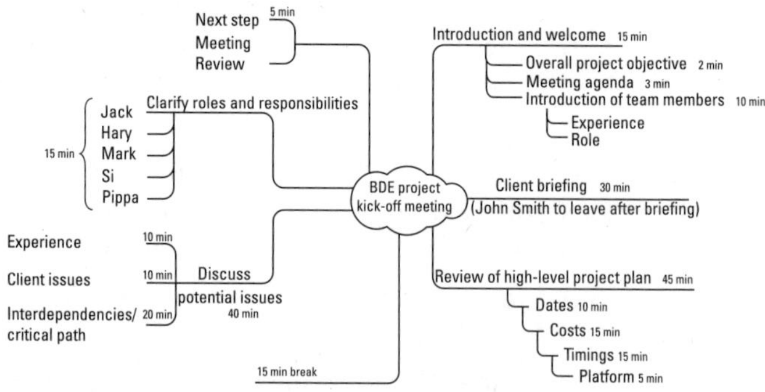

Figure 2-1: A mind-map used to plan an agenda.

If you prefer pen and paper, then sticky notes do just as well. In either case, here's a simple process for getting to the right agenda items:

1. **Write all your ideas down, one on each sticky note.**

   Make each idea start with an action word, so you know what you're doing with this idea. So instead of writing 'accounts', write 'review accounts'. Stick your ideas on a flip chart or mind-map them in any order but don't make a list at this point. That's because quite often the first thing that's on your list stays in the first place, not necessarily because it's a priority.

2. **Cluster all your similar ideas.**

   Once you've run out of ideas, review them and cluster what's similar to see what groupings you have. Throw out any repetitions or very similar ideas by combining them.

3. **Check that each item is aligned with the one-sentence purpose.**

   If the answer is 'yes, this is aligned', keep it. If it's a 'perhaps', put it to one side; you might like to check this with a participant or sponsor. If it's a 'no', throw it out.

4. **Add timings.**

   Write how long you think each item will take and then add up the time you have for the meeting. Then ask yourself 'What else do I need to throw out or amend?' Do a reality-check of your agenda items and timings with a colleague or participant and if you're still unsure, come back to review them a day later. Remember that it's easy to under-budget time.

5. **Think about a rough order and opportunities for breaks.**

   Doing this will mean you can start to put the key topics into a priority order. Don't leave the most difficult item until the end of your agenda and take guests, late arrivals and early leavers into account as you plan.

Quite often, meetings go wrong because the agendas are stuffed with too many items. Participants can't get through them all, and everyone feels overloaded and annoyed, especially if they've had to prepare. Just remember that if everything's important, then nothing's important.

It's much better to reduce the number of items and have a proper discussion about three to five main topics that are worth bringing everyone in a room for. The alternative is to risk frustration and irritation because participants don't have their say.

Collecting the agenda items, doing a rough order and working out timings is the easy part. You then need to review your agenda to make the items work best for everyone's timings. For example, you might not want remote participants in a tough time zone to get out of bed at 6 a.m. if they won't contribute to a topic until 7.30. Instead, you'd place their item higher up the agenda or tell them not to dial in to the meeting until later.

Assessing who's going to participate in your meeting

Make sure that everyone is responsible for something on your agenda or can at least contribute to the conversations. If participants can't own items or at least contribute to them, they shouldn't be in your meeting. There's nothing worse than a silent but deadly passenger who acts as an energy vampire, sucking meeting life-blood out of everyone. The only time the vampire is fully participative is when he hijacks or derails your meeting.

Check who *you* want to come and make sure you are working with people who really need to be in the room. And that doesn't necessarily include people who *want* to be in the room.

Planning your agenda order

So you know what you want to cover, who needs to be there and approximately how long it will take, and you've taken their timings into consideration. You also want to

- **Ensure that participants get something of value straight away so they want to be there on time.** But make sure that what you do is not so important that if a couple of people miss the item, your meeting is wrecked.

  Something of value includes a YouTube video, interesting sector or industry information, organisation updates like big wins or misses, people updates, a relevant blog, or a McKinsey or Harvard Business School article you read. It doesn't always have to be you fulfilling this role: You can share it among the team, which is another incentive for them to arrive on time.

Ice-breakers or energisers are not necessarily of value, so think twice before you use them as quite often they can be cheesy and will actively stop everyone arriving on time.

- **Start with some easier decisions or discussions before you get to the hardest one.** Just like exercise, meetings need a warm-up session so you remember how you all work together and do a bit of practice.
- **Manage breaks so that they don't occur in the middle of a tough but critical agenda item.** There's nothing worse than breaking off from a topic of conversation or getting into lots of side discussions because you've planned an inadvertent break.
- **Place a few items so that you end up with some easy decisions or discussions after a hard one.** Doing this allows the dust to settle and normal relations to resume. You don't want to end a meeting on an angry low moment when goodwill has been lost and relationships are a bit battered.
- **Plan a mini meeting review at the end.** If you don't ever assess your process, how will you know it's good? Or what to do to make it better?
- **Think about participants' energy and focus.** Most people aren't energised or focused at the very start or end of meetings. That's because they still have what they were doing on their minds when they arrive. And they start to think about what's next just before they leave.

  Participants are energised around the main points or the items that affect them the most. And they can't focus for much more than 60 to 90 minutes with peaks and troughs during that time, too. So plan regular breaks and changes of activity. Figure 2-2 shows how to structure a meeting for maximum attention and energy. It also shows you what items to place where to achieve this.

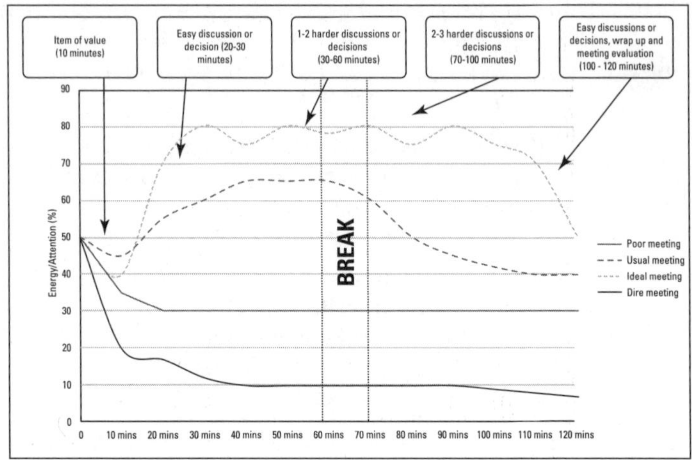

Figure 2-2: Understanding the difference meeting structure can make.

Fleshing out your agenda items

Most agendas are cobbled together at the last minute with very little thought, so if you were going to a restaurant, instead of going to a meeting, you'd be handed a menu that looked something like this:

Drinks

Starter

Main course

Dessert

If you were in such a restaurant, you'd clearly call the Maître'd over and say, 'Yes, but what have you actually got to eat today?' And if you didn't get a good answer, chances are you'd walk out, stick a poor review online and tell all your friends, too. You want specifics of what you'll be served.

But when it comes to meetings which cost us all a lot more than a meal out, we get shy, and we put up with all sorts of agenda rubbish because we're simply too polite. Or too lazy. Or too used to it. Of course, we also do the equivalent of sticking a poor review online: We gossip to all our colleagues.

What we should do, of course, is call time on badly written agendas. Getting together costs money, and that cash needs to be accounted for in all senses of the word. So if an agenda acts as your menu or meeting backbone, that means (well, not to extend a metaphor too far) you gotta put some flesh on the thing! That, in turn, means being clear and specific about

- What's the **precise** topic of your agenda item
- What **action** you want for this item
- Who is **responsible** for it
- **How long** it should take

Making all this super-clear means there is no room for doubt or misunderstanding. Everyone will know when they get into the room exactly what you are there to do, and so you'll have far less ambiguity from the get-go. And therefore you're much more likely to have a productive meeting. And a return visit from happy customers.

Recognising a poor agenda

Imagine that you are planning a usual management meeting to keep projects moving forward, and you want to work out how you could reduce travel costs in your first quarter of the next financial year. For the sake of argument, assume that you have a two-hour agenda in mind.

Figure 2-3 shows what a lousy agenda looks like.

Okay, the topics may not be thrilling, but no-one knows who's responsible for what or what any of the documents apply to. It looks like a super dull session; neither of us certainly wants to come. You've also put the main item as the first item on your agenda, a typical and classical mistake that your planning list should have told you to avoid.

To:	Alan Harting	Marketing
	Petra Kowalski*	Operations
	Lars Jonsson	HR
	Serge Muybridge	EDP
	Anja Weber	Marketing/Sales
	Paul Harrington	EDP: dial in only
Date:	05 May, 10.00-12.00 CET	
Location:	Osprey meeting room	
Dial in:	0808 456 1567 or +44 207 455 8181 (Code 61172122)	
From:	Diane Lytollis	VP Finance (Chair)

Management meeting

1. Travel costs reduction
2. Marketing update
3. HR updates and furniture
4. Accounting software

Figure 2-3: Example of a poor agenda.

Structuring a Great Agenda

So what does an ideal agenda structure look like? Well, Figure 2-4 shows how you could put together the same meeting to try and maximise attention and energy bearing in mind all the points from your planning session.

You can see that this agenda has clear logistics, actions, responsibilities, minutes and timings. That means it's a document you can always go back to if topics get off -track because it's what you all committed to in advance.

Reviewing a good agenda

Figure 2-4 is not a perfect document because nothing ever is. But we're sure you'll agree with us that it's a heck of a lot better than the agenda shown in Figure 2-3 because it's clear *who* is responsible for *what* and what is going to happen at every single moment.

To:	Alan Harting	Marketing
	Petra Kowalski*	Operations (Time)
	Lars Jonsson	HR (Minutes)
	Serge Muybridge	EDP
	Anja Weber	Marketing/Sales
	Paul Harrington	EDP: dial in only

Date: 05 May, 10.00-12.00 CET,

Location: Osprey meeting room

Dial in: 0808 456 1567 or +44 207 455 8181 (Code 61172122)

From: Diane Lytollis VP Finance (Chair)

AIM: To find three measures to reduce travel costs by 10% in Q1; CRM update, article selection, furniture investment, accounting software

Nr	Item	Who	Minutes	Timing
1.	Introduction and new customer update	AW	5	10.00 - 10.15
2.	Announcements			
	(i) Update: CRM trial software: what the pros, cons and next steps are	ST	10	10.05 - 10.15
	(ii) New stationery supplier: how to order our office stuff	PK		
	(iii) Auditor's visit on June 17: what you need to do!	DL		
3.	Decision Items			
	(i) Articles for in-house magazine: select top 3 items (see pre-reads**)	AW	15	10.15 - 10.30
	(ii) New office furniture: decide investment (see YouTube + web links**)	LJ		
4.	Major Decision Item (Chair AW)			
	Travel costs – the headlines: analysis and insights (see pre-reads**)	DL	50	10.30-11.20
	3 actions to reduce travel costs by 10% in Q1: brainstorm, review and decide	All		
	(Serge to facilitate this section)			
	Break		5	11.20-11.25
5.	Discussion Item			
	New accounting software implementation – pros and cons for sales	DL	25	11.25-11.50
6.	Actions and review	LJ	5	11.50-12.00

* AW to remain until 10.30

** See attached zip file

If you want to amend/add anything to the agenda please tell Paula McDonald by 22 April.
Please confirm attendance to Helga Schröder by 20 April.

Figure 2-4: Example of a better agenda.

We're also sure you're thinking 'wow, that's a lot of work.' And it is to start with. But if what you want is to attend great meetings, then you'd better give great meetings, too. That means you just have to write tight and focused agendas, which, of course, get faster and easier to do the more you practice.

Now you'll notice some other things about the agenda shown in Figure 2-4. There

- Are clear upfront logistics
- Are readily available supporting materials
- Are clearly allocated roles and responsibilities
- Is no agenda item called Any Other Business

Including meeting logistics

All meeting agendas need to contain this critical information:

- Where it's happening and in which room (it never hurts to add a map if you have new participants attending)
- When the meeting will start and end
- Who will be there
- Who has responsibility for what items
- Who else has been invited – outside the usual participants
- What timings are for which items
- When breaks will happen and for how long
- What needs to be read in advance and where to find it

Ideally, all this information is sent out in a calendar invitation. That way, everyone coming doesn't have to search for it, and it just pops into their diaries automatically. The advantage of an electronic invitation is, of course, that replies are immediately collated, and there's no extra work to do.

Supporting materials

We've all been in meetings that begin with the chair, leader or facilitator handing out reams of paper as you come in or projecting a series of hideous slides in font size 8. Irritating and de-energising? Naturally. The meeting then becomes a group reading lesson with the person in charge staring at their laptop, the wall or the screen. Whatever they are doing, they are not paying attention to the energy in the room or the outcomes everyone has come to achieve.

We'll say it again. Meetings are not good forums for sharing lots of information. So give everyone pre-reading in advance of the actual meeting. The more preparation time you allow your participants, the better prepared everyone will be for your meeting, so allow everyone at least 48 hours before you get together to prepare.

And if you have large documents to read, it's important to highlight that they are big. If you don't need everyone to read everything, indicate which sections or pages are vital. If there's sensitive information, you might need to send passwords in a separate mail or send out hard copies in advance.

But don't send a 5,000 page report and the management accounts the night before and expect everyone to have read them in detail. That's unreasonable. Defer your meeting instead.

Allocating roles and responsibilities beforehand

The advantage of assigning roles and responsibilities ahead of time is, of course, that there are no surprises. As most of us don't like surprises at work, you're making clear who needs to prepare what, with what documents, and who will be leading on all the different items.

In addition, you need to know

- Who'll be writing minutes, when they'll be circulated and after what process
- Who'll help keep timing and ensure that the process stays on track
- Who will be chair or facilitator if there is a conflict of interest and who will help point this out

This ensures that the governance of your meeting is always robust and rigorous.

Understanding the ramifications of AOB

Traditional meeting etiquette always includes the dreaded phrase 'any other business' (AOB) at the end of an agenda. But our hearts always sink when we see this. That's because AOB

- Allows anyone to raise any issue just at the end when everyone wants to leave and when attention is starting to wane. AOB always gets discussed when there's very little time and therefore meetings slide instantly into over-running. That is one of the main reasons people get to hate their meetings.

  You can greatly increase your chances of success and reduce others' frustration just by eliminating AOB from your agenda.

- Gives everyone an open invitation to re-run the meeting you had last week, to raise a closed issue for the umpteenth time, to put an irrelevant topic on the table or to drop a bomb on the group. There's always someone with an unwelcome axe to grind, and it's better that your meeting isn't their forum.
- Means that participants don't have to bother thinking about agenda items well before the meeting. Why should they if they can do thinking at the very end? This is the most powerful reason for getting it off your agendas.

Our strong recommendation is to remove AOB: It will make your meetings focused, shorter and force everyone to think before they turn up.

Writing really simple agendas

You might be thinking 'Wow, you're asking me to do a lot of work, and I'm only having a really simple meeting.' For example, you might want to update your team on your critical projects and share information about who's doing what. (Notice that this is a simple one-sentence objective!) If that's the case, then this can serve as an agenda. Just make sure that you

- Tell everyone how long they each have to talk.
- Clarify the end time so the meeting doesn't drift.
- Keep the session on track.

It's easy for teams to start having sub-meetings and then to waste everyone's time. So make sure you stay focused.

There's just one more thing you need to take into account – when is the best time to have your meeting from your participants' energy perspective.

Planning For and Managing Personal Energy

You not only need to think about meeting energy and attention and how you can manage it. But you also need to take into account the natural energy cycles or circadian rhythms everyone experiences, especially if you're meeting regularly with the same group of people.

We all have natural rhythms, which include the times when we feel more focused and more energised, or more 'up' and on the ball. And they include those moments in the day when we feel less focused and less energised, when we're more 'down'. Remember, this isn't about emotion, just energy. After all, that's why we talk about *down time.*

During your *up time,* your brain is firing on all cylinders, and you can give a subject your best attention and input. But during your down time, your brain feels more sluggish, and it's difficult to have new ideas, problem-solve or be creative.

If you're having a series of meetings with the same people, you can use this to everyone's advantage by working out the majority of your participants' up or down time. You can then plan brainstorming or problem-solving meetings during most people's up time and regular update meetings during the majority of people's down time. That way you're helping everyone work in line with their natural rhythms.

You work out up and down times either on a spreadsheet that you can circulate or a simple piece of paper. Here's how:

1. **Draw a graph and on the *y* (vertical) axis, mark off 0 to 100 in 10s to represent your energy level as a percentage.**

   A 100 per cent would represent firing on all cylinders, and 0 per cent would mean you were asleep!

2. **Take the *x* (horizontal) axis and add your work hours in one-hour increments.**

   Find a day when you can regularly assess your energy. Do this from the moment you get to work by marking an *x* where the percentage of energy you feel matches the actual time.

3. **Plot a series of dots hour by hour over the day to show how your energy increases or decreases; then connect the dots.**

4. **Draw a dotted line in your personal top 25 per cent range.**

   This dotted line represents your peak productivity zone. Do the same for the bottom 25 per cent.

5. **Highlight your top 25 per cent time ranges on the side of your graph or make them clear on your spreadsheet.**

   These are your peak hours, when you are at your best compared to the other times of the day. During these hours, you do your best thinking and get lots of great work done.

6. **Mark up your down times in a similar way.**

7. **Invite everyone attending your meeting to do the same.**

   You'll get a graph that looks something like Figure 2-5, showing the team's top energy times.

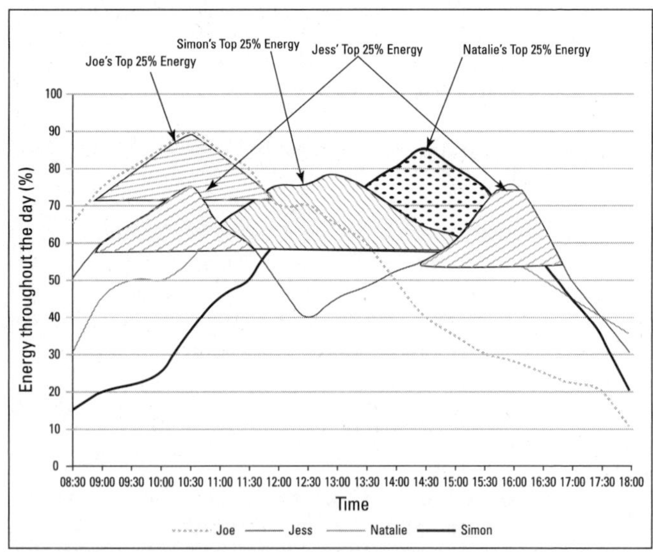

Figure 2-5: Showing a team's top energy times.

In Figure 2-5, taking this team of four and thinking about when they are most and least energised, it's clear that they should have problem-solving meetings between 10.30 and noon and information-sharing sessions towards the end of the day.

Double-Checking Your Preparation

So you've planned your objective, your agenda and your timings. Before you hit the Send button, just check that you can tick the following:

- Am I happy with the objective of this meeting?
- Are my sponsors or stakeholders aligned and informed?
- Does the agenda make logical sense?
- Does the agenda work in terms of focus and energy?
- Is it clear who's doing what and when?
- If I received this agenda, would I want to read it?
- If I got the pre-work, would I want to read it?
- Have I sorted out all the logistics?
- Have I maximised the natural energy cycles of the group?
- If I was invited to this meeting would I want to come?
- Have I sent everyone a calendar invitation?

Now you're ready hit Send; just remember to include yourself if you too are going to attend the meeting!

Chapter 3

Planning Your Workshop

In This Chapter

- Understanding more about workshops
- Identifying your stakeholders
- Planning and managing your design

So you decided you're going to run a workshop because you want to bring everyone's brains together to investigate an issue, solve a problem or learn something. And here's what you're on a mission to avoid: a super-dull day that, although it's been labeled a workshop, is really a reading lesson of endless slides covered in hundreds of words written in font size 4. (Remember that power corrupts. But PowerPoint corrupts absolutely – everyone's brain and their will to live.)

You want to design a day that feels loaded with zing and zap, that gets results and that has people saying that they can't wait to attend your next session because they were so energised and engaged throughout the whole process. What does that take? Yup, a lot of planning and preparation.

This chapter helps you think through everything you need to plan and prepare to deliver a great day. If the whole thing works smoothly, that's because there's a huge amount of work you've put into it. Just remember that if you're running a workshop you've got a lot at stake – including your reputation.

Understanding What Workshops Are All About

Whether you're focusing on how to solve a strategic corporate issue or planning a scrapbooking event, all workshops have some fundamental similarities:

- **Participants:** You'll generally have more than five participants, a number that means everyone gets personal attention and the chance to contribute. Any fewer, and you may not get the dynamic or output you are after. Over 12 people, and you start to get a different session as some people hold back and group work becomes very different.
- **Purpose:** It's clear why everyone is there and what you are all aiming to do as you work together.
- **Outcomes:** You will all know, articulate and agree on what success and failure looks like, both collectively and individually.
- **Interests or needs:** If the purpose and the outcomes are clear, you'll have a group of people with overlapping or similar interests and needs. They therefore should want to be in your room and want to help you make the day successful.
- **Culture:** A great workshop allows participants to open up and feel good about doing what they are doing. The more culturally aligned you are with the people you are working with, the more likely you are to have a great workshop because participants feel safe to talk.
- **Sharing:** When participants share their thoughts, they contribute to the process, and then they own it. Your design has to help make that happen.
- **Time-limited:** A workshop may last a few hours or a few days, but it's clear what will be achieved by when.
- **Expert leader:** Workshops are led by people who either have a real experience in the subject in hand or who are fabulous at managing a people process – because that's what a workshop is.

Recognising when you might want to run a workshop

You should consider running a workshop when you are

- Training or developing employees' professional skills.
- Implementing a new process that people have to learn how to use.
- Investigating an issue to find out what's happening, why it's happening and how to fix it.
- Solving difficult problems that are blocking projects or creating conflict and you need everyone's input.
- Understanding or developing a new idea or technique or explaining its importance to a group of people.
- Beginning a change program, and you want to help everyone understand why you're doing it, what to expect and how they can join in.

If you're facing any of these situations, you'll have to bite the bullet and think about whether you should have a workshop. Use the checklist in Table 3-1 just to make sure.

Table 3-1 Shall We Have a Workshop?

Do Plan a Workshop If . . .	*Don't Plan a Workshop If . . .*
You have a business critical issue to thrash out.	Not having it makes no difference.
You're stuck until you've dealt with stuff as a group or team.	It will end in a massive fight.
A problem will be solved fastest by getting together.	It's not been properly planned.
You need to learn new leadership skills.	Your stakeholders are against it.
You're kicking off a new project and have lots to clarify.	A key decision-maker can't be there.
It's the most efficient way of demo-ing a product or system.	A webinar would do just as well.

Following your decision: Making a project plan

Once you've made your decision to hold a workshop, you need to make a practical project plan. Just remember that the larger the group or the more senior they are, the higher the stakes, so the more robust your plan needs to be.

So take your time to think through how you will

- Identify your stakeholders.
- Plan your workshop content.
- Take care of logistics.
- Do any follow-up after the workshop.

You can download all the questions that will help you build a great project plan by going to `www.dummies.com/go/rungreatmeetingsworkshops.com`. But whether you build a really detailed plan or simply work from ten bullet points of things you need to do to have a great workshop, your starting point is to identify all your stakeholders. Everything else, including your success, flows from that.

Identifying Your Stakeholders

Stakeholders include anyone with an interest or concern in the workshop you are going to hold. So an obvious stakeholder who you need to keep close to is your sponsor. He or she is the main supporter of your workshop and will be advocating for you behind the scenes.

Your other stakeholders could be limited to just the people going to attend your session. Or they could include a very wide group if you are addressing a strategic issue. If that's the case, you'll find that there are a many interested parties who want to be consulted on what you're doing, and you need to take advantage of their interests and knowledge. That's because without doing this, you run the risk of being derailed and incurring reputational risk.

So you need to get supersonically clear about whose fingers you need to have in the workshop pie you are trying to bake. Failing to do this will result in as many fingers in your eye later down the line because you failed to get important people on-board at your planning and design stage.

To define your stakeholders, do the following:

1. **Make a list of everyone with an interest in this project and write each name on a sticky note.**

   For example, the list could include the participants, your boss, their boss, direct reports, other teams affected by the output of the day, vendors, suppliers, customers or clients. These are your primary stakeholders.

2. **Check if there are any secondary stakeholders you need to add to that list.**

   For example, think about regulatory bodies, unions, the local community, pressure groups, the media, educational organisations or your competitors.

After you have a full stakeholder map, you are ready to categorise your stakeholders to find your key players.

Finding your key players

If you've identified a lot of stakeholders, you might be feeling a bit flabbergasted because you've realised that you have so many of them. To make life easier, check first that they have real power in what you are trying to do. Power can be outside or inside your organisation and comes from the sources shown in Table 3-2.

Table 3-2 Sources of Stakeholder Power

External	*Internal*
Hierarchy	Hierarchy
Influence over outcomes	Influence over outcomes
Control of strategic resources	Control of strategic resources
Possession of knowledge and skills	Possession of knowledge and skills
Influence in the environment	Control of the environment
Influence in implementation	Involvement in implementation
Benefits from the workshop outcomes	Benefits from the workshop outcomes

Once you've thought about power, reflect on your stakeholders' level of interest in what you're doing. Use the matrix in Figure 3-1 as it will

- Help you check power one more time.
- Categorise your stakeholders to find the most important ones.
- Ensure that you have a clear direction for working with everyone.

So take all the sticky notes you've written and plot them on the matrix in Figure 3-1. Your sponsor will obviously be a key player and should be in this quadrant.

Level of Interest

Power	Low	High
High	2. Keep happy	1. Key players
Low	4. Minimal effort	3. Keep informed

Figure 3-1: Stakeholder categorisation tool.

Now you can clearly identify who and in which order you should really target your efforts as you plan your workshop:

1. **Key players:** They are the focus of your stakeholder management time and effort. Above all, they need a really good listening to as you plan your workshop.
2. **Keep happy:** These people need to be pleased with what you're up to. Remember that if they aren't happy, their level of interest can quickly change.
3. **Keep informed:** You need to put in more effort here on the communications front. Stay sharp because if a large group starts to feel uninformed, they can get more powerful.
4. **Minimal effort:** Yay! Here is the group who'll give you very little trouble as you plan your workshop – unless, of course, the landscape changes.

Meeting your sponsor and any key players

Your sponsor will already have told you what they want to achieve, and, of course, some sponsors have much more clarity than others – as do key players. Right now, you need to prepare to consult to them and lock down your outcomes. But before you do that,

- **Revisit your sponsor's and key players' interests** and decide what you think their positions will be. Will they be for what you want to achieve in your workshop, against it or neutral? Are there any hidden agendas involved? This will help you plan your approach.
- **Decide in advance** if you want ideas and input or feedback on what you're going to do.
- **Have a rough high-level plan** so that your sponsor and key stakeholders know what will happen, by when and who's involved. Don't get dragged down into the nitty-gritty if you can possibly avoid it at this stage.
- **Think through** what you would like to commit to and by when in terms of follow-up actions before you meet with them.
- **Start to think about your workshop outcomes** so you can have a productive conversation.

Defining Your Outcomes

Workshop outcomes can be particularly hard to lock down. That's because it's tough to

- Articulate outcomes really well: This takes time, thought and energy.
- Manage sponsors and key players: They will always have conflicting interests and ideas about what you should achieve.

But because it's hard to really thrash them out, workshop designers take the easy route and often go with really sloppy and weak outcomes that tell you nothing. And no one ever knows if you have achieved them.

There is one thing you do need to watch out for as you define your outcomes. We can guarantee that everyone, including you, will want you to get too much done in too short a space of time. So you need some careful consulting with your sponsor about what's possible in the time you have

Here are the questions that you, your sponsor and possibly some key stakeholders need to thrash out to arrive at clear outcomes:

- **What would we like to have achieved by the end of our workshop if we had an ideal situation and open-ended amount of time together?** This helps you widen your focus before you narrow it down in the next step. Make sure you use verbs or 'doing' words so that you immediately start to get to actions and avoid any fluffy answers. Think about the tangible outputs that have to come out of the session; these can include a process, new learning, actions or a document.
- **What specifically must we get done in this particular workshop?** Now you can take this list and start to prioritise it. To do this, simply rank order list of the statements you have already generated and throw out the ones you don't want. You can then take this work to your key stakeholders to show you have already put in your thinking and see if these outcomes align with theirs.
- **Why is it important to get this done right now by this group?** This helps you tie what you're doing to the participants' context and will help you position what you're doing with key stakeholders and your participants.
- **What would success look like?** This is an interesting one, because success may look different to you, your sponsor or key stakeholders and to participants. You need to think this through from every perspective before, during and after your workshop. If you can find metrics to help you, you should. But settling on behaviors or knowledge is fine, too.

You can download a full document that guides you through defining your outcomes more fully by going to `www.dummies.com/go/rungreatmeetingsworkshops.com`.

Checking your outcomes

After you've fully articulated your outcomes, check to see that they are

- **Clear:** There is no room for misunderstanding about what's going to happen in this particular workshop.
- **Specific:** The outcomes apply only to this workshop (or series of workshops) and are the basis for your full design.
- **Appropriate:** Achieving the outcomes is of particular interest to everyone who will be participating.
- **Action-oriented:** Participants should be accountable and responsible for further actions after your workshop, so they have a genuine interest in attending and contributing to it.

Reviewing some good and some bad outcomes

Just so you're really clear, Table 3-3 shows you three good and bad workshop outcomes: What do you notice about the good ones?

Table 3-3 Examples of Poor and Well-Articulated Outcomes

Poorly Articulated Outcomes	*Well-Articulated Outcomes*
To get to know each other better	To understand the core activities of both our organisations, to review areas of potential mutual interest and decide on next steps
Governance for the senior leadership team: how we work together in the cascade	To review how we work and behave as a leadership team when we meet To plan our roles and responsibilities in communicating and delivering change across the organisation

(continued)

Table 3-3 *(continued)*

Poorly Articulated Outcomes	*Well-Articulated Outcomes*
Develop our presentation skills	As a result of this workshop, participants will Know how to structure a clear, logical and well-thought-out presentation Recognise and deal with tricky situations credibly and with confidence Use words, voice and body language to maximum effect Understand strengths and development areas when presenting Have given and received clear and considered feedback

Poor outcomes

Recently a global organisation got the extended management team of a critical business unit together, and I (Jess) was asked to facilitate a half-day session. This was organised by the organisation's HR business partner and sponsored by the senior leader. Because of cost and budget constraint, the extended management team hadn't met face-to-face for two years, and in that time, the team had been reduced from a headcount of 120 to 65 people. So there was a lot of uncertainty and lack of energy around the future and what it might hold.

I had taken the brief from the HR business partner, and in the run-up, I asked to talk to the sponsor and six people – key stakeholders who would be at the meeting. During that time, I struggled to get focus on and commitment to solid outcomes, and I certainly didn't get to talk to six participants. When I reported this to HR business partner, I was told, 'Don't worry. Everyone's okay with what you've planned.' But I wasn't okay and felt very uncertain about what we were doing. Against my better judgment, I ran the session; it was a disaster.

No consulting around the outcomes meant no real buy-in from the team. So I stopped the process after 45 minutes and explained that I wanted to re-contract around what we were there to do. Quite quickly, we worked out that there was a lot of mistrust between various sub-teams. So I asked the group if they wanted to work on this. 'No, not really' was the answer. I checked in with my sponsor who shrugged and said 'No' in front of his team.

I was amazed and couldn't quite believe that I was in this room in a lovely French chateau with a team who would rather live with the pain than address it. But it taught me once and for all that if you can't get your outcomes clarified and aligned with your sponsor and key stakeholders, just don't run a workshop!

Understanding why you spend so much time on outcomes

It may seem like a massive headache to spend so much time working on outcomes. But we promise that if you do this you will dramatically increase your chances of workshop success because you will

- Know that your outcomes are rock solid.
- Be able to show you have consulted well and listened to input.
- Know clearly what you are working towards achieving and how you are adding value, which is especially important if you are planning to calculate the return on investment of your workshop.

Establishing the return on investment (ROI)

On the face of it, it looks simple: Effective workshops, programs or projects should positively change participants' ability to do their job. So you should see increased productivity, reduced costs or decreased time taken to do something. And that should be measurable.

But the problem with calculating ROI is that everyone has a different opinion about what that ROI should be:

- **The Board** may be most concerned with how the investment helps the organisation achieve its goals.

- **Finance** may look at the cost and want to know if there could have been a more effective spend elsewhere.
- **Your sponsor** might be focused on performance and productivity in a particular group of people.
- **Learning and Development** may be focused on program delivery, impact and reputation.
- **Stakeholders** may simply want time to build trust and work more efficiently together.
- **You** might see it as securing your next engagement or series of workshops.

So you need to have several conversations with all your key stakeholders to work out what it is you are measuring and for whom. Whatever it is, is has to be measurable performance data of some kind, and that can be hard to identify – which is often a reason why ROI doesn't get calculated.

Other reasons why it gets ignored include:

- You often can't measure it until **several months** have passed, by which time new projects are underway and business has moved on.
- It ties employees up on something that isn't seen as value-adding as it **takes time and costs money**.
- Everyone's frightened of a **negative ROI**, its implications and impact.

What that really means is that you should calculate the ROI for your larger and not for your smaller projects. These include projects that affect important and strategic aspects of the business.

If your workshops fit into this category, you've got to be ready to work out and consult with your sponsor on

- What data you want to measure.
- What your costs are going to be.
- What you think you'll save as a result of the work you are doing.

What performance data you want to measure?

To measure the ROI of your workshops, you'll need to collect and then analyse performance data. Good data can include project completion dates, customer satisfaction, speed of decisions, accidents, grievances, waste, time supervising, complaints, absence, milestones met, employee turnover, cost over-run, quality/quantity issues and time invested. That's because you can translate all of these into evidence of real financial benefit to the organisation.

What your costs are going to be?

Your costs will include

- Design
- Delivery
- Your salary
- Materials
- Participants' salaries
- Pre- and post-evaluation
- Travel
- Accommodation
- IT support
- Venue
- Opportunity costs of participants' attendance

What are you going to save?

Once you have selected your performance data and done an analysis of your costs, you can

- Estimate what you think the improvement could be (take a look at industry averages and best practice elsewhere to help you).
- Look at current trends and trend lines both with and without the investment you are about to make.
- Identify the overall cost.

- Work out a conservative monetary value for the improvement you hope to see.
- Deduct the costs from the benefit.

Now you have a rough ROI.

Just remember that you'll need to come back to this analysis after you've done your full implementation. But having it to hand with help you get buy-in from tougher stakeholders because numbers speak louder than words. These numbers will act as your key deliverables: in other words achieving them will be markers of your success.

At about the same time, you should also be starting to think about your design.

Getting Ready to Do the Design

The design of your workshop is critical, but you're halfway there with having solid outcomes. We recommend a three-stage process:

1. **Think about all the information** you need that could affect the design.
2. **Plan all the workshop's activities,** the timings, objectives and materials on a one-pager to start with.
3. **Write up a running order** of every activity in some detail, including what you'll say.

There are three key benefits for doing the design this way. It will

- **Result in a strong design** because you will have really had to think things through, and a strong design can help you manage weaker facilitation skills while you're learning them.
- **Help you learn your stuff** before you lead it, so your delivery is really smooth. That means you won't constantly be referring to your notes.
- **Make you think it through** in a level of detail that means you'll realise where potential weaknesses lie.

You start getting ready by gathering all the information you need.

Thinking it through

You need to find out or work on some key information that will materially affect your design before you start thinking about what you'll do during the day itself.

People stuff

When thinking about people, you need to consider

- **How many participants will attend your session?** What you'll plan for six people will be very different than what you'll plan for 18 of them. Over 15 people, and you might like to work with a co-facilitator or get additional support.
- **Is their attendance optional or mandatory?** If you've got some prisoners in the room, you'll be starting on a back foot, and buy-in will take longer. It's essential to know this before you start your design.
- **How well does everyone know each other?** If your participants don't know each other well, they will take longer to warm up.
- **Will anyone have any special needs?** This covers any disabilities you need to take into account and any animosities or sensitive issues you should know about beforehand.
- **What knowledge do they have of the subject?** If you've got any specialists in the room, you'd better think through how to co-opt them and use their expertise to help get the group on-side. If they are novices, then you know how you need to pitch your material.

Time

When thinking about time, you need to consider

- **How much time do you have to deliver what you need to?** Remember you can get through a lot of 'why' and 'what' in a short period of time with many people in the room (think lecture). You can't get through very much 'how' (think practice). More frequent but shorter interventions are better than one long one, unless you are trying to solve a problem. Then you may need to just hammer away until you're done.

- **How much time will you build in for participants to think?** It's really easy to let this slip, especially if you are new to design. But if you don't allow any thinking time, your workshop will simply feel like one activity after another, and participants won't understand how they connect or what these activities mean to them as individuals. Then they'll get annoyed with you.
- **How will you deal with slippage?** Many activities take longer than you think, and participants like to explore things in greater depth than you might plan. How will you build slippage into the schedule? There's nothing worse than having a workshop leader say, 'We haven't got time for this' or 'Moving quickly on.' So what will you plan that you can dump if you need to?

Sequencing stuff

When thinking about sequencing, you need to consider

- **How will you ensure that everything you do has a start, middle and conclusion?** If you don't do this, your activities will feel unstructured.
- **How will you vary activities so they don't feel the same?** Even if you need to have three brainstorming sessions, you'll have to do them differently, or your participants will lose the will to live.
- **How will you plan for changing energy?** You need to recognise that energy changes through the day so, for example, consider getting everyone moving after lunch, not sitting down doing deep thinking. They'll simply fall asleep.

Planning the start

When planning the start, you need to consider

- **How will you open and immediately give your participants something of value?** Far too many workshops open with introductions. How dull. Your workshop isn't a party; everyone can get to know each other during breaks or afterwards. If you want your participants to be committed from the start, make it easy for them to commit!
- **How will you clarify expectations?** This should take between 10 to 20 minutes, depending on the size of the group. It's something that new designers often miss, but

it's really important because it's when you agree with the group about what you will and you won't do. Moreover, you need to refer to expectations throughout your session to check you are delivering against them.

Considering whether to stay on-site or go off-site

There's a lot to noodle on before you start – especially the location. Where are you going to hold your workshop?

Well, of course, budget is the first thing you'll think about, but this shouldn't be your major influencing factor. You don't have to hold an off-site meeting or workshop in a swanky hotel. We've run sessions in village halls, tents, bars, coffee shops, gardens, woods, fields, barges and on beaches.

Cheap and cheerful can be even more effective than being near phones and colleagues, so think as widely as possible about places you could go. Table 3-4 lists some additional thoughts you'll want to consider as you make your decision.

Table 3-4 On-Site Versus Off-Site Locations

Off-Site: Pros	*On-Site: Pros*
Little distraction from the usual work hassles (no calls or interruptions)	Practical and cheaper from a kit and cost perspective
People are often more willing to have different conversations	Resource available when you need more information or support
Easy to relax and get to know each other more informally after	Level of comfort and familiarity with the surroundings
New venue can more easily mean new attitudes and fresh starts	Swift re-entry to work

Checking out the workshop room

If you can't check out the space because it's not nearby, call someone who has run a workshop there before. You might have looked at photos of the space, but they can be misleading. And some venues are better than others, even if they have a series of rooms all located next to each other. Light and air are key factors that make people feel more positive. And a windowless, poorly-lit, small and stuffy room just reduces energy and focus if you've got to be there all day.

Check that there is enough space for people to move around. Many meeting rooms that are allegedly for eight people are so cramped that you have to stay seated except during breaks. This will obviously affect the activities you can plan.

Doing Your Design

You've done your research that was the easy bit. Now you've got the harder process of thinking about what you'll actually do on the day.

Getting in the right frame of mind

Here are three keys for getting your approach right as you begin the one-page design:

- Think of your workshop as a **shared experience,** which is co-created with your participants.
- Recognise that you are there to **facilitate a conversation,** not to provide all the expert knowledge, even if you are the so-called 'expert'. Added together, everyone else brings a lot more years of experience to the table than you do.
- Plan to keep referring to the **practical applications** of what you're going to cover.

If you do this, you'll help build in the most effective tone and style as you set about the design.

Working on and with your personal style

This sounds as if it should be a given. But it's not. One big mistake new facilitators and trainers often make is to slip into 'teach' mode because it feels safe, and it emphasises expertise. The problem is that people often associate teachers with school, and this brings out the worst in many of them. They don't want information pushed into them and much prefer a Socratic approach, which involves having the information pulled from them with thoughtful questioning.

So what's your preferred style when working with a group? Take this mini questionnaire to find out.

1. **Someone comes to you from the group during lunch and says that they have been asked by everyone if they can change the content for the afternoon. You say:**

   a. 'I can't do that. We agreed to the plan beforehand.'

   b. 'I propose we do the first activity and change direction after that.'

   c. 'How do we set about making it work for you?'

2. **A participant comes into the room and asks where to put their heavy coat and suitcase. You warmly**

   a. Tell them to put everything under the table at the back of the room.

   b. Recommend that they put it where no one can fall over either and where they won't get in the way.

   c. Invite the participant to put both wherever they think most suitable.

3. **You are facilitating a group, and the session has been running for some time. You notice energy is low. Would you say**

   a. 'Everyone is looking tired. We'll take a ten-minute break.'

   b. 'I propose we take a break: what do you think'?

   c. 'I think energy is low. What do you want to do about it?'

4. **You are facilitating a group who is trying to reach a decision on an important issue by consensus. Two of the nine team members have a different point of view, and you've reached an impasse. Would you say**

   a. 'You seem unable to agree on a way forward as you wanted to. What should we do?'

b. 'You can't reach consensus so we'll leave the decision for now and come back to it this afternoon.'

c. 'We've got a majority agreement. I recommend we go with that.'

5. **You have been asked to step in to facilitate a team an hour ahead of their meeting. You would**

   a. Ask the team members what they expect of you before the meeting starts.

   b. Explain your role to everyone and get on with the information you have.

   c. Let the group have their meeting and offer input when you are asked for it.

6. **One key person, Jim, walks out of your workshop in anger and frustration at the way a discussion is going. Your response is to:**

   a. Ignore the situation right now and deal with it in the next break, which will be in 15 minutes.

   b. Say, 'how about someone goes to find Jim and talks to him?'

   c. Say, 'Jim left the room because the discussion made him angry and frustrated. What shall we do about it?'

7. **A participant is being very challenging in your session. You notice that this is irritating the group and affecting group dynamics. Do you**

   a. Confront the person head-on in front of everyone.

   b. Pull other participants in to help you manage this behavior.

   c. Put it to the group that you adopt a new ground rule for managing negative comments.

8. **You are running a skills workshop and worried about timing. Your participants are late coming back from breaks because they are making 'urgent' calls. One has gone missing. Do you**

   a. Set up a new penalty system for latecomers.

   b. Re-contract with the group about timings.

   c. Suggest to them that it's their learning that's being affected and they need to take responsibility for it.

Now score your results by adding up all the Ds, Ss and Fs. Then discover what this means in the following sections.

1: a = D, b = S, c = F   **2**: a = D, b = S, c = F

3: a = D, b = S, c = F   **4**: a = F, b = D, c = S

5: a = S, b = D, c = F   **6**: a = D, b = S, c = F

7: a = D, b = S, c = F   **8**: a = D, b = F, c = S

More Ds

This means you currently have a tendency to be more directive – in other words, more like a teacher. This style works well for children but is less effective for adults because it doesn't encourage experiential learning or ownership. You want participants to attend your workshop and then take action.

The times you want to use this style are when you are giving participants safety or process information. Then you need to be very directive.

Aim to spend a maximum of 10 to 15 per cent of your time in directive mode.

More Ss

This tells you that you prefer the suggestive mode, which lies between being directive and being facilitative. It's a suitable style for new groups who are uncertain how to behave together or who may not gel quickly. Staying here does incur the risk that the group won't take responsibility for itself or its outcomes.

Aim to spend no more than 15 to 20 per cent of your time here and mostly at the start of your workshop.

More Fs

You are a true facilitator who likes to enable others to take responsibility for the process that they are in. You understand the nature of working collaboratively with people to help them get the best out of themselves as individuals and as a group. Knowing how to get the group to own what they are doing is a skill you have mastered; you understand that you are there to simply guide the process.

Aim to spend 70 to 80 per cent of your time in facilitator mode.

In case of a tie

If you end up with a tie, ask yourself what style would be most useful to the group you are about to work with. Then aim to use more of it.

Recognising all the different activities available

There are only so many activities you can do in a workshop, and they include

- Listening to someone presenting information
- Talking or practicing a skill, tool or technique in twos, threes or small groups
- Sharing peer experiences through structured and unstructured group discussion
- Brainstorming and presenting ideas back to the group
- Learning a new technique and practicing it to give and receive feedback
- Watching a video and reviewing and drawing learnings from it
- Role playing a situation to learn from it
- Working with actors who role play a scenario
- Reviewing a case study to see what others have done
- Rote learning
- Working through written exercises
- Taking tests or competitions as individuals or smaller groups
- Making or designing something together
- Doing a paper-based or computer-based simulation individually or as a group
- Reflecting on outcomes or learning

Bear in mind if you are designing a content-rich workshop rather than a content-free one (see Chapter 2), the more you get participants to work through activities themselves, the more invested they will be. And they then learn through their direct experience that you should get them to reflect on. That's what *experiential learning* is all about. (For an article on experiential learning, visit www.dummies.com/extras/rungreatmeetingsworkshops.)

If you want participants to be even more invested, you can also think about how you want them to contribute. What parts of your workshop could they run? How can you get them really involved in the day?

Getting a rough design together

Doing the design takes time. A rough design means planning what happens and when. If you're designing a half-day session, your time will be divided into two main chunks. If it's a one-day workshop, you'll have four: before the first break and after it, after lunch and after the second break.

You've therefore got time for a maximum of

- One big activity before the first break.
- Two big activities before lunch.
- Two big activities before the second break.
- One big activity after.

In other words, you've only got time for a maximum of six big activities, even if you break them down into smaller steps, because each major activity needs a full debrief and some reflection time. If you refer to your outcomes and you have about five or six of them, these will help you plan your big activities. And, as a reminder, if what you're doing is thought-provoking, your time may well run over, so you need to have some flexible sections that you can drop without damaging the overall integrity of the whole day.

Be careful not to plan any big activity that is disrupted by a break; you never get the same energy back when you restart it. Instead, juggle with the timings without being silly. You don't want to work from 8.30 to 11 a.m. and take a 15-minute break only to stop for lunch at 12. That will just annoy your participants. If it happens like that and you contract together in the room, that's one thing; if you plan it, that's quite another.

To get your rough design:

1. **Review your outcomes and make sure you have them to hand.**
2. **Take some sticky notes and write down each activity on a sticky note.**
3. **Put them into a rough order.**
4. **Check that you are building in variation in terms of participants standing, sitting, plenary discussion and smaller group work.**
5. **Add timings.**
6. **Imagine how you would facilitate this workshop; does it make sense?**
7. **Check that all these activities will achieve the outcomes you have set.**
8. **Think, would I want to attend this session as a participant?**

Now you're ready to write up your one-page design.

Writing up your one-page design

When you're ready to write up your one-page design, here's a quick caveat. When you're new to design, it's easy to make what you do far too complex. Simplicity should be your underlying theme. All you need to do for your one page-design is open a Word, Mac or Google document; we prefer a writing program rather than one used for numbers or presentations because they are much easier to work with when you need to change stuff around.

Open your document in landscape and, first of all, transfer the outcomes you are aiming to achieve. That way, they will always be top-of-mind.

Then create a four-column template that looks like Table 3-5.

Table 3-5 Outcomes to Achieve

Timing	*Activity*	*Objective*	*Materials*
8:30–8:40	Opening bang	To interest the group and provide value	TED talk: for example, Hans Rosling on data
8:40–8:45	Explain outcomes	To clarify content	Flip chart
8:45–9:00	Gather expectations	To understand needs	Sticky notes
9:00–9:05	Review agenda and connect to expectations	Get buy-in from the group	Flip chart
9:05–9:30	Review what we like about current planning procedure (paired exercise)	Create a positive working dynamic	White board

You get the picture. It's pretty simple to do, and as you write it up, check two or three times that your activities map onto your outcomes.

Start with something positive and don't plunge too early into what's really hard for the group to do. This is because, like all athletes, the group needs a warm-up and because

- The group needs to feel each other and work together efficiently in this new context with you as leader.
- You need to watch and understand the group's dynamics before you give it something hard to work on. And you need to see who's for the session, neutral or against it, so you can manage the group well and help bring everyone in.
- They need to feel successful as individuals and as a group so they build their energy and appetite for the tougher stuff later on. If they fail at something difficult early on, it's much harder to pull things back.

So make sure you plan 30 minutes of easier stuff, even if you're only running a half-day workshop.

After you've written your one-pager up, check for simplicity and success. You can do this by

- Reading it aloud to yourself to figure out whether it makes sense.
- Asking yourself whether the methods you've chosen meet your stated objectives.
- Imagining everything happening in your head, such as – what could go wrong and how you could prevent it
- Giving it to a participant or key stakeholder and asking their opinion.
- Thinking again, would I want to attend this day?

Breaking the ice

It's a hand-on-the-heart moment right now as we confess to you that we hate ice-breakers. We simply can't see the relevance of telling you about our favorite vegetable, of drawing a picture that represents our hopes and fears, or getting you to find out what's a lie about us and what's not.

Instead, and just like meetings, participants should get something of value straight away, something that will make them sit up and think, 'I really want to be here.' Ice-breakers feel very 20th century to us. But an extract from a TED talk, a market insight, team statistic, a witty video, a real-live senior leader in your workshop . . . well, that's different. That's what creates fizz and attention, not some crummy old bingo game.

About TED

TED brings together incredible speakers who originally came from Technology, Entertainment, Design – hence TED. But now the remit is much wider, and all sorts of fascinating people present. Speakers have to talk about their ideas in 18 minutes or less and the best performances are available for free, with more being added all the time. All of the talks are subtitled in English, and many in other languages too. Visit `www.ted.com` to find out more.

Structuring your stuff

I (Jess) designed my first workshop more than 15 years ago. But, of course, I still remember the complete tizzy I was in as I hadn't got the faintest clue where to start or how to go about it. I had taken on a new job from someone going into retirement, an unflappable character called Mike. Mike gave me piece of invaluable advice when it comes to workshop design.

'Start by writing down the morning and afternoon breaks and then plan lunch. Decide you want to end 15 minutes early as no one hates you for ending early, but they really resent you going on too long. It just shows you can't manage timings. But once you've planned coffee, lunch and tea, your day is divided into four sections; all you've got to do is manage your activities within those four sections. And never do anything complicated at the end of the day. That's a recipe for disaster.'

Thank you, Mike. I remember this advice every time I do a new design.

Writing your detailed running order

Sorry to say, this boils down to three things: blood, sweat and tears. There's no getting away from the fact that you just have to lock yourself away and do it. If you've got the one-page design, it's not difficult to do; it's just time-consuming. That's because we find that they run between 15 to 25 pages.

If this is your first workshop and you're coordinating the content, looking after the logistics and facilitating at the front, you'll need to think about the 8:1 rule: For every hour of delivery, plan on at least eight hours of preparation in terms of thinking and design time. So how do you arrive at a fully fledged design?

Just take the one-pager and add lots more details about

- How to run every activity
- What you might say as you set it up, run and debrief it
- How long each step of your activity will take

For a sample part of a running order that works on goals, go to `www.dummies.com/go/runninggreatmeetingsworkshops`.

Writing a running order is not something you can do when you're being interrupted. So turn your phone off, find a quiet place and give yourself several blocks of time.

You're probably questioning the value of writing a running order if it's so tough. But you're doing it because

- When it comes to delivery, it's easy. You will have spent considerable time embedding everything in your head as you write up your running order.
- When you or a colleague want to run this or something similar in the future, it's easy. You've got all the details.
- When it comes to signing off what you're doing with your sponsor or key stakeholders, it's easy because you really know what you're talking about.

One final hot tip for running orders: Never ever hand these out to any of your stakeholders. It's way too much detail, and, frankly, they don't need to know it. You do. You consult using your one-pager instead.

Getting sponsor sign-off

After you've written everything up, it's time to check in with your sponsor (as well as any other key stakeholders) and run them through what you're going to do. We recommend sending your one-pager through in advance of a meeting or calling with a brief agenda that includes

- Outcome review and check-in written on your one-pager (2 minutes)
- Content overview (20 minutes)
- Location discussion (3 minutes)
- Next steps (5 minutes)

Doing this will ensure that sign-off is very quick. Just check that signed-off means what it implies, and that there are no other actions you need to take other than reporting back after the workshop.

Supporting materials

Some sponsors want to review your supporting materials as part of the sign-off. If this is the case, make sure you have them all ready and that you've sent them through in advance, too. Our experience is that the content often isn't the issue; it's internal brand guidelines that take up the most time. So check with marketing that you are compliant before you attach them to an email.

Joining instructions

Your joining instructions, which some people call invitations, should include (not necessarily in this order)

- **Why the workshop is happening:** This should be a mini overview of why this session and why now.
- **What participants have to do to prepare:** Make clear if they have to read or bring anything.
- **What the outcomes will be:** They should have no surprises on the day.
- **What a mini agenda will include:** Don't send your one-pager; just give them six to seven bullets of what you're working on together.
- **What else to expect:** This should include any guests who'll be there, video sessions they may take part in and so on.
- **Where to go and when:** Remember to add the location, room, time and date.
- **What to wear if participants need to dress differently:** Be super clear about this. There's nothing worse than participants who can't take part in something because they are dressed in unsuitable clothes.
- **What to do if they have concerns:** This should just be your contact information.

Make sure you write your joining instructions in an upbeat and welcoming manner because for many people, this will be their first introduction to you.

If you are running a strategic or high visibility workshop, you might want your sponsor to send out the joining instructions because if they come from her or him, they set a totally different tone.

You can download sample joining instructions at `www.dummies.com/go/runninggreatmeetingsworkshops`.

Building your skills and getting good at group work: Next steps

Well done because now you've done all the hard preparation. Your aim should now be to skill yourself up to work with your group as effectively as possible. To do that, you'll need to

1. **Refresh** your questioning, listening and observing skills.
2. **Understand** how to apply them to group work.
3. **Become more aware** of what happens in groups.
4. **Rehearse** what you'll say on the day.

That's what Chapter 4 is all about.

Chapter 4

Getting Ready for the Big Day

In This Chapter

- Developing your essential skills
- Understanding groups
- Rehearsing your stuff

You've done all the hard graft to prepare for your meeting or your workshop, but this is just the beginning. If you want to lead truly great meetings and workshops, you need to spend time developing the skills that will support you. We know you can't do this in a matter of a few weeks or days. But you can start to think more mindfully about these skills, practise them in different settings and think about how they work for you.

Then you can apply these key skills so that you become more aware of what happens within a group. It's essential to grow your awareness of what's going on in a group if you're going to do great work.

Finally, you need to do your personal preparation. The amount of personal preparation you now do will really affect how you come over on the day and whether or not you achieve your outcomes. To give you an analogy from school: You've attended all the classes, made fabulous notes and handed in all your essays, but you haven't yet done the revision for your exam. And the exam date is already in the diary.

This chapter helps you pass with flying colours because you work on your skills, rehearse what you want to say, know how you want to look and decide how you want to be in the room.

Developing Your Essential Skills

There are some key communication skills you need to use when you get people in a room to inform, discuss, decide or learn something. These skills include

- Asking good questions to stimulate conversation.
- Listening to participants' answers and the overall conversation in play.
- Observing what's really happening in a room.
- Staying neutral.
- Synthesising what's being said.
- Capturing main themes for thinking about more or acting on.

To make sure your session runs really well, spend as much time as you can using these skills in your normal working life. That way, they will start to come naturally to you. We recommend taking one skill a day and making a mini plan to try it out a couple of times during work; then just before you stop for the day, think about how you used this skill. What could you keep doing because it worked well? What would you like to build on so that it works even better?

Doing this will give you the valuable opportunity to work on your core skills before you go live. In other words, you'll de-risk your session, which has got to be a good thing.

Asking good questions

For the past 20 years, research has shown that the way in which a question is asked can have a profound influence on the personal processes involved in formulating answers. In other words, the questions you ask in a group context really matter because they will affect the responses you get.

And as you know, it isn't easy to ask good questions when you're working with a group. Of course, there's no such thing as the right question; it's just that some questions work better than others. For example, if we were to ask you, 'Are you enjoying reading this book?' you can see our premise is that you are. This is called a *leading question* because it leads you to answer it in a particular way. What's not helpful is that your answer might be false or at least slanted; common politeness could mean you just wouldn't say 'no,' especially if we've only just met.

If we really wanted a genuine answer to what you think about this book, we should ask you, 'What do you think of this book so far?' This is a simple *open question* as opposed to a closed one. And open questions are really great tools to work with in meetings and workshops.

Open questions aren't better than closed ones. They simply serve different purposes.

Closed questions

Closed questions lead to yes or no answers and feel safe to use because you stay in control of a conversation; there's no risk of someone else taking it over. So in the context of group work, closed questions are really useful to check data as they provide quick and easy answers, especially if you want to check

- Understanding
- Process
- Mind-set
- Energy or activity completion

Table 4-1 lists a few example questions for you.

Table 4-1 Examples of Closed Questions

Purpose	*Examples*
Check understanding	Are you with me? Is that clear? Do you want me to say that again?
Check process	Have you understood? Do you want to start? Shall we stop?
Check mind-set	Are you happy to continue? Would you like to take a break? Are you uncomfortable with the process?
Check energy or activity completion	It seems to me energy is low. Is that the case? You've finished the task, haven't you? Let's stick with this. Is that okay with you?

You can see that the first word of the question that signals a closed question include words like are, is, do, have, shall and would.

If you look at the questions checking energy or activity completion in Table 4-1, you can see these are slightly different. Here you've got what are called *tag questions,* which involve making a statement and then encouraging everyone to agree by adding a couple of words. For example, 'You're going to read this whole book, aren't you?' If you're sure of your ground, use them to indicate you have noticed something and want the group to know it.

Closed questions are really useful for checking what's going on.

Open questions

Open questions are more likely to give you longer answers and can feel scary when you use them. That's because you hand control of a conversation to a speaker. And since you never quite know what anyone is going to say, that can feel uncomfortable, especially when you're new to group work. But open questions are a vital tool if you want to ensure real discussion and are a must for

- Developing a conversation
- Understanding any situation
- Exploring thoughts and feelings
- Problem-solving and creativity

Use open questions when you want to really understand and find out what's happening.

Table 4-2 lists a few example questions for you.

Table 4-2 Examples of Open Questions

Purpose	*Examples*
Develop a conversation	What do you think about this?
	How did that happen?
	Tell me more about what's behind what you just said.

Purpose	*Examples*
Understand a situation	Why is that so important? How might that have come about? Describe what led up to this.
Explore thoughts or feelings	What are you thinking about it? How are you feeling at this moment? Tell me why you're in this frame of mind.
Problem-solve	What might you do about that? How could that be approached? How could you fix this situation?

Open questions start with what, why, how, tell me and describe. What you're doing is finding out more and encouraging exploration. To do this, you will find that adding warmth and positivity helps the group, especially as they start to work together.

Probing questions

Use *probing questions* to help you find out more detail or get to the root of something. If you sense that there's more to something than you've been told, try these questions:

- What **specifically** is the real issue at play here?
- What **exactly** did you mean?
- How **precisely** did you get them to agree?

The key words that indicate you are probing are the ones in bold. You're not a prosecution lawyer, so you can soften these questions by adding phrases like

- I'm interested to understand. . . .
- Please can you tell us more about. . . .
- Can we take a quick dive into what you just said?

Reflective questions

Reflective questions ask your participants to examine what they think about something, analyse it and think it through before they answer you.

You need reflective questions especially when you are asking participants for their expectations. For example:

- What do you want to have achieved by the end of this session?
- What would you like to do differently?
- If you had an answer, what would it be?

Hypothetical questions

A *hypothetical question* is really useful if you want your group to explore possibilities and approach something differently. Telling the group to 'think out of the box' never works, mostly because none of us can actually see our boxes in the first place. Instead, try a hypothetical question or two. Don't go overboard with them as they can get irritating.

Hypothetical questions are also extremely useful if someone makes a wacky suggestion, and you don't want to say to them, 'Frankly, I think that's nuts.'

Examples of hypothetical questions include

- If you could get radically better at this, what would the implications be?
- What if you were to go down that path. Where might it lead?
- How might Bill Gates/Mother Theresa/Nelson Mandela approach this?

Hypothetical questions simply encourage people to take a different perspective on an issue.

Neutral questions

If you really want to find out an individual or a group's point of view, you need to create a safe space for everyone to speak in that will encourage them to talk. That means avoiding making judgments or pointed comments about what they think, regardless of your opinion. That means keeping the language of your questions neutral.

Here are two examples:

- **Don't ask,** 'What on earth led you all to do that?'
- **Do ask,** 'I'm curious about why you all decided this was the best course of action.'

- **Don't ask,** 'In what way did you think it would help anyone?'
- **Do ask,** 'What was the positive outcome you were hoping for?

Scaling questions

Scaling questions help you gauge the feelings participants have for any activity before, during or after it. They are particularly useful once a group has concluded some work. That's when you ask

- On a scale of 1–10, 1 being very weak and 10 being fantastic), how do you feel about this result?
- On a scale of 1–10, how much would you like to extend this session?
- On a scale of 1–10, how keen are you to proceed?

Note that if your participants give you only a 6 or 7, ask them what it would take to move that score up a point or two. There may be nothing you can do, but you should at least find out because 6 isn't a brilliant result.

Testing yourself

If you want to check how good your questioning technique is, see if you can turn these negative closed questions into more neutral or positive open ones. If you find it hard, it's just because you're not used to using open questions. And that tells you that you need to practise some more.

Here are some questions to practise changing from closed to open:

- Is Harry going to be late again?
- Have you done it yet?
- Did he react negatively to what you said?
- Did you drop the ball on that one?
- Shall we stop now?
- Have you understood the implications?
- Are you fed up?
- Do you really want to go there?

You can download some suggested answers by going to `www.dummies.com/go/greatmeetingsworkshops`.

The tone of voice you use when asking a question makes a big difference. The most benign question sounds like a judgement if asked critically. A tough question can be heard as a softer one, if asked in a softer curious tone. Watch others to see how this works in practise.

Because questioning is such a fundamental facilitation skill, practise it as much as you can before your session. This includes

- At meetings
- On the phone
- In interactions with colleagues
- With family at home
- Out socialising with friends

Becoming skilled at asking good questions is something that will help you in all areas of your life, so it's really worth getting good at it.

Listening to others and the overall conversation in play

At a literal level, listening to others is about receiving information, extracting meaning from it and responding to it. You've been doing that since the day you were born. Literally. Because listening is the first thing you do as you learn to speak.

Interestingly, listening is the communication skill you use the most, but are taught the least. The result is that is we're often not mindful about how we really listen, and we believe that we are fully engaged when we're not.

That's because there are so many barriers to really tuning into someone else and a group. To name a few:

- **Poor habits:** We're just not used to listening well.
- **Physiology:** We're tired, hungry, frustrated or plain grumpy.
- **Pride:** We think we know better.
- **Assumptions:** We think we know what the speaker is going to say.

- **Close-mindedness:** We don't like someone or their subject.
- **Defensiveness:** We protect our egos from anything damaging and some messages we just don't want to hear.
- **Boredom:** We find the topic not in tune with our taste or interest.
- **Culture:** We don't like the way something's articulated; often more words result in less listening.
- **Distractions:** We love our phones, our tablets and our gadgets!

This is quite a list. And it tells you that it's much easier *not* to listen than to give anyone your full attention.

But listening isn't, well, just about listening. If you're listening, first of all you don't interrupt others. People who are more powerful tend to talk over colleagues, but if this is something you habitually do (and you know who you are), then it's time to practise simply shutting up. No one likes attending a session run by someone who loves the sound of their own voice. It's not a meeting you're holding, but a monologue.

Instead, you need to start focusing on hearing what's been said. As you'll know from your experience, most of us hold very little information in our heads. What's worse is that we're often distracted from the stuff we're trying to focus on as our own thoughts continuously bubble up. So although we might be listening, we've stopped really *hearing* what's being said.

On top of that, we filter what we do hear through our experience, culture, environment, education and preconceptions, so we often hear things as we would like them to be, not as they actually are. All of this gets in the way of working with others in the context of a meeting or workshop.

And that's not to mention the impact that poor listening has on your participants.

We know from our research that being listened to is closely correlated with feeling happy at work. The catch is that listening intently is not just tough. Frankly, it's exhausting; giving someone a good listening to takes a huge amount of energy and focus. That said, if you're going to ask great questions, you'd better be prepared to listen to the answers.

Well before you run your session, work out what stops you from listening, the risk of that happening during your meeting or workshop and then how you will manage it. The exercise in Table 4-3 can help you do this. If anything scores 6 or under as you think it through, please think carefully about what you'll do. You need to stay as connected as you can with everyone in the room. And that means managing yourself.

Table 4-3 Managing My Barriers to Listening

Times When I Don't Listen	*Risk of This Happening at My Event? (1–10 Scale)*	*How I'll Manage Myself*
I find it difficult to listen to someone talking about. . . .		
I get irritated by speakers who. . . .		
As a listener, I switch off when. . . .		
When I'm listening to someone speaking, I find myself spending most of the time. . . .		
I am easily distracted when. . . .		

Once you have identified the key triggers that prevent you from listening really well, plan what you'll do, identify the times you can practise prior to your workshop and think about the level of listening you want to get to.

Recognising the levels of listening

So what does the research say about listening? Last time we looked at theories of listening, there were dozens to choose from. Any angle you like, you'll probably find. If you're more keen on the practitioner angle, here's our model of listening that we've found practical and easy to use.

We reckon there are four levels of listening.

Level 1: Listening to yourself

When you are at level 1, most of your attention is focused on your own internal voice and thoughts. In other words, your listening spotlight is shining almost 100 per cent internally. This is the state we're often in when we fail to listen to others.

If you want to go up a level, you need to become aware of what happens when you go internal, why and when. The exercise in Table 4-2 can help you. At this level, you are not ready to work with a group or even be a participant yourself.

Level 2: Active listening

Active listening is characterised by

- Asking **questions** of others.
- Being able **to summarise** back to them what they have said.

When you do this, your main focus is on the words that others say. At this point, your attention spotlight is starting to become more externally than internally focused. The result is that you are able to check your understanding because you can reflect back the essence of a verbal message.

This is the most basic level of listening you need to have if you're working with a group of people, and it's what inexperienced facilitators tend to focus on because they are more worried about content and process rather than people.

Level 3: Active listening+

Active listening + includes an ability to

- Watch others' **body language.**
- Notice very **specific words** they say and the **intentions** behind those words.
- Observe everyone's **tone of voice.**
- Track **interactions** between people.
- See **who says what** and who doesn't.
- Know **who's with you** and who isn't even if they aren't speaking.

At this point, you are much less focused on your inner spotlight because your attention and energy are so much more externally focused. When you lead groups, you should aim to get to this point fast. You can do this if you spend time after each group interaction assessing your levels of listening.

Level 4: Deep listening

Deep listening takes time to develop, but when you are really skilled at working with a group, it will come easily to you. It involves

- **Having speedy awareness of interpersonal dynamics:** You know what's going on for the individual and the group really fast because you are so good at reading the overt and covert signals people send each other. Reading a room fast means you can quickly work out what's happening and what to do with it. (See Chapter 7 for more on dealing with difficult behaviour.)
- **Having great judgement:** Because you can read a room so skillfully, you know how to judge activities and energy really well. Most of all, you understand when to let the group work something through without interfering.
- **Working with hunches and feelings:** You are prepared to take risks and try something out you may not have done before. Because you are grounded in yourself, you know when to put your feelings on the table. You are aware that doing this helps the group move forward. At this level, you know that if you're experiencing a strong feeling, others will be, too.
- **Tuning into your gut:** When you get personal ah-ha moments with the group (and you become aware of your spotlight), you are ready to share them if, and only if, you think it's appropriate. You always use these insights for the benefit of the participants.
- **Understanding the people and the process:** Because you are listening at this level, you know exactly how individuals within your group are feeling and you are acutely aware of where they and you are in the process, too.

At level 4, you are listening to all internal and external information to help the group. This is true mastery. Figure 4-1 gives you a visual that will help you understand the concept of your attention spotlight and levels of listening.

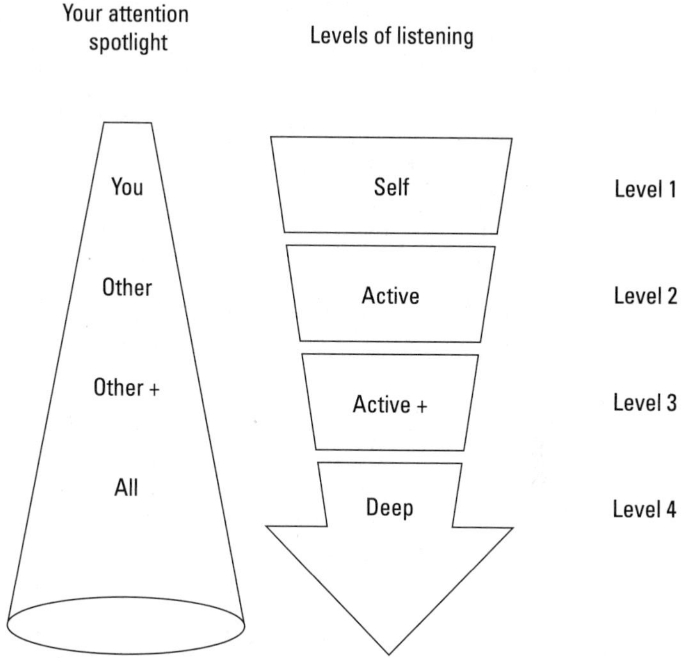

Figure 4-1: Attention and the levels of listening.

You'll be greatly helped with your listening skills if you combine them with your observing skills, too.

Observing others

When you are leading a meeting or a workshop, you not only have to pay attention to the process and what's happening in the room but also to additional signals you are getting. Those glances you and others get – the rolling eyes, the big sigh, the person who won't meet your gaze – are all really useful stuff that you may or may not need to act on. That means paying attention to body language, facial expressions, energy and voice.

Body language

Body language can tell you a great deal about other people's state of mind – or it can be totally misleading. To get better at reading others before your event, start wondering about how someone might be feeling and then test your guess-work out by asking a few questions. Next time you are with a group of people at work, watch out for individuals who are

- **Leaning forward or writing things down:** You can probably assume that they are engaged.
- **Sitting slumped back in their seats or leaning back with their hands folded behind their heads:** What message do you think they are trying to convey?
- **Shifting uncomfortably:** Why might that be?
- **Hunched over their smart phones:** Why has this taken precedence?
- **Avoiding eye contact:** What might they be feeling?
- **Fiddling or doodling:** This might not be because they are bored. How can you tell?
- **Nodding as others say things or covering their mouths in some way:** To what extent are they really listening?

This will help you grow your awareness of what's happening to an individual and to a group. If everyone's displaying disengaged body language, it's time to do something different. If everyone looks engaged, keep going!

Just remember that body language is part of an overall communication package and to read it well, you need to combine what you see with what you hear. For example, if someone says, 'Gosh, I'm interested,' but everything else tells you he isn't, they probably need to be asked a probing question or two to find out what's really going on.

You'll also need to think about your own body language as you get ready to work with your group. *Tells* are our personal indicators that, amongst others, we are experiencing a stressful situation. When we're nervous, we all have some special tells that can include

- Standing with crossed legs
- Standing with folded arms
- Clutching one arm
- 'Washing' our hands
- Tucking hair behind an ear repeatedly

- Fiddling with a pen
- Scratching or touching our heads or faces
- Jiggling a leg

The last thing you want to do is make others aware of your nerves and make them feel uncertain about what you're doing as a result. So if you don't know what you do when you're feeling uncomfortable or under pressure, start to pay attention. This is the stuff you're going to have to do your best to control when you're leading the room.

And just remember that practising positive body language will help you especially if you

- **Use your hands** as this will automatically bring more modulation to your voice. Your hands will help underline and emphasise a verbal message and help with energy and enthusiasm.
- **Smile and use open body language.** This will help the group relax as everyone feels your warmth.
- **Stand tall or sit up straight** as this shows you are confident in what you do. Remember that your breastbone should be tilted up, not down, as this helps posture. Try this in a mirror to see what we mean.
- **Give lots of eye contact,** especially to people who might make you nervous. You need to check in with them to see how they are doing just as much as everyone else.
- **Relax your hands, shoulders and jaw.** Shake out your hands to get rid of tension, so it doesn't travel up to your shoulders; you want them relaxed, so you don't get headaches. Massage your jaw to take tension away and then roll your shoulders forward and back to make sure you are as relaxed as possible.

If you practise this as you prepare, you'll really help yourself on the day because you'll have reinforced these techniques beforehand.

Facial expressions

Facial expressions matter because we tend to react to what we read in others. So if you scowl at someone in a meeting or workshop because you don't like what they are doing, in all probability, they would notice this and might ask you what was wrong or make a change in some way.

Reading body language

A few years ago, I (Jess) was standing in my daughter's primary school reading the school notice board. I was looking for a kitten to buy and was quickly scanning the board before heading into work. As I was standing there with my thumbs hooked into my belt, the headmistress, who I hadn't noticed, approached me and said, 'What are you feeling so aggressive about?'

Not surprisingly, I was really taken aback. I'd been day-dreaming about finding the ideal black kitten and had images of a purring little thing in my lap, so I asked the headmistress what had given her that impression.

She replied that she'd been on a body-language course that week and been told that standing with your thumbs hooked into your belt was a sign of aggression. I said that it was fine to have an assumption, but that before she decided that this was the gospel truth, could she please test it out first. I simply had no pockets, and that's where I usually stuff my hands!

We tend to make our facial expressions really clear at critical social moments. So we smile when we meet someone new and shake their hands. And we look shocked or surprised when we get difficult or amazing new information.

There is an important caveat.

What you read on someone's face may not be what they are genuinely feeling, perhaps because they don't want you to know or because they come from a different culture. In other words, don't make too many assumptions. When you do, please test them out.

One place you can get more genuine information is through reading people's eyes, which is why eye contact is so important. Eye contact helps you

- **Take turns in conversation:** You know when to start and stop by looking at someone.
- **Know if someone likes you:** It's hard to look at people you don't like.
- **Show interest or involvement:** If you're bored, your eyes glaze over, and your eyes become less focused.

In Western cultures, if we don't get eye contact from someone, we automatically think they don't like us, or they are rude, disengaged or tired. But too much eye contact without glancing away from time to time can feel patronising or aggressive. So aim to look at a speaker or listeners about 80 per cent of the time in the context of running a meeting or workshop.

So what can you interpret through eye contact? If people are interested in what you say, their pupils widen. When they are bored, their pupils contract. So before your session, try asking a few friends about things they love. Then ask them about their tax return and just watch what happens to their pupils. Getting good at reading interest and disinterest before your session will help you maintain momentum in your session.

Finally, the surprising thing about eye contact in a meeting or workshop is that, because you have so many things to think about and do, it can take quite a lot of your focus and personal energy to maintain.

Energy

If you can observe your participants in action in other settings, that's great; you'll get a feel for who they are and their energy levels. Mostly that's not possible, so instead, start to pay attention to what high energy expressive people do and to what low energy expressive people do. Table 4-4 shows you what to look out for.

Table 4-4 Observing the Energies of Others

High Energy Expressive Tendencies	*Lower Energy Expressive Tendencies*
Larger and more gestures	Smaller and fewer gestures
Louder	Quieter
More interruptions	Fewer interruptions
More likely to take the lead in group work	Less likely to take the lead in small group activity
Focused on contributing at all times	Focused in high-value contributions
Happy to be a spokesperson	Reserved when a spokesperson
Vocal	Thoughtful
More modulation in their voices	Less modulation in their voices

If you happen to have a majority of low energy expressive people and you're the opposite, it can feel quite draining and can sometimes bring the atmosphere down for the higher energy expressive people in the room.

On the other hand, if you are a lower energy expressive person, you'll need to cater for your opposites by having enough activities that involve pairs, small groups and working at flip charts so that you feed others' energy levels appropriately.

Voice

Your voice is affected by

- **Learned patterns of speech:** These are influenced by education, culture, context, accents and practise.
- **Pace:** The speed at which you speak affects how much others listen. Faster speech indicates energy and enthusiasm; slower reveals you're more serious.
- **Modulation:** This means the general up-and-down of your voice or the music of the words you say. It's really dull listening to someone who speaks in a monotone. It's more interesting listening to a well-modulated voice.
- **Emphasis:** Emphasis helps with modulation. It's about picking key words in a sentence and saying them with punch. Try saying the previous sentence aloud both with and without punch, and you'll understand what we mean.
- **Articulation:** Articulation means how well you say your words. Mumbling doesn't help with understanding, especially if you are working with people whose first language isn't English.
- **Intention:** If you want to be warm, you'll set out to smile more, which will make your tone sound warmer. Positive emotions are catching, and if you are intentionally positive, your group is more likely to be, too. Of course, this is particularly important if you are managing a remote meeting or workshop.

Getting into some more detail about your voice, your tone or the quality of your voice is affected by your

- **Natural pitch:** Pitch refers to whether you have a high or low voice. Recent research indicates that people tend to prefer and give more authority to lower voices.

- **Resonance:** This is about the richness of the sound you make. The more resonant the voice, the easier it is to pay attention. Voices tend to be more resonant when they are low.
- **Breathiness:** Some people just have breathy voices, but breathiness can also indicate nerves.

In physiological terms, your tone is controlled by the diaphragm, the intercostal muscles between the ribs and the muscles in your throat. Tone can tell you a number of things about others' state of mind, in particular their emotions and mood because it's so affected by context and nerves.

You can use your tone of voice to show intent really effectively – for example, when you want to be sarcastic, funny, dominant or submissive. We all change our tone when we're speaking to people of higher – and lower status; just think about how you talk to a baby and then a boss. Lower tones are associated with authority and truth. When Mrs. Thatcher became British Prime Minister, she had a lot of voice training to lower her tone – so to speak. Higher tones are associated with nerves, pressure and requests.

We use softer tones when we want to be friendly, a rising tone to ask questions and a higher tone when we're under pressure. That is especially noticeable in first meetings when nerves can make us speak higher and faster. Think dating if you don't believe us.

What does all of this mean? Well, when you are leading a meeting or workshop, it's important that you pay attention to others' tone of voice to diagnose what's happening for them, and manage your own tone of voice to help influence the group.

If you want to get better at managing your voice tone, try

- **Singing in the shower** to find out how high and how low you can go.
- **Recording yourself** and listening to what you say when you're under pressure. You can simply do this with a smart phone.
- **Asking for feedback on your tone.** Use the checklist in this chapter and get a friend or colleague to score you from 1–10 on each of them.
- **Humming to build resonance.** Try extending the time you can hum for.

- **Breathing exercises.** Great breathing helps with tone as any singer will tell you, and that means practising. If you want to download a breathing exercise, visit `www.dummies.com/go/rungreatmeetingsworkshops`.

As part of your preparation:

- Start to see what you like and dislike in others' vocal tone, remembering that we like others who are like us.
- Think about what you'd like to do more of and less of with your voice and experiment with it when you rehearse what you're going to say.

Understanding Groups

People love to join groups and be part of them for three main reasons:

- To build close relationships
- To belong to something bigger than themselves
- To get stuff done successfully

That means they have personal aspirations tied up in the group's success. And the implications of this is that you have to be really alive and alert to what's happening for the individuals, to individuals as part of the group and the group as a whole.

No pressure there then.

The real issue is that, at first glance, it's complex stuff and occasionally baffling into the bargain. For example, we've run the same session in an identical way in the same organisation on the same day and got different results. That's because of what goes on inside a group and the interactions that happen between a bunch of people who are put into a group setting.

So if the very idea of leading group-work is making your stomach lurch, here's some stuff you need to know and that you can develop before you go live on the day. And it's where you can really put your listening and observing skills to good use to watch out for:

- What the group's norms are
- How the group communicates

- How decisions are made
- Whether the group is doing real work
- How well the group is gelling
- What your role is in all of this

Working on understanding these before you lead your meeting or workshop will mean that you are much more aware of what's happening amongst a group you are facilitating.

Understanding group norms

All groups have norms, which are the spoken or unspoken rules about what is and what isn't acceptable behavior when everyone gets together. Common norms include

- Not interrupting each other in meetings
- Making sure everyone can speak freely
- Avoiding talking about feelings, dealing with conflict or addressing difficult topics
- Sticking to an agenda or simply freewheeling

Here are some things to think about that will help you identify the norms as you start to listen and observe groups at work prior to running your event:

- What are the norms for this group?
- How well does everyone understand them?
- How well are they enforced both verbally and nonverbally?
- Who breaks the norms?
- How much power do norm breakers have in this group?
- How do the norms help or hinder the group?

Two typical problems that affect norms are

- No one really knows that they are.
- No one takes responsibility for enforcing them.

As you look through the rest of this section, keep in mind that everything referred to will be affected by norms, starting with how the group communicates.

Communicating in a group

Communication in groups happens at two levels:

- What's going on above the surface and is very visible to everyone
- What's going on below the surface and which is less visible to you and potentially to the group, too

The more you tune into what's happening above and below the surface, the better you'll be able to work with the group. As part of your preparation, start to notice

- Who talks most and least?
- What's said and what's not said?
- Who interrupts whom?
- Who brings up difficult topics or avoids them?
- What happens as a result?
- What impact does individual power and influence have on the group?

Because lots of communication is driven by norms, you may have to develop new norms with a mature group if you're going to achieve your objectives. And if you're working with a new group, then you'll need to help establish those communication norms by quickly setting ground rules. (See Chapter 5 for how to do this.)

Two typical problems that affect communication are:

- Everyone talks, but no one does anything.
- There are silent but deadly participants.

Decision-making

Some strong characters can both hog the limelight, try to make the group do what they want and drive all decisions. Other people spend a lot of time trying to always achieve consensus. Ideally, they use a mix of approaches because there isn't a one-size-fits-all way of making decisions.

Meanwhile while you're getting up to speed on how groups work, here's what to look out for in terms of decision-making:

- How clear are the rules for decision-making for this particular team or group?
- Who tries to drive decisions without getting group buy-in?
- How long do decisions take? If they feel painfully long, could the process be quicker?
- How do they work with process?
- Who brings everyone back on track?
- How do they support each other's suggestions or decisions?

See Chapter 9 for more on helping groups with decision-making.

Two typical problems that affect decision-making are

- Decisions get constantly revisited.
- Nothing is ever decided!

Surfacing issues and concerns

Lots of groups appear to be doing good work on the surface. But then you discover that underneath that they are skating around on presenting issues rather than root causes. This happens for a number of reasons:

- Issues haven't been well-defined or well-articulated.
- No one recognises that deeper issues are at stake.
- A minority group or someone less powerful is raising the issue or concern.
- The group is immature or hasn't learned to work together, so it doesn't know how to deal with it.
- There are assumptions flying about that the issue isn't important.

When this happens, you can guarantee that at some point the group will experience frustration at best and conflict at worst. In other words, the group needs to take the time to investigate the issue and do some good and honest work together. So here's what you need to look out for:

- How insightful is this particular group about what it is doing?
- What assumptions is the group making that may need challenging?

- How does the group put tough issues on the table and then address them?
- Who says, 'I have a major concern or worry?' How is that individual then heard?
- How safe and comfortable does this environment feel so that everyone can really speak up?

Two typical problems that affect whether issues and concerns are surfaced are

- Tasks are always prioritised over people.
- People feel shy to call a spade a spade and then go digging!

Doing real work

When issues are surfaced and concerns addressed, groups have a better chance of doing real work and making significant progress. When that happens, it's a delight.

But sometimes you can think real work is taking place when it isn't. What you've got is surface work dressed up as real work or a few dedicated individuals carrying the load.

Real work takes emotional investment and means everyone takes part at all times. To understand whether real work is happening in a group, take a look at

- How committed is everyone to investigating and solving their problems?
- Who holds back?
- What real insights or breakthroughs does the group achieve?
- Where is the group getting stuck and unstuck?
- How do group members talk about feelings?
- How energised overall does this group feel?

Two typical common problems that affect doing real work are

- Lack of motivation.
- Group buy-in isn't addressed.

Assessing the gel factor

When a new group of people comes together or meets to do things in a different way, everyone has to learn to work together in another capacity. When group members gel well, it's a sign that there's a high level of trust, that individuals can take a risk with thoughts and feelings, and that it's safe to talk freely. It's fantastic working with a group that's gelled well because they achieve such a lot.

To really understand how well a group has gelled, notice

- How formal or careful is everyone being?
- What level of real work is being done?
- How much humour is at play?
- What appetite and energy does everyone have for group tasks?
- Who is helping whom with what?
- What level of challenge and support do group members show each other?

Typical problems that affect groups gelling are

- Other more pressing stuff to deal with.
- There isn't real work for everyone to do

In your preparation period, notice the differences between groups and teams that have gelled well and those that haven't. What do you think makes the difference? This will help build your self-awareness.

If you'd like to know more about how to deal with all these difficult people and situations, turn to Chapter 8.

Building self-awareness

You can help prepare to lead group work by growing your awareness of the perspectives, judgements, beliefs and biases you have on the topics and group you'll be dealing with. You need to do this because whatever negativity you have, it's bound to affect the work you're planning. In other words, if you're blonde and have an aversion to blonde jokes, someone will be sure to tell one.

In the same way, if you have a belief that a group or an individual will be difficult, he will be. What you do is create a self-fulfilling prophecy, which means that you'll tend to see behavior through a certain lens. Remember one of the things you are aiming for is to be in a neutral position so that others can take positions while you guide the process.

To check your self-awareness about the group and topics you'll be leading, ask yourself

- What do I think about this group or individuals within it?
- How do I feel about the topics I am working with?
- How will I manage my personal beliefs in the context of the session I am managing?
- How will I put my professional beliefs to one side to work best with this group?
- What will I do if my thoughts and feelings get the better of me?
- Who might put me off, and how will I manage this?

Typical common problems that affect self-awareness are that

- You aren't aware of your own relevant beliefs and judgements.
- You fail to notice how this affects the group.

If you really start to notice what happens in other teams and groups before you deliver your session, you'll quickly recognise what good and bad looks like. That way, you can start to visualise how you'd like your day to run. Doing this will also make your practise easier because you'll already have been thinking through how you would like to position things. And, of course, this will also help you write your agenda or your running order. (Refer to Chapter 3 for more information about this.)

Practising What You'll Say

If you're leading a workshop, you've got your running order written, which will help guide you through what you want to say.

If you're managing a meeting or think you might forget something important, you'll need to make notes for key things you want to say. Don't write these notes out longhand, (you're not making a speech), but do think about using cue cards instead with key words and phrases on them.

Rehearsing

Then it's a question of finding a quiet space and like an actor, practising what you're going to say, so the difficult bits are on the tip of your tongue. We think that practising three times is about right to embed the process and an approximate form of words.

Please don't use your running order like a script. It isn't a script. The danger of learning a script is that you

- Forget what you want to say and have to rustle through a huge sheaf of notes.
- Get flummoxed when conversation takes an interesting and valuable diversion because you find it hard to know or remember where you were.
- Focus on delivery at the expense of the conversations, which is where everyone gets real value.

Instead, imagine the group in front of you and say what you are going to say out loud. Rehearsing in your head alone isn't enough and means you are more likely to forget key parts of the process. But, by all means, do this as part of a deliberate visualisation process.

Rehearsing what to say

I (Julia) was recently asked to observe a trainer and review her delivery. As she had ten years of experience and knew her stuff, I was looking forward to spending the morning with her.

Imagine my surprise when I saw that she didn't ask the group for their expectations; she didn't seem to know what activity was coming next; her instructions were unclear; and her feedback to the group on tasks it did was really weak. For example, she said to one person that what he did 'was nice.'

During the lunch break, I asked her how she prepared for her workshop, and she told me that she made a mind-map and ran things through in her head. I asked if she ever prepared by saying things aloud, already knowing that her answer would be no.

Real preparation means saying aloud what you're going to say in the room and doing that more than once.

Visualising your session

Visualisation is a fantastic tool that can help you think through what you'll be doing and how you'll come over especially in the difficult bits. These tricky times include

- Managing your opening
- Setting the context
- Clarifying expectations
- Giving instructions
- Explaining anything difficult or emotional
- Debriefing a task or exercise

To really visualise your session, think about how you'd like to come over. Start by deciding on three attributes you would like your group to see in you. For example, you might select warm, professional and fluent. These will determine how you want to behave.

Ensuring that you are warm, professional and fluent, play out a tricky scene in three different ways:

- **Being yourself** and imagining looking at participants through your own eyes.
- **Being a participant** and seeing yourself doing your delivery.
- **Being a third wise person** observing you in the room working with the group.

As you do this exercise, ask yourself

- What else do I need to do to ensure I am warm, professional and fluent?
- What else might participants need from me to ensure I am warm, professional and fluent?
- What else is the third wise person telling me to do to ensure I am warm, professional and fluent?

Now just run through it all one more time, visualising it going as well as it possibly could.

This will give you the confidence to know you have prepared everything to the best of your ability. Now you're good to go!

Part II

Running Great Group Sessions

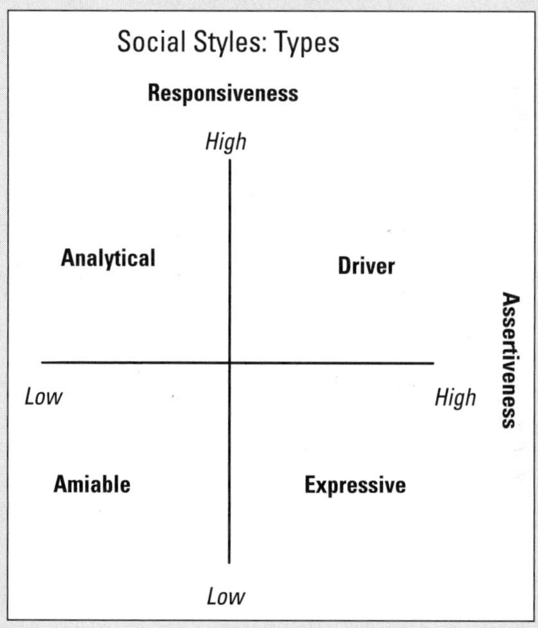

Find more tips about running great group sessions at www.dummies.com/extras/rungreatmeetingsworkshops.

In this part . . .

- Get your meeting or workshop off to a great start.
- Stay on the right track during the course of your meeting or workshop.
- Know what to do when things go wrong.
- Touch base with your attendees after the big event.

Chapter 5

Handling the Start of Your Session

In This Chapter

- Managing yourself
- Kicking the session off
- Making decisions
- Understanding who's in your room

The day of your meeting or workshop has dawned.

By meeting day, you'll have put in so much thought and preparation that you should be looking forward to getting going, even if you are feeling a little nervous.

What really matters in the hour or two before you start is that you manage yourself as well as you can in the moments leading up to your kick-off. That's because a great start is much more likely to lead to your overall success. A shambolic beginning is much harder to overcome and means you have to work more than twice as hard to overcome any negative impressions.

Now research differs in how long you have to make that great first impression, but it's anywhere between three seconds to three minutes. So as soon as they see you in your room, your participants will be thinking, 'Is she in control?' 'Does he know what he's doing?' 'Do I like her?' 'Do I trust him to lead this process?'

Getting off to a great start means you have to be as planned, organised and managed as you can be and ready to manage the people who turn up in your room.

This chapter helps you do just that.

Managing Yourself

Starting with the right personal energy is key, and everything else flows from there. That means taking yourself seriously by going to bed early. Then you'll feel refreshed enough to be running on more than just adrenaline. You can be absolutely sure that you'll wake up, your stomach will loop-the-loop and you'll get a surge of energy. You should welcome this energy because it gives you the wherewithal to perform at your best. It's hard to be sharp without adrenaline, and feeling it tells you that you care about what's going to happen.

To manage an adrenaline rush well and not let it overpower you, just remember that nerves and excitement produce a similar sensation. So say to yourself, 'I'm excited about today' rather than 'I'm nervous.' Mind and body are so tightly connected that thinking about nerves will just increase those butterflies in your stomach and build even more negative energy. Thinking about excitement will help you find a more positive mental attitude and help you stay in control.

If you combine this positive mindset with your new breathing techniques, you'll give yourself every chance of staying really focused and grounded (see Chapter 4).

You can also try a technique from sports psychology. Research in this field shows that a motivational inner voice that says, 'You can do it!' works much better than an instructional inner voice. That bossy instructional inner voice says things like 'Remember to stick to the agenda,' but it doesn't work as effectively in terms of results. Find a personal mini pep phrase and then use it.

Wearing the right clothes

We've all turned up at a party in the wrong clothes and know how uncomfortable this feels. So think through what you want to wear on the big day well before it happens. The secret is loose and comfortable.

Table 5-1 describes what not to wear and why.

Table 5-1 What Not to Wear and Why

Item	*Why*
Pale blue shirts	Show serious sweat patches. Stick to white instead.
Un-ironed clothes	Appear sloppy and as if you don't take yourself seriously.
Sleeveless tops	Remember that armpits aren't pretty for most people and are offensive to some.
High heels	Bear in mind that you'll be on your feet all day. Sore heels and toes are distracting.
Casual wear (T-shirts and trainers)	Look as if you can't be bothered to think about your presence in the room.
Visible underwear	Undermines your credibility and authority.
Short skirts	See yourself bending over and think about how that might challenge you or the group.
Really formal wear	May be harder to have different or difficult conversations while in a jacket and tie.
Loud clothes, big jewellery or too much flesh	Are just distracting and may create the wrong impression.

Of course, if these items are all fine for you or the culture of the organisation you are working in, then you can ignore all this advice. But the reason you need to think about clothes is that you don't want to put any additional barriers in your way. It's tough enough as it is.

If you are worried about getting it right, here's what you can do. First, dress more formally than informally; you can always remove a jacket or tie, but you can't upgrade on the spot. Second, notice the dress code of others as you plan your session. Then you'll know if you need to arrive suited and booted or in a jacket and open shirt.

Checking your materials

If you're going to run meetings or workshops regularly, it's worth putting together a kit-bag that includes

- Chisel-headed marker pens for you and your group
- Blu-tack or tape that doesn't damage walls
- Sticky notes
- Pens for participants to make notes
- An extension cable for your laptop and some tape to stick it down so you don't trip over it
- Mini speakers for any videos you want to show
- A memory stick with any presentations or videos
- One set of all the materials you are going to need

Preparing a kit-bag means you'll have everything you need to run your event just in case materials are lost, not ready or haven't arrived. Make sure it's ready the day before so you can focus on more important stuff.

Eating the right food and drinking the right drink

Whether you're leading your session in the morning, afternoon or evening, you need to have fuelled up, so have a light meal before you start. Rich and heavy food can make you feel sick and tired – quite literally – while sugar might give you a quick boost, but won't carry you through a longer working session. If you simply can't eat beforehand, take fresh or dried fruit and nuts with you. As you relax into your session, you'll get hungry and be glad you have them.

Please don't be tempted to drink a lot of coffee or have a couple of sodas. Caffeine on top of adrenaline won't help you think clearly. Your heart rate will speed up, and it becomes harder to stay cool, calm and collected.

There's another reason to avoid caffeinated drinks. It's thirsty work being in charge of a room, managing yourself and everyone else. That means you'll need to drink more water than you usually would for your voice to remain strong. Drink a glass of water well before you start and have some to hand as you begin, and then your voice won't sound sticky after half an hour.

You'll also find that you'll be really hungry shortly after you end when your adrenaline levels start to return to normal. That's when you'll be pleased you have some healthy snacks, and it will stop you falling into another sugar and coffee trap.

Getting there early

Remember that your performance begins from the first minute you arrive on site and ends only when you leave. Most people think that the start is when their first participant enters the room. Wrong. Reputations are ruined beforehand by being rude to technicians trying to fix projectors, behaving coldly to administrative staff who can't find your stuff or speaking unguardedly on the phone. You are in full-on professional mode as you drive through the gates or walk through the door to sign in.

Setting up the room can be stressful so mentally prepare for that. We always allow an hour to get the room ready and plan for the first participants to arrive 15 minutes before your kick-off. Giving yourself this amount of time means that you can

- **Deal with any curved balls** like occupied or locked rooms as well as mislaid materials.
- **Set the room up as you want it,** move tables and chairs and make sure the room is clean and tidy. Even if you asked for a certain layout to tables and chairs, it often doesn't happen. Make sure you lay your materials out so that they look inviting.
- **Check your laptop or other audio-visual kit** to see that it works.
- **Ensure that additional materials are available;** for example, flip chart paper, sticky notes, pens and paper.
- **Liaise with catering** if you have ordered drinks and refreshments.

If you're ready 15 minutes before the meeting, you'll have the time to take a calm moment and visualise how your session will go.

Imagining yourself doing well

Once you've prepared the room, take a minute and a few deep breaths. Inhale and exhale deeply and see yourself leading a great process, being really fluent, answering all the questions, engaging with the group and doing a wonderful job. Imagine all the participants walking away saying, 'We had an excellent day, and this was a really good use of our time.' Psych yourself into this active and positive mindset for two to three minutes, and as you do so

- Feel yourself grow tall.
- Remind yourself that you are really prepared.
- Remember that what you're doing is important for this group right now.

Now you're ready to meet your first participants.

Meeting and greeting everyone

You're going to have to take your cue from everyone coming into your room here and try to be culturally appropriate. The options you have range from a polite nod as people walk through your door to hugs and kisses, even if you don't know your participants. All you need to do is respond warmly and without surprise to whatever you get.

If you've never met your participant, you need to

- **Stand** as each person comes into the room if you are sitting. It's the most polite and engaging thing to do.
- **Shake hands firmly or simply approach, smile and nod** (in the Middle East, for example, touch may not be acceptable).
- **Introduce yourself** with your name if you haven't met.
- **Repeat each person's name** as you meet, so you learn it; you'll learn it if you say it.
- **Invite this person** to get refreshments and find a seat.
- **Introduce the person** to anyone who arrives if this is easy for you to do.

It's always interesting to see who asks where to put their coats and bags. This is a signal to you that he or she is handing over responsibility to you. It's up to you to decide if you want to be directive or not. In the same way, when people ask you where they should sit, you can be specific – or not. This depends on the level of control you want to establish from the start.

If you are leading a regular meeting and everyone always sits in the same place, you might deliberately decide to mix it up a bit so that new relationships get formed. The easiest way to do this is to write all the names on folded A4 pieces of paper so that they can't be ignored. Or simply meet in a different room.

By the way, don't be surprised when the room or seating fills up from the back. This is usual, even if you lay out all the materials at the front! All you need to do is invite everyone to move closer to you as you start.

Kicking Off the Session

This is when your agenda (see Chapter 3) or running order (see Chapter 4) comes into play, and you'll go straight into doing an opening bang and adding something of value. We recommend doing this before you talk about the objective, your outcomes, your agenda items or any roles. That way, you immediately get everyone's attention.

Don't wait for late arrivals if you can possibly help it. If you wait until your latecomers get there, then you are punishing the people who arrive on time, and you are sending a message that you'll tolerate poor behaviour. Start on time.

When a late arrival turns up, get another participant to summarise what you have been doing or discussing. That way, you are getting the group to manage itself.

As you get going, you'll need to

- Create an open atmosphere
- Outline the agenda
- Clarify expectations

- Set up ground rules
- Allocate roles and responsibilities

But don't worry; it's all a step-by-step process that is pretty simple to follow.

Creating the atmosphere you want

If you've been warm and welcoming as everyone has come in, the chances are that you can just carry this over as you start to establish your relationship with the group.

As you take the stage to begin your session, you essentially have two options. You can create

- **A more formal start** where you stand and invite the group to begin work using more official language – for example, 'Shall we begin?' or 'Shall we start proceedings?'
- **A more informal start** where you sit down or lean on a wall and invite the group to start work. Then you'll use more colloquial language – for example, 'Let's go.'

Try not to mix up formal with informal or the group won't quite know how to read you or what to expect.

Opening your session

If the group doesn't know you at all, the best introduction is one done by someone else (for example, your sponsor). Whoever introduces you should explain

- Who you are
- Why he or she wanted you to run the session
- What your expertise or position is

It's much tougher for you to explain why you are so magnificent for the job.

By the way, even if you have the most expertise in the room, we think that it's better practise to acknowledge that everyone else's experience probably adds up to much more than yours in terms of years. Then say that what you are there to do is to help facilitate a conversation and that you are really looking forward to hearing what everyone else has to say.

Remind participants that they are likely to learn as much from the people sitting next to them as from you, which is why it would be helpful to participate fully in the day.

Explaining your role

At this point, you need to let everyone know what your role is and what you will be doing in terms of

- Guiding the process
- Giving instructions
- Explaining information
- Facilitating discussion
- Offering feedback
- Chairing the session
- Giving input into decisions
- Taking part in activities
- Handing over the chair from time to time
- Allocating roles and responsibilities to others

You need to let everyone know if you will be performing a variety of roles, so the group doesn't get confused about what you are doing. After you explain what you'll be doing, you then move into what you'll all do together.

Outlining the agenda

All your participants will have seen an agenda of sorts beforehand. That's because you'll either have sent it or some joining instructions out in advance. But the reason you want to run through it again is to briefly make clear

- **Why you are getting together** – the objective of your session.
- **What you are going to cover** – how you intend to meet that objective.

Once you have everyone agreeing to this skeleton form, then you have permission to go ahead and add flesh to the bones. But before you do that, you need to do your housekeeping.

Housekeeping

Your housekeeping involves

- Clarifying where exit routes are in case you need to evacuate the building or when alarm testing may happen.
- Pointing out where useful facilities are located.
- Explaining all your break timings and where refreshments are.
- Finding out any hard stops or phone calls that your participants have to stick to.

The benefit of doing this is twofold: Participants know when they can make calls and answer emails, and you show that you are aware of their needs and are attending to them. They'll feel this even more when you then clarify their expectations.

Clarifying expectations

Regardless of your session, you need to spend some time investigating your participants' expectations. That's because you can quite often get curved balls thrown at you about what others think you will and won't get done during your time together.

So even if you've articulated what you're going to do really well both on paper beforehand and out loud as you start, here are the two simplest options. Ask everyone what would have to happen to say that this get-together had been a fabulous use of their time and then do one of the following:

- **Ask everyone to say their answers out loud:** This option is fine for up to six or seven people. Make sure you write down what they say, so you can refer back to their expectations as you move through the session.
- **Get everyone to write down two to three concrete expectations or outcomes on a sticky note.** Do this option if you have more than seven participants. Otherwise, this five-minute activity will take way too long. You need to make sure that these expectations or outcomes are concrete and actionable; otherwise, you won't be able to deliver them. Table 5-2 illustrates this.

Table 5-2 Understanding Good and Bad Personal Expectations or Outcomes

Bad Personal Expectations/ Outcomes	*Good Personal Expectations/ Outcomes*
Review our strategy	Understand what we need to deliver to the business to meet our numbers over the next 18 months
Have difficult conversations	Learn and implement a framework and process for having regular difficult work conversations
Do better team work and have fun together	Establish team governance; clarify our working behaviors and procedures

You get from bad expectation to good expectation by asking probing questions, such as

- What precise outcomes do you want to have achieved as a result of reviewing the strategy?
- What deliverables must we have clarified by the end of the day?
- How will we know we have done this?
- What exactly do you mean when you say better team work?
- What do we need to achieve today to make that possible?

These are the kind of questions that will lead you to something concrete and solid that you can actually achieve.

Let's talk about fun. Because lots of participants talk about 'having fun.' As far as we're concerned, this is what we call a *tar baby.* It looks attractive to children on a beach, but, in fact, it's sticky and can only lead to a hideous mess if you hang on to it. In other words, 'fun' is a bad idea as an expectation. Not that we want to be killjoys, but here's why:

- **What's fun to you is probably dead dull for everyone else.** If you don't believe us, come over to try three hours of meditation, which is 'huge fun' to one of us or custard pie throwing – ditto.

- **Who owns the delivery of this fun?** If it lands on your shoulders and you're expected to provide it on top of everything else and at the last minute – well, good luck.

Don't get us wrong: We love fun. But right now, it's not part of what you're trying to do. Don't do it and do say that this is outside the scope of today's session. Save fun for the bar afterwards. If the group gets stuck in and knows how to help, everyone will enjoy what they are doing anyway.

Or try this. If someone asks for fun, get him to explain what this means, get the group to agree and then ask your funster to take ownership for it.

Allocating roles and responsibilities

We like to co-opt members of the group to work with us. That means asking members the following:

- Who can help with **timings** and give you checkpoints every hour?
- Who will help call **breaks** when energy gets low?
- Who will help **write** on flip charts?
- Who will **take notes** or type them if you need a record?

Doing this means that lots of people have an active role in the process, and it takes the pressure off you to do everything. And you'll find that your participants love being involved and contributing to the group's success.

There's one special role that needs more attention – that of a wingman.

Working with a wingman

A *wingman* is a pilot who flies behind and above the leader in a formation of planes. That means she can spot trouble as it happens and help the whole formation avoid it. A meeting or workshop wingman can help you do exactly the same because her role is to

- **Focus on what's happening with the group and the trajectory of the conversation.** She can give you a quick reality-check for what's happening and what else you might need to do.
- **Point out when you're going down a time-wasting rabbit hole** and get you back on track as the meeting happens.
- **Stop anyone running sub-meetings and side conversations.** Your wingman should help you shut these down.
- **Serve as temporary leader** if you want to take an active part in the discussion yourself and know you can't stay impartial, focused and tuned into everyone else.
- **Back you up when there are tricky issues.** Your wingman should be there for actual and moral support.

In other words, a wingman is a key person who can help you lead a great session because they keep a constant eye on what's happening. Just make sure that as part of your ground rules, all the participants know who your wingman is. That way, you are transparent about what you're doing.

Setting up ground rules or a code of conduct

Ground rules or a code of conduct are there to help you articulate how the group will work together and put boundaries around what is and isn't okay. The following sections cover some typical questions that ground rules or a code of conduct can help manage.

Standard ground rules

Standard ground rules include answers to

- How to deal with phones, tablets, laptops, timings and calls
- What active participation means
- When to raise issues, questions and concerns
- How to contribute to a conversation – in other words, no interrupting or talking over each other
- How to cascade any relevant information to others and how to support each other in the process
- How to manage confidentiality

Confidentiality can be a tricky one because quite often information needs to be cascaded out. What you don't want is that the details of a conversation are discussed outside in a 'you-won't-believe-what-she-said' manner. That's disrespectful and needs to be knocked on the head from the get-go.

So how do you enforce ground rules? Ideally, everyone assumes responsibility for them, though, if you like, you can decide on an enforcer or an MC. The point is that if you have thought through group norms and then don't stick to them when they are tested, there's no point having them in the first place. And you can pretty much guarantee that the most senior or influential person in the room will think that the rules don't apply to them.

When someone infringes your code of conduct, take this person to one side in a break and remind him that he signed up to it at the start. If it's the most senior person, remind him that you are looking to them to be a role model. And explain to any rule breaker that you are open to a renegotiation, but until that happens or there's an emergency, then the group's ground rules apply.

Ground rules for tougher stuff

If you want to ensure that tougher stuff is handled as effectively as possible, we recommend adding a pause, rewind and fast-forward button:

- **A pause button** helps the group take a break or a breather when things get tough. Anyone can call a pause on his own or another's behalf.
- **A rewind button** means that you can deal with any second thoughts or missed opportunities. You might want to limit these to one each, so you get work done.
- **A fast-forward button** means that anyone can suggest you speed stuff up and increase the pace at which you're going or drop a topic as it isn't useful.

Decision-Making

One important topic deserves its own section because it can be complicated. That's decision-making. How you're going to decide needs to be dealt with early on if your meeting or workshop is going to involve a tough or complicated decision.

Decisions can be difficult to make because they involve a final choice based on both rational and emotional information. And frequently, the consequences of those decisions aren't clear. But in a group setting, as time becomes more limited, pressure and tempers often rise. Being accountable for choices and responsible for their results isn't easy.

Don't be surprised if any group you work with gets heated around tough decisions. Something that will help both you and them get perspective is recognising what's happening and reflecting this back to the group.

Understanding the decision-making process

Making a decision involves the following steps:

1. **Sharing all the relevant information.**

   This step is ideally done before you all meet to save time.

2. **Disputing and testing the relative merits of the information the group has.**
3. **Getting to an emergent decision by clarifying what you can and can't agree on.**
4. **Consolidating final agreement so that the group can move forward.**
5. **Imagining explaining the decision to your stakeholders.**

   This helps get the group to test it from outsiders' viewpoints.

6. **Implementing the decision.**

   The group should decide what the immediate actions are to drive the decision forward.

A big risk that may face a group is believing that they don't have all the information they need to make a decision and therefore deferring it. There is *never* enough information to make a tough decision. If this is your group, challenge them on what 'enough' means. Wanting more information is a terrific Get-Out-Of-Jail-Free card that allows the group to do nothing.

Just remember when you're working with a group to arrive at a decision, you will really help when you

- Articulate where the group is in the decision-making process. This will mean that if it gets stuck somewhere, you can explain what's happening, so that everyone can move on.
- Explain that making a really quick decision may ultimately result in an agreement that is superficial, inferior or both.
- Point out that taking endless time to decide will reduce morale and increase frustration because everyone will feel a lack of progress.

Well before you even get to a decision, you and your group will need to decide how you're going to decide.

Understanding your decision-making options

Table 5-3 describes the six basic ways to make a decision. None of them are better than others; they each have their own use and context.

Table 5-3 Six Ways of Making Decisions

Method	*Process*	*Risks*	*Benefits*
Consensus	Talk until everyone agrees	Takes time; some people may not genuinely commit	Gets everyone engaged; leads to buy-in
Majority	Discuss options; vote on a position	Some people may be unsupportive afterwards and continue lobbying	Saves time
Expert	The person with the most knowledge decides	Experts may discount others' useful ideas as 'not invented here'	Means the most able person drives the decision

Method	*Process*	*Risks*	*Benefits*
Command	The leader decides	Not everyone is bought in; fall out afterwards	Is useful in crisis
Consult	Individual and group conversations before and during the event	May not lead to a decision; good for getting ideas	Gets ideas and support prior to a decision
Force Majeure	No one decides; circumstances dictate	You have a suboptimal outcome that no one selected	Forces change

The main point in deciding which method you want to use is to

- Reach a positive and easy agreement before dealing with a much tougher one.
- Get commitment to a process.
- Allow you to make real progress when it comes to decisions.

Here's what often happens: The group decides that it wants to use consensus as the best approach, so it wants everyone to get to 'yes.' But then you run out of time trying to make that happen, so it turns to a majority decision instead. This peeves some members of the group who feel that they haven't been listened to, so they become passively or actively resistant, and all the good work is undone.

If you think that there's a risk this might happen, get the group to select two methods. Then you have Plan A and Plan B if the group can't reach consensus.

Working with weighted decision-making

Research has shown that when decision-making reaches a certain level of complexity, it becomes harder and harder to make a choice. That's because most of us can only keep a small number of variables in our heads at one time. An excellent way of managing a difficult decision is to use the *weighted decision-making technique.*

This technique works much better than simply generating a 'pros and cons' list because it gives you some kind of objectivity and is more likely to lead to a clear result. What you do involves two steps.

Step 1

Step 1 in the weighted decision-making process consists of the following:

1. **Think about the decision you want to make.**
2. **Define your key characteristics.**
3. **Give a weight to each key characteristic.**

   This must add up to 100 per cent.

Table 5-4 shows you how it would work if you were trying to decide which of three offices you should move to. You can see that the decision you are trying to make is in the title, and the key characteristics are listed down the side. The weight for each key characteristic adds up to 100 per cent.

Table 5-4 Select the Best Office

Key Characteristics	*Weight*
Cost	30%
Parking	15%
Public transport	15%
New building	15%
Windows	10%
Cafeteria	10%
Local shops	5%
Total	**100%**

Once you have done this step, you can move to Step 2.

Step 2

To follow this office example through, you would

1. **Write the name of each possible office on the left hand side of a spreadsheet (your y-axis).**
2. **Write all your criteria along the top (your x-axis), with the weights underneath each one.**
3. **Allocate a score to each of your criteria using any scale you like (1–10 is the easiest).**
4. **Multiply everything up, and you reach a clear answer.**

Figure 5-1 shows you how to work this through.

		Cost	Parking	Modern	Transport	Windows	Cafeteria	Shops	
Options	**Weight**	30%	15%	15%	15%	10%	10%	5%	100%
Location A	Raw	10	2	8	3	6	2	10	
	Weight	300	30	120	45	60	20	50	625
Location B	Raw	8	8	7	1	9	7	5	
	Weight	240	120	105	15	90	70	25	665
Location C	Raw	6	5	5	3	10	6	7	
	Weight	180	75	75	45	100	60	35	570

Figure 5-1: Weighing your criteria.

As you can see in this example, it's easy to see which building is the best bet.

Using a weighted decision-making approach is brilliant because it saves lots of time, and it reduces conflict. You'll really help reduce conflict in a group if you are attuned to who's in the room.

Recognising Personalities in the Room

One of the things that's hard to learn is not to get thrown for a loop by the behaviour of others when you are leading them in a group context. This section of the chapter helps you in two ways:

- **To better understand the behaviour of others.** This will mean you recognise and work more easily with others' responses in group situations. And if you meet individuals' needs, you're more likely to have a successful session.

- **To work with how others learn.** This will help you plan for and manage people's learning preferences. It's essential to understand them for any workshops that require participants to learn.

Working with Bolton & Bolton's Social Styles

Bolton & Bolton's Social or Behavioural Styles is a brilliant tool that helps you analyse and act on the different behaviours that occur in a roomful of people. If you are going to work regularly with a group, it's worth taking the time to think through who the members are in terms of their Social Styles. That way, you'll know what makes them tick well in a group setting.

According to Bolton & Bolton's model, 75 per cent of others' behaviour is different to yours in terms of thinking, communicating and making decisions – in other words, all the core things you do in a meeting.

Understanding where your strengths are and recognising those of others will help you flex what you do. That way, you can work as effectively as possible with everyone in group situations.

So what are Social Styles? They refer to a stable pattern of observable interactions that a person uses with others. They don't take values, hopes, dreams, motives, feelings, attitudes or experience into account. But they do reflect patterns by which someone meets their personal needs and manages themselves in groups.

There are two key dimensions to understanding Social Styles: Assertiveness and Responsiveness.

Assertiveness

Assertiveness is the degree to which someone's behaviour attempts to influence the thoughts or actions of others. You can see this illustrated on the horizontal part of the matrix in Figure 5-2.

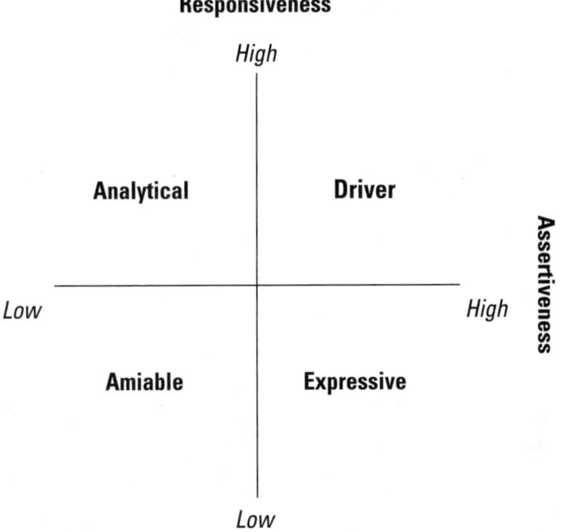

Figure 5-2: Assertiveness, responsiveness and the social styles.

Table 5-5 lists some behaviours associated with assertiveness in a group setting.

Table 5-5 Understanding Assertiveness

Less Assertive People Tend to . . .	*More Assertive People Tend to . . .*
Be more 'ask' oriented	Be more 'tell' oriented
Be more supportive	Be more directive
Respond	Initiate
Demonstrate less energy	Show more energy
Speak less rapidly	Speak more rapidly
Gesture less vigorously	Gesture more strongly
Decide less quickly	Decide more quickly
Be less confrontational	Be happy to challenge
Be less direct	Be more direct

It's important to remember that assertion is a continuum. This does not mean you are aggressive if you are on the right side. And if you're on the left, it doesn't mean you are submissive. It means you get your needs met differently.

Responsiveness

The second part of the matrix deals with levels of responsiveness in a group situation. This means the degree to which you are comfortable with expressing emotions.

Table 5-6 describes some of the behaviours that characterise responsiveness.

Table 5-6 Understanding Responsiveness

Low Responsiveness People Tend to . . .	*High Responsiveness People Tend to . . .*
Disclose feelings less easily	Express feelings more readily
Be less interested or skilled at small talk	Be comfortable and interested in small talk
Be more task-oriented	Be more people-oriented
Be more structured with time	Be less structured with time
Be concerned with thinking	Be concerned with feelings
Be precise and specific	Be more imprecise and general
Use facts and data	Use opinions and hunches
Be more disciplined	Be more personal
Appear more reserved	Appear more friendly
Be thought of as more serious	Be seen as more playful

To assess your preferred style, try the following:

1. **Think about which of the behaviours you tend to use when working in a group situation and tick all the ones that apply to you.**
2. **Plot yourself on the matrix in Figure 5-1 to find your primary style.**
3. **Ask a couple of colleagues to do the same for you.**

   That way, you get feedback on you as you are rather than you as you would like to be.

4. **Observe what you do when you work in a group and think how this helps or hinders you.**
5. **Think about what irritates you about others when you do group work.**

   This will probably be the opposite of what you do in both Assertiveness and Responsiveness. These will be the people you find harder to manage when you are leading group-work yourself.

If you are going to run effective meetings and workshops that get the best out of everyone, here's how to work with each of the four types.

- **Supportive:** Their focus is on people, so relationships matter to them. Meetings need to have enough time to build connections not just get work done. Don't hurry them along and make sure you are warm and friendly as they will respond positively to this. They tend to be risk-averse from a people perspective, so be ready to deal with this.
- **Analytical:** They focus on facts and data. Liking everything to be right, they expect you to be disciplined in your approach, just as they are. They want to understand the process and know that it makes sense. They, too, are risk-averse but around facts and data. You might find that they are reserved in their overall approach to group work.
- **Expressive:** They are all about the vision and big picture. Loving ideas, they are quick to respond with ideas and thoughts when working in a group. You'll find that they are social, supportive, enthusiastic and warm. But you need to make sure that your pace feels right to them. You'll lose them if you're too slow.
- **Drivers:** In a group, these are the people who make things happen. They are all about the action and have a just-do-it-now approach. Happy to take risks to achieve results, they can speed group work along. They will tell you if you move too slowly and can show impatience with others. Finishing a task first or taking part in a competition really gets them going.

If individuals perceive that you are helping them meet their needs as you work with them, they'll love your sessions. So at the start, observe who's in the room, so you can adapt what you do to incorporate everyone's preferences and flex your behaviour to match others when you need to.

Remember that you'll miss the mark if you use a Driver's style with a Supportive person or an Expressive style with an Analytical person. So pay attention to what you think their preferred styles are and match where you can.

Meanwhile, here are some things to remember about Styles:

- **There is no best or worst Style.** All of them have advantages and disadvantages, and all are effective when they are appropriate.
- **We tend to have one main Style and a subsidiary,** even though we can all use all of them.
- **Inner reactions and outer responses may differ,** so test your assumptions out.
- **Your challenge is to handle people who are very different** to you.
- **Styles don't explain everything.** There are plenty of other influencers at play.

You can download a document that will give you more detailed insights about working with different types if you go to `www.dummies.com/go/rungreatmeetingsworkshops`.

Now Social Styles help you manage information sharing, conversations and decision-making interactions. But you'll also need to take Learning Styles into account when you are asking your participants to absorb new information that you want them to digest and then use.

Working with Honey & Mumford's Learning Styles

While there is a huge amount of research into the way people learn, one of the most practical and easy-to-use approaches is that of Peter Honey and Alan Mumford. They indicate that there are four types of learner:

- Reflectors
- Theorists
- Activists
- Pragmatists

Like Social Styles, Honey & Mumford suggest that there isn't one learning style that's best, and that everyone will use all four approaches with a preference for one or two. The benefit of recognising your preferred learning style is so that you understand what to do to manage everyone with different learning needs.

Here's a summary of the four Learning Styles:

- **Reflectors: Prefer observing and thinking.** They like to learn from activities that allow them to watch, think and review what has happened. They may not have instant answers because they want to absorb expert information and analysis and come to a conclusion in their own time.
- **Theorists: Prefer understanding reasons and concepts.** They like to think problems through in a step-by-step and logical manner. They won't buy into an activity unless they feel it's grounded in a strong and clear rationale. They are good at asking probing questions and disciplined in their approach.
- **Pragmatists: Prefer having a go.** They really enjoy applying something they learn to actual and immediate practise to see if it works. They need obvious links between the task you provide them with and a real work problem.
- **Activists: Prefer doing and experiencing.** They love the challenges of new experiences, being involved with others and role playing. They like anything they can do that helps fix things. They can be easily distracted as they are open-minded and willing to give everything a go.

Table 5-7 illustrates the learning activities associated with the different learning styles.

Table 5-7 Learning Types and Preferred Activities

Type	*Learn Most When . . .*	*Preferred Activities*
Reflectors	Doing pre-work before attending a workshop Observing others Reviewing what has happened and given time to think	Case studies/exercises to do in advance Background information and data Role play done by others

(continued)

Table 5-7 *(continued)*

Type	*Learn Most When . . .*	*Preferred Activities*
Theorists	Probing and testing information Being put in complex situations they can test theory in Working through structured situations with clear briefing and objective	Case studies Problem-solving situations Discussion Application of theory Watching expert videos
Activists	Doing simulations and tasks Being thrown in at the deep end and made to get on with activities Chairing meetings and leading discussions	Brainstorming Role play Group discussions Competitions Problem-solving
Pragmatists	Seeing the link between the activity and work Learning and practising new techniques Getting feedback Seeing a model they can emulate	Case studies Problem-solving Exercises Role play Feedback sessions Videos

To take care of each learning style, what you'll need to do is

- Offer reading ahead of the session for your Reflectors.
- Position expertise or underlying principles carefully for your Theorists.
- For the Pragmatists, make the link between what you're doing and work.
- Do a hands-on practical exercise for your Activists.

- Ensure there's feedback built in for your Pragmatists and Reflectors to add value to.
- Debrief by drawing out the theory in practice for your Theorists.
- Make sure there's enough assimilation time afterwards for your Reflectors.

That way, you'll cater to everyone's needs as you move through your workshop. The benefit of doing this is that you build trust with individuals. Then they'll be more willing to extend their comfort zones because you are aware of what makes them learn most easily.

Chapter 6

Continuing Your Meeting or Workshop

In This Chapter

- Steering the day
- Leading discussions at the front of the room
- Making sure that you manage process issues
- Reviewing your meeting or workshop

You've started your session really well and set yourself up for success. What you now need to do is make sure that you keep a constant eye on what's happening in the room. To do that, you need to keep an eye on the process so that your meeting or workshop stays on track and goes as you planned it.

You do that by paying attention to how you lead your session so that you keep focusing and shaping it as well as you can. Like driving a car, you don't allow anything to drift. That means being very aware of how the group is reacting to what you are doing and being explicit about the journey you are on.

Even if you've done the most detailed preparation and got the group going really well, mishandling the process is the first thing that can let you down. If the process gets lost and people are uncertain about what they are doing and why, then your participants won't just zone out in the room. They'll actually leave it.

This chapter helps you keep everyone on the ball and with you all the time.

Managing Process

As you start your meeting or workshop, you always run through the agenda, probe expectations, create ground rules and allocate roles (See Chapter 5 for more detail.) Doing this helps you manage the frame in which you and the group work and sets up a strong meeting process.

During your session, you need to keep this process and your purpose explicit when you move through items, sections and activities. Otherwise, your participants lose sight of why they are doing what they do, and what you do will start to feel random.

To make sure you keep the process explicit at a big-picture level, you need to explain

- **What** you are going to do
- **Why** you are going to do it
- **How** it helps you meet your objectives

And to make sure that everyone knows what's happening at a detailed level, you need to

- Check in
- Signpost
- Summarise
- Link
- Paraphrase
- Write up key information well
- Give clear instructions

This following sections review them all in turn.

Checking in

When you check in with a group, all you are doing is verifying what you believe has taken place. You need to check in when you think the group

- **Has finished an activity,** so you can move on.
- **Wants to spend more time on something,** so group members cover it in depth.
- **Has arrived at an insight or decision,** so you reinforce that this is the case.
- **Wants to change direction,** so group members get maximum value from their session.
- **Needs a break,** so group members can re-energise themselves.
- **Has an emerging difference of opinion between members,** so you can deal with it.

And you need to check in with an individual to see that you have fully understood what they have said.

You check in by saying things like

- It seems to me that we're getting lots done. What are your thoughts?
- How's the pace for you? Should we go faster, slower or is this okay?
- This conversation appears to have shed light on a difficult situation. What are your perceptions?
- I think we might have arrived at a consensus right now. Is that right?
- I'm really pleased that you got to grips with this technique, and it looks like you are using it quite naturally. What's your opinion?
- I believe we're done with this. What do you all think?

What you are doing is simply stating what you have observed and seeing if participants have reached the same conclusions. The reason you need to do this is because your participants often get so involved in what they are talking about or doing that they'll lose sight of the overall experience. You are the only person who can draw the threads together for them. And a key way of doing this is by signposting.

Signposting

Signposts are small phrases that help participants

- Stay engaged because they understand what you and the group are doing.
- Get clear about how everything hangs together.
- Draw meaning from an activity.
- Connect continuously with where you are going.

That's why they are called signposts! Without these really important phrases, it's easy to get lost in what's happening.

Table 6-1 shows how signposts work in practice.

Table 6-1 When and How to Signpost

When You Signpost	*How to Do It: Typical Phrases*
To set up what you are going to do	I'm now going to explain how you're going to brainstorm.
To connect the group back to what you did earlier	This is a key marketing insight for the customer needs we explored earlier.
To connect one section or activity with another	Having looked at the symptoms, we'll now turn to the causes.
To signal you will tackle a subject later	We'll get to that in half an hour once we've finished this.
To shut a subject down	We agreed earlier we're not going to deal with that today, so now we'll move on to. . . .
To conclude	In conclusion, we're going to adopt the first idea and come up with a project plan in the next month.
To summarise what's important	To summarise this: There are three main points. . . .

Saying you're going to summarise and then doing it is one of the most important signposts you should frequently use.

Summarising

Summarising is a tool that helps everyone understand where they are in your group process. Moreover, when you summarise, you

- **Maintain a sense of momentum,** even if you get stuck in certain discussions or activities. Coming back to what you have achieved emphasises that you have got work done.
- **Check everyone's understanding** because saying things one more time is likely to flush out any misalignments at the time. It's much better to check now than stall later.
- **Show the group that you know what's happening** and where you are in your overall process.
- **Reinforce the key points** of any discussion or activity. Saying things once is generally not enough to ensure that important stuff is really heard.
- **Embed actions or learning** because if you hear three times that Joe is responsible for something, everyone is likely to remember it.

In other words, you can't summarise often enough. Failure to summarise is a rookie mistake. Without it, you lose people, and they often feel frustrated.

If you think you're going to forget to summarise, write yourself a sticky note and place it somewhere you'll see it.

Linking

The best link that happens is when your participants pre-empt you by 30 seconds by asking a question that helps you segue to the next topic. That means you have done a great design, and your activities flow logically.

If this doesn't happen, you need to

1. **Summarise what you've just been doing.**
2. **Signpost you're finishing one thing and moving on to another.**

3. **Explain how what you're doing next connects to the previous activity and builds on it.**
4. **Connect what you are doing to your objective or outcomes.**

We know that this may feel a bit laboured, especially if you're not used to doing it. But your participants will be absolutely clear about what you are doing and why, whether you're in a meeting or workshop. And that will mean they are much more likely to go with you and stay with you throughout.

When people don't understand why they are doing something, they can easily turn into difficult people. You want to avoid that at all cost.

Understanding why meeting process matters

When we're recruiting new trainers, facilitators or team coaches, we always ask them to come in to run a short session for us. To set them up for success, we share all the competences and behaviours we are looking for and ask them to observe one of our most experienced people in action beforehand. To make certain they are clear about what we think good looks like, we ask them to identify the competencies and behaviours they see during that observation.

Recently, someone came in to run a short 30-minute session. He was warm, friendly and prepared. The omens looked good, and we were all ready for something great.

But we didn't get an objective or an agenda, we weren't asked for expectations, we didn't understand why we were doing the activity he'd set up or how we could use it. There was no take-away. By the end, we were all thoroughly confused and disappointed.

What was really interesting was the effect this lack of process had on the group. Everyone went from interested and engaged to de-energised and fed up in just 20 minutes. And then the session simply fizzled out.

He asked for feedback. So we said what had been missing in terms of process. His response was 'That's a bit harsh.' But process matters; without it, you'll never have a great meeting or workshop.

Stating what's been said: Paraphrasing

Obviously when you're leading a group of people for any purpose, you'll be listening to what they say. (For more about this, see Chapter 4.) To show that you are hearing and integrating this understanding for yourself and the group, you need to *paraphrase*. This means re-stating what someone says using your own or similar words.

For example:

John: 'We had three major outages last week, which resulted in 176 per cent extra voice mails, 268 per cent more complaints and a swamped delivery team working 16 hours a day, so everyone's been doing double shifts. We still haven't responded to everything, and we have no idea how long it's going to take us because we can't retrieve critical information from the system. It's horrendous.'

You: 'So what you're saying is the outages meant a lot more work for the delivery team, and you're still struggling with a huge extra workload and a sub-optimal system. That means your work on project X must have ground to a halt.'

The reason you do paraphrase is to show that you've heard someone and, if you need to, put what was said into perspective. In the preceding example, the perspective you add is talking about the impact on project X.

Suppose that while project X is important, what you want to deal with right now are the three major outages. To do that, you'll need to accurately write down what John said on a flip chart. Listening to him means not only paraphrasing after he's spoken, but, while he's talking, identifying the key information he's giving you to write it up.

Writing up key information on a flip chart

A novice would write every single painful word down that John said. Please don't do that. That's because it

- **Takes far too long:** Time is money, and sitting in silence while you write is boring as well as time-wasting – especially if you write slowly.
- **Doesn't help the group:** You help the group move forward when everyone distils the essential information.
- **Means your body will probably be more angled away from the group than it needs to be:** You'll be less connected to everyone, and you'll miss crucial eye meets.
- **Means you have to write down everything that everyone else says:** You can't do it for one person and not others.

You're not running a writing session; you're running a meeting or workshop.

So in the preceding case involving John, you would select the only key information to write on a flip chart:

- 176 per cent extra VMs
- 268 per cent more complaints
- Problems:
  - Workload
  - System

Then you'd check in with John that he's okay with this. If he and the team agreed, you might also put Project X in a parking lot. (See the section on parking lots later in this chapter.)

Meanwhile, Table 6-2 lists some more tips for writing on a flip chart.

Here's a brilliant tip for writing on a flip chart: If you've got something complex or that has loads of numbers that you want to share, don't automatically build another complicated slide. Instead, semi-prepare a flip chart and pencil the complicated stuff in beforehand. No one will be able to see what you've written, even if they are reasonably close, and you'll look like a genius when you stand up and magically produce a bunch of numbers or a complex chart. It's a much more powerful way of delivering information, and it looks like you're super confident on your feet.

Table 6-2 Do's and Don'ts for Writing on a Flip Chart

Don't...	*Do...*
Write upper case: IT'S MUCH HARDER TO READ (bad), LOOKS SHOUTY (bad) AND CHILDISH (worse).	Write lowercase: it's much speedier, so you waste less time, and you always use less paper.
Write everything down or you lose the main points.	Capture key information only.
Use red or green marker pen; you can't see them from a distance.	Use black or blue pens because they are easier to see.
Write with dried-out pens as it looks careless and cheap.	Get white board and flip chart pens and use both appropriately.
Buy scented, pink, orange or purple pens. They are girly, hard to see at a distance and give some people headaches.	Buy chisel-headed pens as they improve everyone's handwriting.
Use long words if you have poor spelling. Abbreviate them instead.	Practise so you get used to writing on a flip tidily.
Talk to a flip chart as you write and bend over as you reach the end of the page.	Stand to the side of the flip chart as you write, so you are angled towards your audience.

Giving clear instructions

Why do groups find instructions hard to follow? They just do. We think it's because people fall into TV watching mode and start watching you, so they abdicate responsibility for themselves. Everyone also assumes that all the others are paying attention, so they don't need to.

Using a flip chart properly

There's nothing more irritating than being part of a group who does good work that's captured on a flip chart. Then that work is simply ignored as a fresh sheet of flip chart paper is turned over only to hide the previous good work.

Hang the work up or don't do it at all.

If you post the work around the room, you're much more likely to reference it and signpost as you move through the day. If you hang it up in a logical order, then participants will feel you are making logical progress, too.

Make sure you have an agenda flip chart near you, so you can signpost easily. Even if you have a frequent agenda in your slide deck, participants can forget where they are, and you'll be able to remind them.

We recommend that you write flip charts up in advance as much as possible. It saves time on the day. Among the most important flips you should write up ahead are the instructions for the activities you plan.

To give good instructions, make sure you

1. **Have written them up in advance.**

   That way, you are not writing on a flip chart and explaining them at the same time. If you are watching the group as you explain, you'll be more easily able to see who is confused. If you are giving instructions on a slide, use only one (rather than two), so your group can see everything at all times. If you need multiple slides, print everyone a copy of what to do.

2. **Demonstrate what has to happen in front of the group.**

   For example, if you want participants to swap worksheets in pairs, take a worksheet and physically exchange yours with a participant, making sure that everyone can see you doing this.

3. **Check that everyone knows what to do.**

   Get them to nod their heads if they think they have understood. If they shake their heads or look confused, run through the instructions again.

4. **Invite one participant to explain the instructions back to you, especially if you are inviting them to work outside your plenary room.**

   Then you can be really sure everyone knows what to do.

5. **Encourage everyone to take a photo of the instructions on their phones so that they can check what they are doing.**

   Just agree that they won't start dealing with emails if they turn their phones on. Agree to put them in flight-safe mode instead.

6. **Find out where everyone is going if they leave the room.**

   That way, you can walk around to be certain they all know what to do.

Don't assume, even when you have done all this, that your participants will do what you ask of them – especially if they are pretty senior. In fact, the more senior the participants are, the worse they are at following instructions because they always have a personal assistant telling them what to do, showing them where to go and generally holding their hands!

Facilitating Group Discussions

Facilitating a group conversation can feel really scary if you've never done it. You worry whether people will join in, if they'll argue or perhaps that you won't understand what they are talking about.

The mistake that novices make when they start to facilitate group sessions is to focus on activities and worry about *what* they are doing. The main thing to get right is *how* you are doing things and ensuring that they are clear and that they land for the group.

All you need to remember is this: Like everything else you do in a meeting or workshop, facilitating a group conversation is a process. And as a process, you'll have a clear beginning, middle and an end.

Facilitating a conversation in a group simply involves the following:

- Introducing a discussion topic
- Getting input to the topic
- Allowing a conversation to move sideways

- Shutting up
- Dealing with an elephant in the room
- Challenging comments skillfully

Introducing a discussion topic

If you've run through your agenda at the start of your session, everyone knows that you're going to tackle a topic. Summarise that you've come to the end of the previous one, signpost that you are moving on and make an introductory comment.

Imagine, for example, that you are having a meeting to talk through budgets for next year and that Jane, a member of your team, has sent a draft budget out in advance. Here's what you could say:

- Jane, can you run us through the main points of the budget, and then we can discuss our fixed and variable costs?
- Everyone, Jane sent around the budget. What are your high-level thoughts about our fixed and variable costs?
- Before we get into the detail of our costs, let's have one thought from everyone about the overall fixed and variable costs.

Any of these questions will kick-start a discussion.

Getting input to a topic

One problem with group discussions is that they can turn into dialogues for the most vocal people in the room. If you are worried about this, as you start your session, remind everyone that if, for example, 12 people are in the room for an hour, then everyone has five minutes maximum to speak.

If you still get a couple of people monopolising the air time, validate the speaker: 'Thank you, Bill, for your input. To summarise, you think the budget is too light on costs. Jo and anyone else, what do you think?' Then simply wait. Don't look at Bill (or he'll pipe up again) and stay silent until someone else speaks up. Make sure you thank this person for the contribution, listen to and build on what was said to encourage other contributions.

If the group is still holding back, try this:

1. **Get everyone to write their thoughts down on sticky notes, one idea per note.**
2. **Talk through their thoughts in pairs.**
3. **Move around the room listening in and noting down what people say as they do the paired work.**
4. **Debrief their sticky notes in the whole group.**
5. **Draw the more shy participants in by asking them to repeat what you heard them say.**

This is, by far, the easiest way to help everyone speak up.

When you're working with a group that's struggling to get going, you might also want to let a conversation move sideways just to get everyone to open up. For example, you could ask, 'What about our IT costs? Who here thinks they need a new laptop in the next 12 months?' That would be bound to get the group going, even if it is sideways.

Allowing a conversation to move sideways

If you think a discussion is moving sideways and potentially drifting away from what you originally planned, don't worry. If it's adding value or helping make the group work, let it happen. You have a plan to move away from the plan.

If it's about yesterday's soccer scores, then, of course, you'll want to get your topic back on track.

In both situations, all you need to do is

1. **Recognise that you have moved from A to B.**
2. **Summarise what has been said (if it is of value) or close it down (if it's irrelevant).**

If you notice group members are going off track but they are deeply engrossed in what they are talking about and it's super useful, you might want to let the conversation unfold. In that case, you simply need to shut up.

Shutting up

The most powerful and productive meetings or workshops will be those when you don't do the talking. Your group does. You should aim for the 80:20 rule here. That's 80 per cent them talking and maximum 20 per cent you.

The more your participants talk, the more energised they'll be, and the more they'll get out of their session. You don't need to jump in and control the flow or direction of the discussion. Just listen and ask questions that will drive the conversation further and the insights deeper.

Having the courage to be silent, to not fill a pause, is much more powerful than jumping in, however much you are tempted to. So be brave. If you ask a question, make sure you don't then answer it for the group. Simply hold your silence until someone volunteers.

If no one responds, don't ask another question because then people will wonder which question to answer. What you can do is say, 'That wasn't a rhetorical question, and I'm sure one of you has an answer.' If you smile and are warm as you wait, someone will give you an answer.

You don't empower anyone if you answer your own questions; you are there to guide the work, not to do it.

By the way, staying silent is particularly important if you're going to handle an elephant in the room. You'll find that there are a lot of pauses when you deal with the difficult issue.

Dealing with an elephant in the room

Call it what you like – grabbing the bull by the horns, putting the fish or cards on the table. Everyone's scared of getting into a group and someone saying something unspeakable that results in the nightmare outcomes of silence or violence. Hand on heart, that almost never happens. But here's what you can do to help make the discussion as constructive and productive as possible.

The point is to do it lightly and elegantly rather than making heavy weather of it. Focusing on your process will help you manage really well:

1. **Set a positive intent.**

   That way, you can remind the group if things get tricky that this is the point of the discussion.

2. **Get the group to discuss two positive things and one negative things that have happened over the past few months or weeks.**

   Do this on separate sticky notes, one per idea, so you can review them as a group.

3. **Debrief the positive themes first and then the negative ones without any comment from you.**

   Simply thank people as they offer their thoughts.

4. **Ask group members what they observe from this input and discuss it.**

   At this point, someone is bound to mention the elephant. If no one does (and we've never seen that happen), then you can bring it up.

5. **Remind the group of the positive intent that you already set out.**

6. **Start brainstorming what would have to happen for the elephant to have disappeared and things to be working super well.**

   Make sure that these are actions that are as concrete as possible.

7. **Evaluate the best actions and get the group to decide what's next.**

8. **Ask the group what else has to happen for you all to be sure that the situation has been resolved.**

   That way, you are double-checking you have done the job.

Dealing with comments skillfully

There are two kinds of comments you need to deal with straight away:

- Positive ones that help the group move forward
- Negative ones that can sometimes sound really stupid

Positive and helpful comments

When you get positive input from someone in the group, you want to acknowledge and reinforce it. Use someone's name, repeat what was said and show you appreciate it. That way, they are more likely to continue with their contributions.

You might also like to find them during a break and thank them for what they are doing because they are helping you make the session work.

Negative or unhelpful comments

Okay, so someone says something that you think is really dumb. People do that mainly for two reasons: They want to derail you, or they simply haven't thought something through.

Either way, don't ignore what they say hoping they'll stop (because they won't). And, however irritated you are, don't respond by saying, 'What a stupid comment' or 'Why on earth do you think that?'

You don't react like that because:

- **Your judgements don't help the group** move forward. In fact, they may unintentionally have the opposite effect.
- **You put other people off** from saying something because they don't want to lose face in front of their peers.
- **You risk turning the group against you.** There are more of them than there are of you and even if they don't like a group member, they will still generally side with them against you.

Instead, ask the person who made the comment or suggestion one of the following questions:

- What's behind your thinking?
- I am curious how you reached that conclusion?
- How might that work out in practise?
- What do you think the consequences of doing that would be?

These questions will help an individual work through something themselves and show the group that you are dealing with the situation.

In all probability, if someone is being difficult, this isn't the first time the group will have seen such behaviour. (For more about this, see Chapter 7.) It's highly likely that someone will side with you to help you deal with the difficult person.

Managing Process Problems

There's rarely a meeting or workshop when everything goes absolutely according to plan – when conversations don't get bogged down, when new stuff emerges or when your participants get involved in conversations that need exploring in more detail.

The danger of all of this is that other topics then get squeezed, and people feel rushed, tired, distracted and frustrated by what does or doesn't happen. That's what an unplanned and disorganised meeting feels like. This section helps you deal with some of the tougher stuff so that you stay on course and

- Manage time
- Deal with rabbit holes
- Use parking lots
- Open up old issues or close new ones down
- Manage energy
- Manage guests
- Deal with unexpected situations
- Revisit expectations

Managing time

You can, of course, push the speed of a group discussion without ever saying, 'We need to do this quickly' or 'We're running out of time.' In fact, you should never ever use these phrases even if you've covered only half the topics you wanted to get through and have 30 minutes left. That's for two important reasons:

- **They create uncertainty and discomfort** in participants who worry about what they haven't done.
- **You should have managed time better** and given the group choices about what it was doing. You should therefore never get into this position.

Of course, that's easier said than done because when participants really get into a topic, they can easily go off-track. What you need to do is to listen hard, so you know that's happening and simply point that out to the group.

Say, for example, that you are facilitating a conversation about next year's strategy. You might be doing this in a meeting or in a workshop, depending on the depth of your discussion. During your session, you are planning to talk about *what* to do rather than *how* the team might deliver on that strategy.

At the start of your meeting, you decide that you want to focus at a high level, rather than talk about delivery. But just because you've said it doesn't mean that your group members won't go there. On the contrary, they will because everyone will be thinking, 'How do these options affect me?' and 'What will that mean I have to do differently?'

That means you need to listen hard for the direction a conversation takes, so you don't risk running down a rabbit hole.

Dealing with rabbit holes

Rabbit holes are those conversations that are frankly irrelevant to the topic in hand. For example, in the preceding example, you'd need to point out when a conversation started to focus on *how* to deliver the strategy rather than *what* the strategy should be. Now the group might need to focus a bit on the *how* to fully explore their choices. But individuals shouldn't be getting into too much nitty-gritty. Otherwise, they will be working at an operational level rather than staying strategic.

But how do you recognise the difference?

You simply ask yourself, 'How is this conversation adding to our overall objective?' If your personal answer is 'It isn't,' then throw this observation back to the group. The group will be pleased you helped it stay on track because no one wants to waste their time.

Using parking lots

Sorry to mix our metaphors here, but a parking lot can stop groups running down rabbit holes. A *parking lot* is where you put an important topic that the group needs to discuss – but not right now.

To create one, all you need to do is write Parking Lot on a piece of flip chart and note down each topic as it arises. Hopefully, you'll never have more than a couple of ideas – often, you'll have none at all.

But you do need to create a parking lot when you hear the group coming back to an off-topic issue two or three times because it's important and affects them. When this happens, try the following:

1. **Recognise that the subject matters to the group.**
2. **Point out that it needs discussing.**
3. **Remind everyone that it's outside the objective of this session.**
4. **Put it in your parking lot.**
5. **Get the group to decide what happens next.**
6. **Work out who owns each idea.**
7. **Move on with your agenda.**

Parking lots are useful for

- **New information** that may or may not affect the group
- **Issues that affect some individuals** but not the whole group
- **New ideas** that are useful but not right now
- **Previous meetings** that don't need re-running

Putting all of this in a parking lot will help you keep your session on-track and make sure you have a results-oriented meeting. No one wants to chew over old or irrelevant stuff.

Opening old issues up, closing current ones down

From time to time, you'll have to deal with some sticky issues. We mean *sticky* in both senses – either difficult to tackle or won't go away.

But if you've discussed a difficult issue in some detail and reached a resolution with the group, then the discussion is over. It's time to move on, so it will be important to get everyone to agree that once you've dealt with it, that's that. Game over.

There is, of course, an exception. That's when you or the group gets new information that materially affects a decision in an urgent or important manner. You can check with the group if this is the case simply by using the Eisenhower Decision Matrix (see Figure 6-1), which was first popularised by Stephen Covey. You do this by getting a majority vote on urgency and importance by scoring both of them on a scale of 1 (not at all urgent or important) to 10 (very urgent or important).

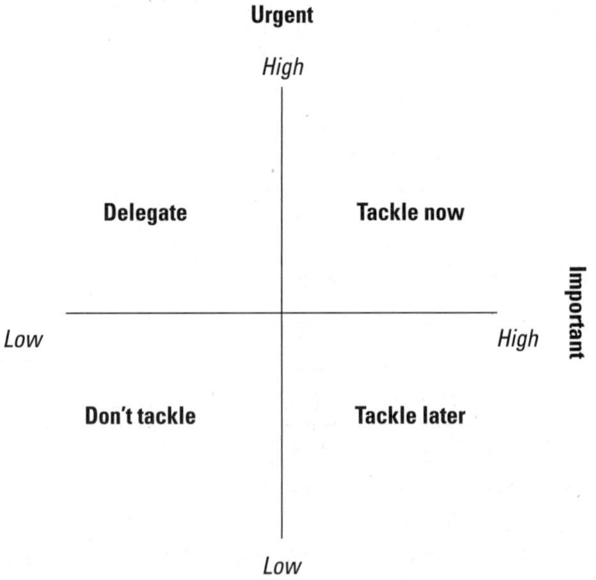

Figure 6-1: Working with the urgent-important matrix.

If the new information is neither urgent nor important, then it's easy to move on, and you'll save time, effort and energy if you do.

Managing energy

Whatever you do to plan for and manage others' energy in advance (see Chapter 2), you will inevitably have some people who are more tired than others. They are jet-lagged, they've been working late on important projects, they've been up all night with a baby or they've been getting ready for your session. All you need to do is notice that they are tired. To manage this in the moment, you might like to

- **Plan a few extra 5 minute breaks.** Invite people to leave the room or go outside, but discourage them from checking emails.
- **Lead some stretching exercises or do something physical in front of the room.** If you can't stand that idea, get someone else to or find a video on YouTube.
- **Keep people moving.** If you stand or move around, it's energising. Sitting for hours is really exhausting.
- **End 15 minutes early.** People hate you for running over, but whoever complained that you ended early? So end early – always, even if it's only five minutes.
- **Be wary of using music.** What we love, you'll hate, and vice versa. And something anodyne like jazz or classical music won't necessarily be energising.

Of course, inviting a guest to your meeting or workshop can really create a big buzz, and it's something special that participants frequently look forward to.

Managing guests

If you've briefed your guest well (see Chapter 3), you'll know what she is going to say, and you'll have seen all her slides. Just make sure you also do the following on the day:

- Remind her of the **name** of the person who will introduce her, so she can thank them publically.
- Reiterate **how long** she has to speak and if there are any hard stops afterwards.

- Refer to what's happening both **before and after** she speaks, so she can make any useful links.
- Recap on how she should **check timings** (technology, you, a clock or buzzer).
- **Introduce her** to the person who will announce her participation, to your sponsor (if they are different) and to anyone who will help with her presentation or AV needs.

So you did everything you could. You briefed your guest, you reminded her about timings, you provided the technology and you waved your arms obviously in front of her and she still won't stop. Your audience is now fidgeting furiously.

What do you then do?

You have to pick your moment and simply intervene. Wait for a pause, a breath and then go for it. Just say that everyone has been really interested in what they have been saying, but, unfortunately, she has only one more minute to wrap up her presentation. If your guest replies, 'I am nearly at my last slide,' say that you are sorry, but politely ask her to end.

It's a technique that never needs a further interruption.

The nightmare external guest

A few years ago, we were asked to help put together and run an extended management team meeting in Italy. As there were 120 people meeting for three days, the sponsor wanted a special speaker who would wow the crowd. So he went to an agency who sent him an American guru at a cost of $50,000 and first-class flights to Europe.

The said guru was going to speak for an hour. We'd had a lot of calls beforehand to work important main messages into the guru's presentation. That was because the sponsor was presenting his strategy for the next 18 months the day before, and we were running leadership skills sessions immediately afterwards. We needed to be absolutely joined up in what we all did.

The event went swimmingly, and the guru's big moment arrived.

At 9 a.m., he springs onto the stage with his music reverberating around the room. Then he announces, 'You've all been in here for an hour, so I'm going to give you a 30-minute coffee break.'

We all turn to stone; you don't get 120 people in and out of a room that quickly, and there wasn't any coffee. The break was scheduled 90 minutes later at 10.30.

Everyone arrived back in the room, and the guru told us all that given what he'd heard in the first hour, he'd decided to change what he was going to say. On tenterhooks, we listened for the agreed key messages. We got two out of the carefully planned five. And there were five for a reason: We were running five follow-up workshops.

We were emailing and making desperate signals at our key stakeholder who was responsible for finding and briefing the guru. She merely stood by the side of the stage and shrugged her shoulders. The guru over-ran by an hour, threw the entire schedule into complete disarray (including the fire brigade – don't ask) and wrecked our careful workshop set-up. Then he flew out before he became aware of the damage he'd done.

Our learning? Well, gurus don't do team-work; that's why they are gurus. If you're planning a big event, make sure you manage the guests and agree with your stakeholder who manages over-running – or prepare to watch a train-wreck take place.

Dealing with unexpected situations

If you're going to be running regular meetings and workshops, you will face unexpected situations that you simply can't prepare for. Here are some of the situations we've faced:

- Locked buildings that no one can enter
- Electricity outages (no lights, no AV and no aircon)
- Groups who have simply disappeared
- Demonstrations that stop anyone from getting to work
- Fire alarms that keep ringing
- Sudden serious illness
- Layoffs halfway through a workshop
- Fisticuffs between participants
- No room lists, no materials and no support
- Double the number of participants turning up

The main thing is to remain calm because then you'll cope.

Here are some things to do:

- **Phone your sponsor.** Consult about what you should do. Text him if you can't get through.
- **Send an email to your stakeholders.** Explain why you have changed direction and give your sponsor a grace period to respond to you – for example, between 10 to 30 minutes.
- **Talk to the group and decide what to do together.** For example, you could decide to take an hour off and then reconvene.

If you want to delay the meeting until another time, get everyone to agree on a date before they leave. Just make sure you keep any work that's already been done, so you have it for the next session.

Revisiting and reviewing expectations

If you fundamentally change what you're doing at any point in your meeting or workshop, you'll need to revisit your participants' expectations. And as you work through your session, you'll need to overtly connect what you do with those expectations. That means that when you get to the end of your workshop, all your participants will be super-clear about what you did to meet their needs. It's as simple as that.

Make sure you revisit and review expectations before you review the meeting or workshop.

Reviewing Your Meetings and Workshops

Why should you review your sessions? Well, if you don't review what you do and get input about how you do it, you'll never get any better at running meetings and workshops.

The reason so many people attend such poor group sessions is that no one bothers to ask how they could be better. A review of some sort is a vital step for improving performance.

Reviewing a meeting

The easiest way to review a meeting is to simply use a scaling question and apply it to the criteria that are most useful your group. Table 6-3 gives some suggestions that you can talk though, evaluate on paper or do online.

Table 6-3 Evaluating Your Meetings

Item	*Score 1–10 (= Poor; 10 = Excellent)*	*Comment*
Agenda		
Preparation		
Content		
Timekeeping		
Listening		
Contributions from everyone		
Distraction factor		
Meeting our objectives		
Clear next steps		
Other stuff		

Using online tools

The advantages of using an online tool to review is that after the pain of setting it up, you can then collate all the information and pull some stats or charts from it to see what trends emerge over time.

The disadvantage is that your participants will have yet another survey to do – so they may not do it, and then you only have skewed information from a few people who love or hate your session.

If you can, you might like to incentivise participants to answer – for example. a book, vouchers or a small treat. Ask them what incentives would work best for everyone and make a group decision.

If you want to find a good online tool to use, you can find plenty – for example, Google Docs, SurveyMonkey, SurveyGizmo, FluidSurveys, QuestionPro and Survey Analytics. Hunt about for the one that will be most useful for you and your needs.

Reviewing a workshop

Reviewing a workshop is quite challenging from a number of perspectives:

- Participants are often in a **hurry to leave,** and even if they answer, your quantitative questions, they may not answer qualitative questions, which give you the richest information.
- Questionnaires often reflect just how much a group **likes someone** rather than the work it got done.
- Obviously none of the important outcomes or learning will have been implemented, so **any questionnaire is a poor reflection of action.**
- Questions are often written to generate positive answers – for example, 'How much did you enjoy this session?' **Good questions are not leading questions.**

Having said all that, a post-workshop evaluation is still worth doing. It's also worth repeating six months later to get a reality-check on outcomes. If possible, you can assess this with a small impact study. If something has worked, there should be real evidence to show that this is the case. That's where all your hard work beforehand investigating the potential return on investment (ROI) comes in. (For more about ROI, see Chapters 3 and 8.)

And ROI is particularly important for you. Then everyone knows that what you did was a brilliant investment of time and money, so they'll definitely want to work with you again.

Chapter 7

Dealing with the Tough Stuff: Troubleshooting

In This Chapter

- Making sure you are successful on the day
- Handling tricky behaviour with aplomb
- Recognising and managing politics
- Dealing skillfully with conflict

If you're lucky, you won't need this chapter because everything will go swimmingly well. But the more you run meetings and workshops, the more likely it is that you'll come across tricky situations that you'll want to handle with aplomb.

There's one thing you can be sure of when you're working with a group: A problem only disappears when you deal with it. When people appear disengaged, bored, tired, withdrawn or more challenging than you'd expect, you've got to address what's going on.

This chapter explores how to deal with those issues.

Managing Typical Barriers to Success

Things mostly go wrong because the design or the delivery isn't what it could or should be. That means your preparation, skills and process management isn't good enough.

Here's a summary of the top five barriers to success:

- **Failing to put together a good agenda** for your meeting (see Chapter 2) **or running order** for your workshop (see Chapter 3). What you do doesn't meet the mark.
- **Failing to use your essential skills** (see Chapter 4) and demonstrating poor questioning, listening or observing. You're not really aware of what's happening.
- **Failing to kick your session off well** (see Chapter 5) by clarifying the agenda, expectations, ground rules or roles and responsibilities. Participants don't feel that you are in control.
- **Failing to work well with the personalities** in the room and irritating your participants as a result (see Chapter 5). People feel misread and misunderstood.
- **Failing to manage the process**, so you don't check in, signpost, summarise, link your topics, paraphrase, write information up well or give clear instructions (see Chapter 6). Participants get lost in what's going on.

No sweat there then. But having said all that, there are times when even with the best will in the world, what you do just doesn't work.

Knowing What to Do When It's Not Working

There are only two main times when you need to be very vigilant to understand whether your agenda or running order meets everyone's needs:

- **Right at the start of your session.** This one is tougher to handle. The group hasn't yet done any real work, so they haven't yet gelled, and you have to think hard on your feet.
- **Any time during the session.** This is obviously easier to handle as you have already got rapport, done some work and, if you're checking in regularly, the group is getting used to telling you what's happening for them.

Of course, in either situation, the group should be ready to help you and each other if it wants a collaborative and constructive session. Most of the time, that's the case, but sometimes it isn't.

All change

A few months ago, I (Jessica) ran a team event in London for a financial services organisation. Fifteen people were going to attend, and the brief was very clear. I put the content together and ran through it with my key stakeholders and sponsor. It was all signed off really easily – too easily as it turned out.

The mood on the day was low-key, but I hadn't expected anything else given the organisation. We went through the agenda, and the team started to fidget uncomfortably, so I asked what the matter was. I found out that the evening before, merger rumors had started to circulate, and suddenly the agenda that focused on strategy and execution didn't look so relevant. Everyone was facing downsizing and potentially reapplying for their jobs.

I asked the group to brainstorm what they would ideally like to do given this new situation. We agreed to continue with the workshop, complete a strengths exercise to start, think about 'What should we as a team be focusing on assuming the merger goes ahead,' followed by 'What are our next steps?' Then we linked the next steps to individuals' strengths.

It would have been disastrous to stick to what we'd planned, and it was pretty simple to change.

At the start of your session – when the group helps you

A mature group who know each other well will tell you right from the start if everyone wants to change direction and do something different. The time when individuals will tell you is when you have covered the agenda and are collecting their expectations, which is why these items are so important.

If that happens to you, here's what you can do:

1. **Check what, if anything, everyone would like to retain of what you planned.**
2. **Brainstorm what they do want to do instead.**
3. **Decide what order they want to do it in.**

4. **Give the group a short break.**

   That way, you can get yourself together and think about how you will cover these new items.

5. **Get agreement when everyone comes back that this is how you will proceed.**

Going through this process means that everyone will be happy and feel that their needs are being met.

At the start of your session – the group doesn't help you

An immature group whose needs may not be met is entirely different, as is a group that is obliged to attend your meeting or workshop. In both cases, you are more likely to have protestors, prisoners and passengers whose input, effort and energy will be low, unlike that of genuine participants (see Figure 7-1).

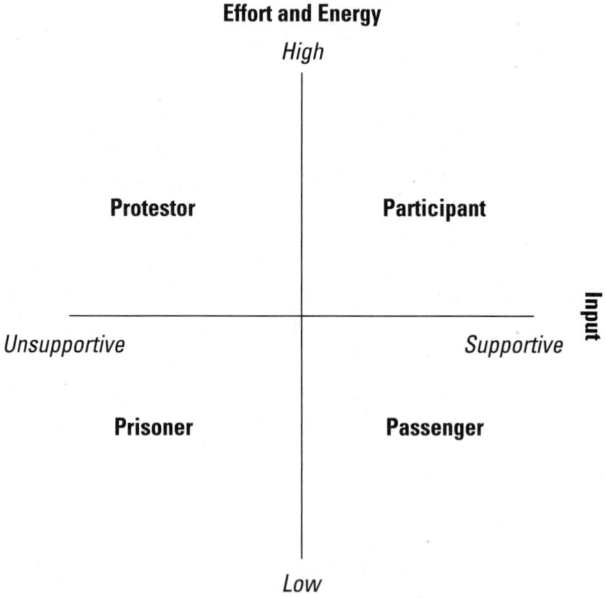

Figure 7-1: Matrix to clarify who you have in your room.

Your protestors and prisoners will arrive sulky and potentially be offhand and curt; your passengers will be withdrawn. If you don't deal with the situation, people will start to use their phones covertly and then overtly. Finally, they'll challenge you outright. Of course, in certain cultures, it's not polite to challenge someone in a position of leadership. In that case, you may just get the silent treatment.

If you find yourself working with this kind of group, then here are some options.

Call a break

During the break, check in with the most influential people in the room about what they think is happening and what needs to change. Then act on the advice you get when you reconvene. You do that by

- Checking with the group that you could be doing something that would be of greater value.
- Getting agreement that that is the case.
- Inviting everyone to brainstorm suggestions for what the group should instead.

Going through this shows the group that you are aware of what's happening and trying to meet its needs. You also show the group that it's safe and productive to speak up.

Acknowledge the situation if your session is compulsory

At the start of your session, say that you are aware that everyone is obliged to be there and then tell them that they aren't. Give everyone a license to leave. It's amazing how doing that reduces the tension in the room because you create choice. Everyone hates being trapped, so if you offer an escape route, you'll find that they all settle down. And if someone does leave, so much the better. No one in the group wants to spend time with a disruptive protestor.

Use sticky notes to work towards a better outcome

An immature group may not like what's happening but may not feel able to speak up to usefully get what everyone needs. In which case try the following:

- Hand out three sticky notes per participant.
- Ask everyone to write down three items (one on each sticky note) that, if dealt with, would represent a good use of their time.

- Get everyone to stand and swap sticky notes (you can do this twice if you like as it increases anonymity and raises energy).
- Share their top three in plenary either by simply sticking them up on a wall or by presenting them, depending on the number of participants you have.
- Count up the ones that have been expressed most often and work out the overall group's top three.
- Get agreement from the group that focusing on these top three would be a better use of their time.

Check with the group that you are on track

If you've changed what you're doing at the start of your session, you need to know you are still on track, so check in from time to time during it, too. We've both run sessions when the group has decided to change the agenda at the start and then revert to what it was supposed to be doing halfway through. If we hadn't checked a second time, we wouldn't have known. It's better to be safe than sorry.

During your session

When things start to fizzle out during your session, it's really important to find out why, especially if you got off to a cracking start. If you've been checking in all along, then the group is much more likely to tell you, so all you need to do is say something like

- It seems to me that we've lost some of the drive or energy we had before. What's going on?
- I'm wondering how useful this is for you and what else we need to be doing?
- What is it that I need to know about the group right now and that you can helpfully share with me?
- How can we most usefully use our time because I'm sensing that it's not like this?

The answers to any of these questions will open up a really helpful discussion.

Here's the main point: Don't keep doing something just because you've planned it. If it's not working, address the issue and change direction.

Dealing with Run-of-the-Mill Difficulties

Here are some typical difficult situations that you need to deal with in an upfront and unequivocal manner:

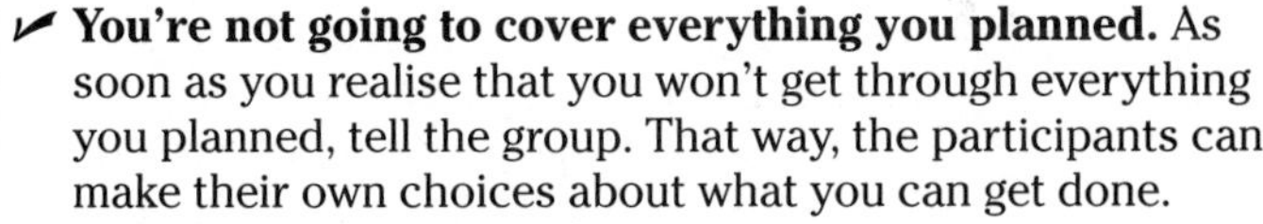

- **You're not going to cover everything you planned.** As soon as you realise that you won't get through everything you planned, tell the group. That way, the participants can make their own choices about what you can get done.

  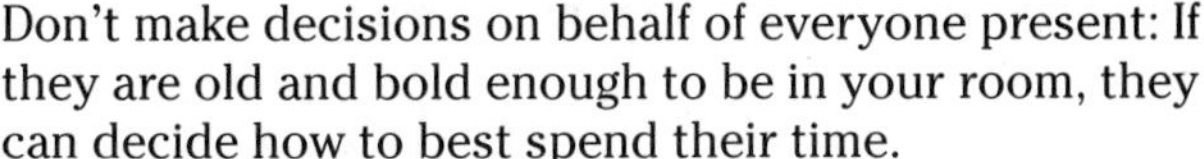

  Don't make decisions on behalf of everyone present: If they are old and bold enough to be in your room, they can decide how to best spend their time.

- **You want to end later than scheduled.** In our view, this is seldom acceptable. However, if you want to end later, put it to the group and get everyone to agree. If one or two people want or need to leave, you gotta let 'em go.
- **You realise you want to include something else.** When you're in a meeting or workshop, you'll often realise that an additional discussion, model or exercise would help the group. If this involves choices about what to do or not do, again, you must tell the group and get its agreement. Never do something that you haven't explained; your golden rule has to be 'no surprises.'
- **They want to end earlier than scheduled.** Put it to the group and arrive at a group decision early on. If your session goes well, don't be surprised if people then decide to stay for the full duration. Getting real value is a powerful incentive to stay.
- **You know what you love and love what you know.** This applies particularly to workshops. There are some people who, when they work with groups, always use the same old model whether or not it's relevant. (For example MBTI, NLP,

DISC, Cialdini, Bolton & Bolton, Johari – you get the idea.) They trot out the same old stuff time and again because it's easy, because they have the slides and because groups enjoy it. Those are never reasons to do anything.

Your obligation is to serve the specific needs of a group at a particular time. If the only tool you have is a hammer, everything will look like a nail – and it isn't. Sooner or later, one of your sessions will crash and burn because what you're doing isn't relevant. Don't dupe yourself that it is.

- **You take yourself way too seriously.** You need to take what you do really seriously. Of course, you do. That way, you'll fully invest in getting everything right. But life means that things don't always go to plan. And if something falls over metaphorically or you do literally, have a laugh with your group at the time. It's much better that your group is laughing with or about you at the time than grumbling and complaining afterwards. So if something doesn't work, smile, say so and move on.

It was a pushover

In my early days working with groups, I (Jessica) was in Johannesburg running leadership development sessions for an IT multi-national. Sitting at the front of the room at my right hand was a heckler named Hendrik. That in itself was unusual; hecklers generally sit at the back.

After about an hour of constant challenges, I said "Hendrik, put up your right hand." And I put mine up to show him what I meant: Shoulder high, as if I was swearing an oath in court. We touched hands, and I pushed.

Now I had done this exercise a dozen times before. Usually, if you start to push someone hand-to-hand, they start to push back, and all you get is wasted energy. That was the point I wanted to make, to show that constantly pushing back gets you nowhere.

Except that this time it didn't work: Hendrik simply offered no resistance. But he was sitting in an unusually mobile chair, and as I leaned my weight into his hand, he suddenly somersaulted flat on his back onto the floor.

There was an audible gasp from the room, and I was appalled by what I'd done. Hendrik slowly stood up. Luckily, he was fine, and in a strong Afrikaner accent said, 'I guess you'll go back to head office and say that the most difficult manager was, in the end, a pushover.' Everyone laughed. And from then on Hendrik was totally on-side.

It takes all kinds of things to bring people round.

Handling Interruptions

Various interruptions arise fairly frequently, so it's worth being able to deal with them quickly so that bad behaviour doesn't snowball.

Phones

Ideally, you'll decide what to do with phones as part of your ground rules (see Chapter 5). And ideally, everyone will decide to switch them off or at least turn them to silent.

You also need to agree that if someone has an important call to take, they'll leave the room. However, if a participant is continuously on calls and it's starting to disrupt the group, you're going to have to point that out and ask them to make a choice about where they want to be and what they want to be doing.

If you forget to agree to phone behaviour when you're doing your ground rules and they start to ring, just stop what you're doing. Get the group to agree then and there how you're going to manage them.

Laptops and tablets

Laptops and tablets are distracting. Even if participants are taking notes, they are bound to be noticing their emails that come in. Or the soccer scores. Or anything else they fancy. If participants are paying attention to written messages, then they aren't really paying attention to what's being said or to others in the room. We defy anyone to multi-task at that level.

If your meeting or workshop doesn't require everyone's full attention, you need to consider who is in the room. Should they really be there?

If you are trying to shape, manage or express thoughts as a group, well, that's a different matter. You will need a laptop or tablet. Just make sure that everyone can see the screen to contribute to the conversation.

To-ings and fro-ings

People pop out of meetings or workshops for calls, breaks and breathers. You don't need to worry why. When they return, you need to bring them up to speed on what they missed. summarise what happened and explain what you are now doing, so you can quickly reintegrate them in the session.

Dealing with Difficult Behaviour

Difficult behaviour can be really tiring to deal with as it tries your patience and is emotionally exhausting at the same time. You'll have to learn to deal with what people think and therefore what they say and do, which are two separate things.

Managing distorted thinking

As you run more meetings and workshops, you'll find that some individuals think and then talk in ways that are unhelpful for them and for the group. They can, often unknowingly, put a negative spin on discussions, limiting themselves and those around them. The group then has to deal with the person rather than the issue in hand, so they waste time.

Table 7-1 describes some of the things you need to listen out for, so you can challenge them.

Table 7-1 Distorted Thinking Patterns

Type of Distortion	*What They Do*
Filtering	Focus on negative details and magnify them, forgetting the positive aspects
Polarised thinking	Speak in extremes; it's all or nothing, black or white, good or bad
Overgeneralising	Talk about always or never while a single piece of evidence results in a general conclusion
Should	Say should, ought and must as they have diehard rules for others' behaviour
Catastrophising	Expect disaster; hear a problem and say, 'What if . . . ?'; this is highly likely when facing change

Type of Distortion	*What They Do*
Blaming	Hold others responsible for choices, problems, decisions and failure
Being right	Concentrate on being right; they know that others are wrong and want to prove it

When you hear this kind of thinking, try these questions:

- What's the advantage of thinking like this?
- How does this help us right now?
- How does it hinder us right now?
- What would be more useful?

If someone persists in their distorted thinking, you will need to take them to one side and explain their impact on the group. Do be careful because they may have low self-awareness and be oblivious to their effect on others.

To help them understand their impact, you can ask them to write down what they want to say before they say it. And ask them to write down every comment of one or two people who move the conversation forward the most. At the end of the session, review what they've written about themselves and others to identify their insights. The benefit of doing this is that it should

- **Increase their self-awareness** as they work in groups.
- **Distract them** as they focus on their impact and that of others, so they'll be much less disruptive.
- **Help them** consider doing something different the next time.

Dealing with difficult individuals

We can all behave badly when we don't want to do something. It's much easier to turn up with a bad attitude and indulge in it than to turn that attitude around. Here are some top tips for dealing with

- Silent participants
- Windbags

- Grumblers and complainers
- Cynics
- Interrupters
- Side conversationalists
- Jokers

Silent participants

People who are silent might be silent for a number of reasons: They're bored, timid, or feel superior. You'll need to find out why they are silent to decide what to do.

Silent participants typically

- Sit at the corner of a table or back of the room, so they are hard to make eye contact with
- Refuse to really engage or comment
- Look bored and sullen if they feel superior; may sigh or roll their eyes
- Look scared if they lack confidence about talking in front of the group
- Say 'Nothing's the matter' when asked if they are okay

To deal with this behaviour:

- Don't ask them directly for their thoughts. Break the group into pairs to see how they participate. Then you can work out why they are silent.
- Ask them if it's you and what you are doing or whether they have an issue with something else. Tell them that if it's you, you're happy to change your approach. If it's something else, ask what they would like to do about it.

Windbags

Windbags are painful because they lack focus so waste hours of everyone's time.

Windbags typically

- Sit where they can give you all the eye contact all the time so they can comment at every turn
- Repeat themselves or circle around what they want to say

- Like to engage and comment on everything
- Dive into too many details
- Off-track conversations
- Irritate everyone else and are often mocked behind their backs
- Are insensitive to others' opinions about them

To deal with windbags:

- Stop looking at them! And don't nod encouragingly either. Turn your body away and stand where you can't easily see them.
- Get everyone to move halfway through your session and put them somewhere harder to make eye contact.
- Tell them during a break that you appreciate what they say and want their help in giving others a chance, too.
- Make them write at the flipchart.

If you are running a really large meeting, you can offer everyone red and green cards to help control windbags. Red cards means 'Stop talking' and green cards mean 'This conversation is important; let's keep going.' Anyone can show a red or green card at any time.

Grumblers and complainers

These participants are really tiring because they moan about the important and the trivial. If everything is perfect, they'll criticise the coffee.

Grumblers and complainers typically

- Sit so that everyone's aware of their grumbling and complaining
- Bang on and on about their work issues; take up more time than they deserve
- Seem unaware of the impact and irritation they cause
- Sit with their hands behind their heads and their chairs tipped back to show that they are more important than everyone else in the room

To deal with grumblers and complainers:

- Make sure you have tight ground rules about positivity.
- Stick to the agenda and bring them back on track all the time.
- Use your parking lot (see Chapter 6), so you show you have heard them.
- Take them to one side and explain the effect that they are having on the group.
- Ask if they could more usefully spend their time elsewhere.
- Don't be tempted to spend more time on them; you'll only encourage them.

Interrupters

Interrupters are really tiresome to deal with because they feel like small children who simply can't wait their turn. And it's irritating teaching adults how to behave.

Interrupters typically

- Sit where they can see most people most of the time
- Interrupt others all the time by talking over them
- Hate being interrupted themselves and may get irritated when that happens
- Worry that they won't be heard, which is why they interrupt

To deal with interrupters:

- Make sure you have tight ground rules about talking over others; refer to them.
- Ask them to 'hold that thought and let *x* finish speaking' every time they do it.
- Ensure you go back to them to find out what they think after *x* has finished.
- Make a very deliberate and lengthy pause when they stop talking!

Cynics

Cynics are devil's advocates gone bad. Devil's advocates test ideas and make clear that this is what they are doing; cynics just demoralise a group.

Cynics typically

- Can only offer negative comments about everything
- Are skilled at deflating everyone's ideas while offering few of their own
- Use phrases like 'It just won't work,' 'We tried it before,' or 'They'll never buy it'
- Enjoy their ingrained negativity

To deal with cynics:

- Ask the cynic to write at the flip chart so they have to focus on other things.
- Make them explicitly focus on the positive and pull them up when they go negative.
- Invite them to support the opposite point of view to test ideas out.

Side conversationalists

Participants have side conversations because they don't understand what's being said and want clarification, want to test an idea out before they try it in the room or because they are bored.

Side conversationalists

- Sit where they can easily chat to others on both their left and right side
- Push their chairs back or lean back to talk more easily
- Irritate others who do want to listen and participate

To deal with side conversationalists:

- Look at or move towards the listener, not the talker. This person will then say, 'John's got an idea' or shut John up.
- Stop talking; both parties will notice the silence.
- Start a small group or paired activity.

We're not great fans of cold-calling people or drawing attention to side conversations by saying, 'Tim, have you got anything to say?' or 'We seem to have another conversation going here; would you like to share it?' It feels a little too like school to us.

Jokers

Meetings without jokers are dull. Because jokers help lighten the mood and get the group to gel, you want them around. But when there's real work to be done, you want less of this behaviour, not more.

Jokers typically

- Wisecrack instead of cracking on with real work
- Look for humour in everything
- Distract other people
- Want to be noticed and appreciated because they are funny

To deal with jokers:

- Appreciate what they do and reinforce their behaviour when it's appropriate.
- Respond to the message behind the façade seriously. If you take them seriously, they often start to do the same.
- Take them to one side if they start to be distracting.
- Focus on using time well so that they get the point.

Asking someone to leave your session

Here's the final card you should always have up your sleeve. And if you give yourself permission to play it, conversely you rarely will.

You can always ask someone to leave the room. If they are being disruptive, preventing real work from happening or annoying others, you are not helping anyone by keeping them there.

So call a break, explain your perceptions and invite them to leave. The group will be so relieved when you do.

There are, however, two occasions when you don't need to deal with a difficult individual or group issue and both concern time. First, when they pop up right towards the end of your session.

Second, when you recognise that dealing with it would utterly disrupt everything else. But in either case, you still need to acknowledge what's happening. And that means being brave.

Tactical seating

If you know you're going to have some difficult participants, think about getting them to sit where you want so they are easiest for you to manage.

Where participants sit has a major impact on the work done and outcomes achieved.

If you want to use name plates to take control, make sure that

- People with strong dislikes or different views don't sit opposite or next to each other. They'll argue more if they do.
- You split factions up so you avoid politics and focus on the work that needs to happen instead.
- Key influencers don't necessarily sit next to the most powerful person – if that's you, move them.

And remember that the table you're going to sit at also affects group work.

Larger meetings tend to use a board room style table or a U shape. Both of them have difficulties that you may need to recognise as you plan your meeting or workshop.

- **Board-room style tables:** Larger, longer tables can make people feel disconnected from what you are doing and therefore more likely to behave badly. It's particularly hard to deal with negative behaviour when it's happening 20 feet away from you. It's also hard to connect and engage with people who are on the same side of such a table but five seats away. You also get less dialogue and less richness of conversation.
- **U-shaped tables:** U-shaped tables can be more intimidating, because a large group means a large space inside the U. But they are much easier for managing poor behaviour. Just stand at the front and then walk towards anyone who's being difficult. They are more likely to stop as you move into their space. And it's easy to stand up to take control, even if you aren't presenting: Simply get up to write something on a flip chart and hey, presto, you're in charge.

- **Round tables:** These are the best because everyone can easily see everyone else, and factions or hierarchies become easier to manage. When you're working at a round table, it's really easy to watch the entire group and to gauge individuals' interactions.

We recommend using lots of round tables for larger group meetings because it's much easier to move around the room and deal with issues as they arise.

Recognising Personal and Hidden Agendas

From time to time, we can all be manipulative to get our own way. But if manipulation is always someone's *modus operandi,* it puts a group or team's work at risk. You therefore need to be aware of both personal and hidden agendas so that you can deal with them.

Tuning in to personal agendas

A personal agenda tends to be more overt and is therefore easier to identify than a hidden agenda.

The chances are that you are dealing with a personal agenda if a participant

- Attends a meeting because it's good for visibility or brown-nosing, not because they are committed to real work.
- Scores political points at the expense of others.
- Puts you down or questions your credentials in front of the group.
- Brings up irrelevant but self-serving topics and frequently talks about them both inside and outside your session.
- Says, 'We all want the same thing' and then clearly doesn't work towards it.
- Manipulates what others say for their own gain.
- Promotes themselves or their interests when it's neither the time nor place.

Tuning in to hidden agendas

Hidden agendas can be difficult to deal with for obvious reasons. That's their point. To understand if you're dealing with something more covert, watch out for someone who

- **Doesn't mention others' good work.** This means forgetting to talk about another team member's effort because that person might then look good.
- **Takes credit for someone else's contribution,** even when they are present. This is the worst kind of trust-busting meeting behaviour.
- **Doesn't confess to personal screw-ups,** even if it would be really helpful for everyone else to understand them.
- **Distorts facts** to make the situation look better than it is for themselves or worse than it is for others.
- **Avoids or delays sharing useful information** so that time gets wasted and others look bad.
- **Promotes a situation from which they will benefit** at the expense of the group or others in the group.
- **Tells downright lies** to advance themselves or discredit others.
- **Refuses to support the group** and doesn't mind if this becomes obvious.

Dealing with personal and hidden agendas

Sometimes it can be hard to deal with this kind of behaviour because it's so surprising. But here's how you can stay in control of the situation:

- **Watch to see what's happening.** Write down the precise words that an individual uses, so you can play them back in private if you need to. See how others in the room react and test the water to see if they feel the same as you do. You may be able to enlist their help by asking them for their opinions.

- **Try to maintain a neutral position** and don't get caught up in the manipulation or emotion of what's happening. This is what he or she is used to; this kind of person loves twisting what's been said or playing the innocent victim.
- **Take them to one side** and explain that what the behaviour isn't helpful and it's disrupting the process as well as irritating others. Don't mention any names, as this will just fan any flames.

Doing this is pretty straightforward. What's harder is when you have to manage recommendations that support someone's hidden agenda.

Dealing with recommendations

People with hidden agendas are as self-serving and political as they can be, so they support people who support them. That means you need to

- **Listen out for who benefits most** from what this person recommends. If the main beneficiary is the proposer or someone close to them, pay attention. Is what they are saying in the best interests of the group?
- **Get the proposer to think through the consequences** of their recommendation out loud. Question them so that it's evident that what they recommend may not be in the group's best interests.
- **Generate different options with the entire group** and then use the weighted decision matrix (see Chapter 5) or force field analysis (Chapter 9) to help you and the group be as objective as you can be. Then it's easier to discount what they recommend.

You'll need to try and tackle personal and hidden agendas because unless you do so, a group can descend into real conflict.

Managing Conflict

Conflict is an inevitable part of group work because conflict only really takes place when people get together. Think about it: Groups are the main place where opinions, judgements and perceptions get aired and shared. Different experiences, skills and knowledge mean that people are bound to come at any issue with a variety of solutions. But it's how you handle conflict that determines whether the group can work through it and benefit from robust discussions that you lead – or not.

There's one thing you can be sure of: Ignoring conflict or making hints to try and deal with it isn't helpful. You're much better off calling a spade a spade and tackling it head on. That means being able to recognise it when it turns up in your room, so you can manage it effectively.

Recognising unhealthy and healthy conflict

If you are dealing with unhealthy conflict, then you'll have a harder time getting the group to work it through. If it's healthy conflict, your job is easier. Table 7-2 shows you what you need to look for to distinguish both.

Table 7-2 Signs of Healthy and Unhealthy Conflict

Unhealthy	*Healthy*
Ignoring or tiptoeing around an issue	Being open about its existence
Muttering and sighing when certain people speak	Having respect and patience for others' views
Making attacks personal inside or outside a group	Closing down unhelpful conversations
Focusing on what can't be changed or the past	Focusing on what can be done or the future
Closing down opinions because they are different	Encouraging a variety of viewpoints and discussions
Looking for blame and recrimination	Taking breaks or timeout when you need to
Getting stuck in minor and irrelevant side issues, which make things worse	Redirecting a conversation when it's off-topic or unhelpful to the main work

Once you know what you're dealing with, then you can start to address it.

Getting the group to understand what's happening

Regardless of whether you are dealing with constructive or destructive conflict, you will need to help a group to

1. **Recognise that there is something to address because it's getting in the way of real progress.**

   That may mean abandoning your agenda or running order and saying that you think there's something to solve first. You'll need the group to recognise this, too; if they aren't ready to work on their conflict, you won't get anywhere. The next step helps make that happen.

2. **Discuss the impact of the conflict on the group and their performance.**

   Get the team or group to talk about the impact of the situation on the group, individuals and any other stakeholders. You can do this in pairs and report back if everyone is reluctant to open up. If they are ready to deal with it, simply have an open discussion.

3. **Agree to a collaborative process.**

   Tell the group that to move on effectively, they will need to work through the following steps, recognising that this takes time, energy and commitment to a resolution.

It's essential to get everyone's buy-in now, or the process won't work. If they won't agree to dealing with the conflict, ask them what they would agree to and work from there.

If everyone's ready to start work, you are can get going on this following process.

Dealing with conflict: A process for a group

Here's a generic series of steps you can use to deal with group conflict. You may have to tweak it to work for you, but it covers all the basic actions you need to work through:

1. **Decide how you are going to decide first.**

   (See Chapter 5 for more about this). Then this part of the session can't get dragged into the conflict, too. You'll also show the group that it can make progress and work collaboratively if they get stuck later on.

2. **Set a higher goal.**

   When you want people to collaborate, remind them that there is a higher goal that they are there to achieve. Get the group to say what this is and keep it posted and visible at all times so that you have a reminder of why they are there and what you are all trying to achieve.

3. **Clarify positions.**

   Ask each person or group of people who are in conflict to clearly articulate the rational and the emotional side of their position:

   - *The rational side of their position:* The more fact-based their reasoning is, the better. And talking about facts can take some of the heat out of a conflict.
   - *The emotional side of their position:* Expressing how you feel about a position and making everyone do this may be uncomfortable. But you are getting to the nub of why someone cares. Here are two useful questions:
     - What are you feeling right now? (You may need to give examples to encourage people to speak up.)
     - On a scale of 1–10, how intensely are you feeling this?

4. **Analyse all the positions.**

   This step is best done in smaller groups using:

   - A weighted decision making process (see Chapter 5)
   - 3WS or Force Field analysis (see Chapter 11).

   They help bring clarity and objectivity to the situation.

5. **Review the output.**

   Get the group to review all the work done and allow them to ask questions as the work gets presented back.

   Don't be tempted to cut this short; this is when people change their minds. Everyone needs to be heard at this point, and you need to ensure that happens. You also need to check that each person who presents feels that they have been heard.

6. **Decide on the way forward following the process you set up at the start.**

   If a group can't reach resolution, you'll have to work out

   - What more information do we need?
   - Who will do what?
   - By when?
   - When do we reconvene?
   - How do we manage our stakeholders in the interim?

These steps will help your group reach a resolution when positions and relationships haven't become totally entrenched. If that's happened, you may need to move more slowly and deliberately.

Dealing with conflict: A process for individuals or factions

Your situation is much harder when you work with a group that has individuals or factions who aren't prepared to concede an inch. When this happens, people get so bogged down in their positions that they forget they are there to work towards a larger goal. Instead, their goal becomes protecting their positions to win the conflict.

Your job is to help them move away from this. You can do that by using the Four A process, which means that you pay close attention to exactly what everyone says, making sure that what's said is what's meant. The benefit of doing this is that you

- Help remove ambiguity
- Reduce heat in a situation
- Allow everyone to speak
- Ensure all sides get heard

You use the Four A process in a very deliberate way by

- **Addressing** what is actually happening in the room and the issue at hand. You do this by observing what you and or your participants see without adding old history, distortions, assumptions, interpretations, or evaluations. You'll need to set up tight ground rules so you focus on this one issue only, and you'll have to model how everyone should express themselves to get the ball rolling.
- **Assessing** how someone might be feeling as the conversation unfolds at each turn. Emotion is information that can easily get in the way of decisions, so it needs to be acknowledged.
- **Attending** to an individual's needs so that they can handle the situation for the better. This is not a linear process and may need going over several times to unearth what these needs are.
- **Asking** for help from each other to move the situation forward. These are best framed as requests rather than demands. A demand escalates conflict; a request doesn't.

The beauty of the process is that it works both for giving and receiving information. It also takes both the rational and the emotional side of any position into account.

Here's how the process works in practise. Imagine that Jack, the head of finance, has announced to the group that there needs to be a 15 per cent reduction in headcount. Harry has had a stand-up row with Jack because he totally disagrees that this should be implemented across the whole organisation. Everyone has been asked to follow the Four A process. Harry is speaking in Table 7-3.

Table 7-3 How to Handle a Tough Conversation

Giving Information	*Comment (Harry to Jack)*
Address the precise issue	'When you said we have to reduce headcount by 15 per cent . . .
Acknowledge and express the emotion	. . . I felt literally sick after all that effort building the team up.
Attend to the need	I need to understand where these numbers have come from and why we need to implement this in the sales team.
Ask for	I want a full rationale for your announcement.'

As leader of the meeting or workshop, you repeat what was said to check and clarify the situation, expanding it to help get to groups with what's really going on. Table 7-4 shows you this process.

Table 7-4 How to Use the Four A Process as Group Leader

You as Group Leader Receiving and Expanding Harry's Information	*Your Comment*
Address the issue	'So when Jack said that you have to lay off 15 per cent of the workforce . . .
Assess and re-express the emotion	. . . it made you feel sick – you have spent years investing in the team, and I can see you are really concerned.
Attend to the need and expand it	As head of sales, you want to know you have the people and resources to land your numbers and build future success.
Ask for help and expand the explanation	What you want is to feel confident you have enough people to run an effective division. Have we understood you correctly?'

Then you would invite Jack to answer Harry, using the Four A process in return.

We recommend you practise the technique first so that you can focus on what's happening in the room rather than the process itself. But you'll find that when you use it, people slow down because they have to think more carefully about what they say and how they say it. That means that they explain themselves more clearly, which is really helpful when you're trying to resolve conflict in a room.

Don't worry if you fail to reach resolution in the first instance. Just check with everyone in conflict that they feel they are making progress by using a couple of scaling (1–10) questions (for more, see Chapter 4). If participants feel that they are getting somewhere, then plan a further meeting.

If, on the other hand, your opposing factions feel totally stuck, suggest that they get a professional mediator instead. Otherwise, you'll run the risk of getting sucked into mud that will stick – including to you. One of the most important things is to know when you don't have the skills to deal with a conflict situation.

The main take-away

The main thing to remember is to be rigorous about understanding where a group is before your session, planning what you do really carefully and paying attention to what's happening in a room. If you do that and keep calm, you'll be able to handle any difficulties that come your way, and feel good about how you do it.

Chapter 8

Handling What Happens Next

In This Chapter

- Thinking about your meeting or workshop
- Pulling together the meetings minutes afterwards
- Working out your Return on Investment (ROI)
- Ending your project

Face it: This chapter is all about the things that most people don't want to do. Follow-up is often hard and dull, and it just doesn't have the buzz that a live session does – but it has to be done.

After any important meeting, workshop or project that involves people working in a room together, you'll have follow-up work to do. That's because, at its simplest, participants frequently want more information or material that only you can provide. You need to make sure you deliver what you promised because that's how you build trust in you and what you're doing.

Now the follow-up you do will be quite different, depending on the focus of your earlier session, because what you do for a meeting can be quite different from what you do when you are running workshops or implementing a large project. This chapter helps you meet those different needs.

But before you jump into what you need to do to keep your sponsors or stakeholders happy, there's important work to do to build your own expertise.

That means taking the time to sit down and think about the session you just ran, how it went and what you can learn from it. It doesn't need to take long, but you do need to do it.

Reflecting On Your Meeting or Workshop

Assuming all went well, you'll be on a high immediately after your session. Then you'll suddenly be whacked. But if it wasn't as successful as you wanted it to be, you'll be feeling disappointed. Either way, what you'll do is focus on what participants said or did rather than on your role in the process. That's not an excuse for little reflection on what you did and how you did it.

As soon as you can, and certainly within 24 hours, you should think through and make notes on how things went. First, you should reflect at a general level, and then you need to think about the specifics. The benefit of doing this is that these reflections will accelerate your professional development so that you develop your expertise more rapidly.

And you won't ever make the same mistake twice.

How did it go at a big-picture level?

To reflect at a high level, ask yourself

- How effective was I in meeting the objectives or purpose of this session and why?
- How did the overall agenda or running order work?
- Who was fully engaged throughout the process and why?

Now you're ready to start thinking about the session in more detail.

What specifically should I keep doing?

To think about the details, drill down into

- What did I like about how I ran each of the activities?
- What went well?
- What would I definitely do again?

This will help you analyse the positives of what you did.

What specifically should I start doing?

This part will help you work through any areas of opportunity and improvement and will mean that you develop your skill and expertise in running meetings and workshops. Ask yourself:

- What could have gone better?
- What do I need to do to ensure that happens?
- What exactly will I do differently next time?

Finally, you should ask yourself, 'What else have I learned from this?' You should be sure to reflect on this, especially if the experience was an important first for you – for example, the first time that you led a team session, ran a large programme, organised a large meeting, took responsibility for the design or worked at a senior level. That way, you'll have insights for your sponsor who is bound to ask you the same question if she does her job well.

At a practical level, make sure you keep your notes somewhere accessible, so you can review them before you run your next meeting or workshop. If you want to download a worksheet with all the self-reflection questions on them, simply go to `www.dummies.com/go/rungreatmeetingsworkshops`.

Then, if it's your responsibility, you can get cracking with writing up the meeting minutes.

Writing Up Meeting Minutes

There are two kinds of meeting minutes: the simple and straightforward, which apply to most meetings, and the longer and more formulaic, which apply to any meeting that needs to stick to strict compliance rules.

Writing up simple minutes

The most important thing is to write an easy-to-read document that readers can skim for all the information they need and scan for their personal responsibilities or deadlines. That means all you need to capture are

- Headlines of topics discussed
- Decisions made
- Actions
    - Who is responsible?
    - What are the deliverables?
    - What are the deadlines?
- Items that were parked for the future
- When and where the next meeting is

Anything more takes too long to write up and means you're writing about stuff rather than doing it.

Other than recording who has to do what by when, Table 8-1 lists some other do's and don'ts to help you with the write up.

Table 8-1 Do's and Don'ts for Writing Up Simple Meeting Minutes

Don't	*Do*
Use complex language and long, waffly sentences	Write bullets; remember many people will be using smart phones to read the minutes
Include emotional or inflammatory comments	Highlight actions, people and deadlines
Skip writing minutes because everyone was there; people forget what they committed to	Stick to the same format so people can always find important information
Use lots of negative language; your minutes will be a depressing read	Write up and send your notes within 24–48 hours so you remember everything

Writing up more formal minutes

These are more appropriate for boards, committees, and trustee meetings or any meeting where there is a legal requirement to write up all meeting information, discussions and decisions. They are usually run by an official *chairperson* or *chair* who presides officially over the meeting and will have certain requirements about how the minutes are written up.

The assumption we have made for this section of the chapter is that you are the minute taker, so you'll be writing up the minutes.

The first thing you need to do when you are writing up more formal minutes is to check the level of detail your chair would like you to include. For example, you need to know if you should write up

- Who proposed or seconded motions
- Who voted for what items or issues
- How decisions were made

Whatever your chair prefers, you must always include

- The date, time and location of the meeting
- Names of everyone both present and absent
- Acceptance or amendments to previous meeting minutes
- Decisions made about each agenda item – for example:
    - Voting outcomes
    - Motions or resolutions passed
    - Items that were deferred
    - The next meeting date and time

The first time you have to take formal meetings minutes can be quite scary, especially if you are worried about understanding and keeping up with what's being said. To make life less stressful, just record the session on a smart phone or iPad. It's polite to let everyone know that's what you're doing and confirm that you're doing it simply to get your record-keeping right. But a recording is really useful, especially if you're worried about reading your handwriting afterwards!

The minutes writing process

Just before the meeting is over, you should look through your notes and check that everything's clear to you. Then you'll feel confident when you tackle the write-up.

Make sure you have set aside enough time to do this while everything is still fresh. Delays act like an eraser to the brain; you'll find there's less and less there the longer you leave it. And there are probably strict regulations about how quickly you need to get your minutes approved and sent.

To write up your minutes:

- Include a short statement of each action taken by the board with a short explanation for the decision.
- Summarise the major arguments before votes or decisions. That doesn't mean write it all up verbatim.
- Use the active voice as much as possible. Anything passive is longer and more boring to read.
- Write in the same person where possible. It's confusing to read a mix of 'we,' 'they' and 'you.'
- Avoid using people's names except for proposing or seconding. You're writing a business document, not a play.
- Attach other documents as appendices. Don't summarise them or stuff them in the body of the text as your readers only want the meat of what was said.
- Read the minutes aloud to see that they make sense. If you stumble as you read, rewrite the sentence because it's probably too long or unclear.
- Use spell and grammar check, so you don't make elementary and embarrassing mistakes.
- Put what you've written to one side to read an hour or two after you've finished. Read your minutes one last time before you send them to your chair. That way, you'll catch any mistakes that you may have missed before.

Distributing and saving your meetings minutes

Your chair will now read, review and revise the minutes to sign them off. Once this happens, you can release them to everyone who attended.

The easiest way to distribute minutes is with a file-sharing system. That way, you're not acting as a post-box, and it's everyone's responsibility to access and read them.

Your minutes will then be reviewed and approved at the start of the next meeting. Immediately after that, make any final tweaks you are asked to, resend them if necessary and store them so they are easy to retrieve. You can do this online or on a hard drive for safety. Most likely, you'll need to file a paper version, too.

Using meeting software

If you're using meeting software, then it will help you to keep everything short, synced and immediately available to everyone, saving you and your meeting participants a whole bunch of time. Here's some of the software available to you:

- **Agreedo** helps you prepare agendas, write minutes and track results. You can capture tasks, decisions and issues and progress with this freemium product.
- **After The Meeting** organises all of your to-dos, action and follow-up items into in a single view that everyone can see and comment on. This commercial software allows you to track progress and get feedback on your meetings.
- **Evernote** does more or less everything that OneNote does, but it's a web-based service with freemium access.
- **Gnote** is a free and open-source note-taking app that uses a Wiki-like linking system to connect your notes together.
- **Google Docs** is a free, easy and simple way to give everyone access to documents you need before, during and after your meetings.
- **LessMeeting** helps you write and share agendas, send invites, track and share attachments, time your meetings, manage notes and action items. You pay by user, by team or by organisation.
- **Meetin.gs** schedules events and gives you access to a landing page for meetings where you can add documents, organise agendas, take notes and distribute minutes.

Remote participants can dial in, and when it's all over, this commercial software keeps everything in one place.

- **Microsoft OneNote is a** general-purpose commercial note-taking tool that lets you integrate your meeting notes with all its other functionality.

Whatever tool you pick, even if it's a blank sheet of paper, it will only work if participants engage with it. That requires commitment to its use. Before you select anything, get everyone to evaluate what would work best in your context and then make a group decision about what is most appropriate for your needs. The good news is that all the tools listed will help with writing up and managing both informal and formal minutes.

Calculating Your Return on Investment

If you're committed to having better meetings and workshops, the first thing you'll do is evaluate what you did (see Chapter 6) and collect happy sheets, or feedback forms, at the end of every session. These are distributed either on paper or using an online tool, and they'll give you an initial reaction to everyone's perceptions.

But that reaction won't demonstrate a return on your investment (ROI); it will simply signal that people enjoyed it, liked you and found interest or relevance in what they did. Calculating your ROI answers the question 'For every dollar we invested, how much have we got in return?' It gives you proof that the huge effort you made was worth it.

If you want to investigate what you did as you work towards finding out the impact of any program you run, you'll need to evaluate your work at several different levels. And doing that is like studying the ripples in a pond. The impact at the centre is obvious to see, but as the ripples spread further out, it's harder to gauge and quantify exactly what's happening.

Evaluating your work

In an ideal world with endless time and money, Table 8-2 shows you what you'd review. We've added an example about muffin sales training to make the process more clear.

Table 8-2 Evaluation Levels

Evaluation Level	*Objective*	*Specific Areas of Focus*
Level 1: Individuals reaction Did they like it?	Assesses action and reaction	Examines liking, relevance and action plans 'I learned a lot, and had fun.'
Level 2: Individuals ability to transfer skills to workplace What did they learn?	Measures learning	Checks the skills, knowledge or attitude changes 'I practiced techniques to ask customers the right questions to sell more muffins.' 83 per cent of respondents strongly agreed with this.
Level 3: Looks at the impact on the department, team or unit How are they using it?	Investigates the implementation	Evaluates change in behaviour and actual application Servers used the techniques in 87 per cent of food sales observed – according to mystery shopper findings.
Level 4: Organisational impact What impact did it have on the bottom line?	Identifies the performance data, business results and ROI	Reviews performance data and business impact Bottom line increase of 24 per cent for muffins post training Cost of training + mystery shopper: $5,000 Increased sales: $25,000 over 12 months ROI: $20,000

(Adapted from the Kirkpatrick 4-level model with acknowledgments to Roger Kaufman)

To evaluate these different levels, you can use

- Questionnaires: Level 1 and 2
- Tests: Level 2
- Peer feedback: Level 3
- Observations: Level 3
- Interviews: Level 2 and 3
- Focus groups: Level 3 and 4
- Internal performance data: Level 4 (see Chapter 3)

The evaluations you do will, of course, depend on the budget you have, so ideally you should try to think this through before you start. Obviously, you can't measure effectiveness fully at all levels for 100 per cent of the people who attend your workshops, especially if you are running a large-scale intervention. For example, in the muffin sales case, a mystery shopper couldn't observe everyone who'd been trained as they handled every sale over the length of a day, so you have to work with your sponsor to set realistic and reasonable targets instead.

Expressing ROI

To calculate your ROI, you look at how the numbers work out by doing a cost-benefit analysis on your key performance data. You can express this in four ways:

- A ratio (benefit: cost)
- A percentage (net benefits x 100)
- A break-even moment in time
- An actual cash amount

You can, of course, report on all four. The numbers that will help you get to your net benefits (total value gained minus total costs) will include those derived from all the different evaluations you have done.

Ideally, you'll need to try and isolate the effects of your work from any other influencing factors. You want to show that the results you got came about from the work you did. You can do this by

- **Using control groups:** You compare and contrast the change in a group that has gone through an initiative with a similar group that hasn't. You use your performance data to show the difference.
- **Showing trend lines:** you can show what would have happened if the group hadn't gone through your process and compare this to the actual change in performance.
- **Isolating contaminating factors:** It's important to try to work out if you have any of these affecting your overall results. For example, the workshops might have been great but, in the case of the muffin sales training, if the store managers were really negative about it afterwards, then the techniques just wouldn't get used.

  Alternatively, there might be a national campaign advertising muffins everywhere, and you can't be sure if it's this campaign or your training that's having such a positive effect on sales. In this case, you need to look at market data for muffins and see what's going on nationally to work out the effect of the campaign against your own uplift in sales.

Whatever numbers you get you'll need to consult with your sponsor and any other key stakeholders who you made commitments to and keep them updated as you start to close your project.

Reporting On and Closing Your Project

What you do to close a project will depend on whether you have been running a one-off but high-visibility intervention or something that is larger scale.

If you've been running a one-off session, simply skim through the following pages and see which actions would be appropriate for you. Then you can make some appropriate suggestions to your sponsor. At the very least, you'll need to be in contact with her for a quick review about what worked and what could have been better.

If, on the other hand, you have been involved with a time-consuming and costly project that has involved lots of meetings and workshops, you'll need to report in some detail about what you did and how it went. Your sponsor will want to know because she has to report back on what you've been doing often at executive level.

If you have a good relationship with your sponsor, you will probably have been keeping her informally and formally updated. The informal updates will be emails or calls; the formal updates will be reports and review meetings.

Reports

The easiest way to keep tabs on any project is with a spreadsheet using a red, amber and green traffic light or dashboard system. At a glance, anyone can see your progress towards milestones and key deliverables.

Your reports shouldn't be complicated but should be regular. As a sponsor, it's much easier to stay connected to what's going on if you get a monthly one-page spreadsheet with a few explanatory bullet points rather than a ten-page report once a quarter.

The last report should make it really clear that you have done everything you set out to do.

Review meetings

Once your programme, meetings or workshops are complete, you'll need to hold a review. In fact, depending on the evaluations you are doing, you may need to hold a series of reviews.

Whatever your review covers, there should be no surprises for your sponsor. If there is bad news to share, you need to do it one-to-one and not in front of a group of people. If there's good news, she should be amongst the first to know so she can spread the good news at senior level.

Good news is that you achieved your outcomes, and you can illustrate that with some key success stories as you close your project.

Understanding project closure

Get a date in everyone's diary well in advance for a final review; then everyone, particularly your sponsor, will be more likely to be there.

To prepare well for this meeting, you'll need to

1. **Review your entire project.**
2. **Write a report.**
3. **Pull together a presentation.**

The review is the part that will take you time as it requires looking through your main documents and pulling together everything you need to sum up the why, what and how of your project.

Reviewing your entire project

Most people and teams are so delighted to have completed their assignments that the last thing they do is a project review. That means that they don't learn from what went well and what could have gone better, which means mistakes get repeated.

If you've done a large-scale or complicated implementation, you can complete a great review by simply answering these 20 questions:

- How did this project go?
- To what extent did we achieve our desired outcomes?
- What worked well?
- What could have worked better?
- What processes, procedures, knowledge and relationships contributed to our success?
- What risks did we take, and how did they work out?
- How acceptable were the mistakes we made?
- What problems or surprises did we encounter, and how did we solve them?

- What major lessons did we learn?
- How did we manage our stakeholders?
- How can we close any gaps that may still exist?
- How closely did we match our time and cost expectations?
- What did our stakeholders feel about us at the start, during and end of our work together?
- How satisfied is our sponsor?
- What do we know from the evaluations we have done?
- What current benefits do we see being delivered as a result of this project?
- What future benefits can we expect – for example, ROI at a later date?
- What would deliver even greater value?
- What do we recommend next?
- What do we need to carry forward into future projects?

You're unlikely to be able to answer all these questions without collecting feedback and meeting with people. That will mean you have to consult with the project team, your stakeholders and participants as you pull the information together.

Right now, you need to be careful of one important aspect of your project: the politics around it.

If you're project has been successful, you will need to make sure you

- **Credit and thank the people who were involved** and make sure that they get the kudos they deserve. You don't want or need to hurt anyone's feelings at this point.
- **Manage those who want to claim your glory** and run around saying that it was 'all their idea' and that they were 'working behind the scenes on your behalf to make it all happen.' Your sponsor or key stakeholders should be able to help you with this.

Sponsor lesson learned

Julia and I were asked to work with a global supply-chain team as it rationalised its hundreds of suppliers and went through a competitive tendering and renegotiation process. The sponsor was the team leader, and he wanted to manage his team's input and expectations, so we wrote draft documents for him to present for feedback and signoff.

Our sponsor told us that all the members of the management team were happy and gave us their thoughts and amendments. And so we prepared for a team of nine of us to run a three-day event. On the evening before, just as we are doing our final preparation for the first day, I was asked to spend half an hour going over the process one final time with the management team. Feeling confident because the team members had been involved in the design, I went to see them.

I was in for a shock.

Unbeknownst to us, our sponsor had wanted to spring a surprise on his entire team; the so-called 'feedback' we'd had were all his personal thoughts and ideas. His team was deeply unhappy about having been kept in the dark. Not surprisingly, everyone wanted to turn everything on its head.

We then had to spend six hours trying to re-engineer a carefully orchestrated event for over 80 people while working with a group of influential and disgruntled stakeholders.

The lesson? Spend time with your sponsor clarifying her role and responsibilities. Make sure you explain *why* what you need from her matters and what the consequences are if she doesn't follow through. It's as simple and easy as this: if she can't deliver, nor can you.

If your project hasn't been as successful as you had hoped, you can be sure that people will be distancing themselves from it and leaving you to carry the can. If that's the case, you need to be particularly careful and think through why your project failed and what could have been done to prevent this.

Projects that involve workshops, training or facilitation typically fail because they are

- The wrong thing to do
- Impossible to deliver

- Poorly managed
- Weakly implemented
- Badly sponsored
- Delivered in a rapidly changing environment

In other words, the wrong person was doing the right thing, or the right person was doing the wrong thing. In either case, the participants fail to benefit.

If an implementation, series of workshops, or change management programme you run looks likely to fall into any of these categories, you'll need to have pretty good answers to

- What went wrong in the scoping or delivery phase?
- Why?
- What could have been done to mitigate the challenges and risks?
- What actions were taken to manage the situation?
- Why didn't these work?
- What else could have been done?

If things didn't go as they should have because of a bunch of mitigating external factors – for example, the market crashed, and your work was cancelled – well, that's pretty black and white in terms of where the issue lay.

But if your project didn't land because people didn't pull their weight or your sponsor didn't do her job as well as she ought to have, you may be in an exposed position. Think about who else you need to align yourself with and get support from so that you aren't hung out to dry.

As you document the lessons learned, you don't need to write down every single detail about what went wrong. Prioritise the top five items and discuss them while being careful not to point fingers at people.

By now, you'll have a lot of information. That means you're ready to write up your report.

Writing up your report

The report consists of two parts: what you write up and how you write it.

What to write up

Your official project report should include:

- A title page
- An executive summary
- A table of contents
- An overview including
  - The purpose of the project
  - The business case
  - Deliverables
  - Cost
  - A high-level overview of work performed
- An analysis section including
  - Results (ROI) and how this compared with objectives
  - Risks, issues and mistakes
  - Lessons learned
  - Information applicable to other projects
- Recommendations
- Conclusions
- Appendices

How to write up your report

Write your report for any nonspecialist reader. That means make the language easy to understand and jargon-free. In addition, you need to make sure that what you write is credible, concise and constructive.

You can guarantee that none of your readers will pick the report up and read it from end to end. They'll want to read the sections that have the most pertinent information. By and large, that means the executive summary, your analysis, lessons learned and recommendations. So

- Make your headlines and sections clear.
- Use plenty of bullets.
- Write in everyday language.
- Make your report visually appealing with graphics and lots of white space.
- Keep your paragraphs and sentences short for easy reading.
- Use an unfussy font.
- Get someone else to check it through for you for clarity and style.
- Write the executive summary and recommendations last – it's always easier.
- Keep your recommendations realistic.

What to include at your final project meeting

After you've written your report, you'll be ready to have a final project meeting. That probably means a final project presentation. Don't simply copy and paste your project report onto slides; the font will be tiny, and your presentation dull. And you don't want to turn your very last meeting into a reading lesson.

Just select the most important items from your report and create a simple slide deck. Then you can present the work you've done, making sure that key players get a chance to shine, too. Make sure that everyone who attends your meeting has access to your presentation and to your report. They may want to share it with others.

When the meeting's over, make sure you go and celebrate with your team. You're all bound to have learned a lot and shared some memorable moments, and it's worth reliving them together before you all move onto your next big thing.

Part III

Building Your Skills

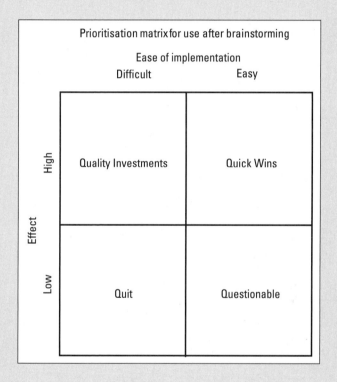

Prioritisation matrix for use after brainstorming

Ease of implementation

Effect	Difficult	Easy
High	Quality Investments	Quick Wins
Low	Quit	Questionable

Find out what you need to know about experiential learning at www.dummies.com/extras/rungreatmeetingsworkshops.

In this part . . .

- ✔ Use role play and case studies to grow participants' skills.
- ✔ Run a focus group like a pro.
- ✔ Using brainstorming and other tools brilliantly.
- ✔ Run meetings when you or others aren't in a room together.

Chapter 9

Building Participants' Knowledge and Practise

In This Chapter

- Working with case studies
- Using role play
- Giving good feedback
- Using video footage

This chapter mainly applies to workshops – and workshops in which you specifically want to accelerate and embed others' learning. Role plays and case studies are two important tools that help you do that.

When you use either of these methodologies, you need to have fabulous facilitation skills, so you are at ease working with a larger cohort of people. That means feeling grounded and confident in your skill set.

The good news is that when you work with case studies and role plays, you extend and grow your expertise by leaps and bounds. This applies not only to your facilitation capability but also to the subject matter, too.

In fact, exactly the same applies to giving feedback as a result of a role play. You'll quickly grow your self-awareness and ability as you learn from the scenario you use and role model the skill for participants to learn it. When you add video feedback in addition, you create rich and deep learning experiences that participants get huge value from.

This chapter helps you understand how to use four important tools that bring learning to life and really engage participants when you use them skillfully.

Working with Case Studies

A *case study* is a descriptive analysis of an event, used to find out why something happened and explore what could be done about it. Case studies are a wonderful way of exploring complex or nuanced topics to which there are no obvious and simple answers. What they provoke are in-depth discussions based on real-life situations, issues and problems. Those discussions lead to insights that are often powerful realisations for the participants who have them. And case studies can fundamentally change the way people think and work. That's why they are used so often as teaching aids in business, law or medical schools.

To get a feel for how you can incorporate case studies into your work, you need to

- Understand what they are all about.
- Know when to use the case study method.
- Think through your purpose in using this approach.
- Use great cases.
- Manage everyone's preparation.
- Work with the group.

Understanding what they are all about

When you use the case study method, you typically have a situation in which

- A decision-maker faces a complex problem with multiple and competing stakeholders.
- There is a context with a bunch of tough restraining factors.

- Supporting information; for example, data, documents, statements, pictures or video that flesh out the situation.
- Participants can access deeper learning, but only through wider group discussion.

Case studies come in many formats. These range from a 'What would you now do?' response to a couple of pages of information all the way through to detailed and data-heavy computer simulations that involve rapidly changing information.

Most cases are 12 to 25 pages long, explaining a situation often from the point of view of a manager or leader who is facing a dilemma. Generally, the case is written so that the reader feels empathy with the problems the central character faces.

In every case, there's always

- An overview of the situation
- An explanation of the main issues
- Relevant background
- A description of the people involved
- A history of the events that led up to the current situation

In fact, most often cases are disguised actual events or a mix of various but similar situations put together to maximise learning.

Knowing when to use the case study method

Cases work really well when you are

- Working with a larger group; for example, over 20 people
- Trying to get everyone to share knowledge, experience and practise
- Wanting to get the group to learn together and interact with and challenge each other in a group setting
- Building skills in problem-solving, analysis and decision-making

The type and length of case you decide to select obviously depends on your purpose in using one.

Thinking through your purpose

Just as you do for your entire workshop, you'll need to think through your purpose or objective in using a case study. Here are some questions you'll need to answer to do that:

- What's the learning I want everyone to draw from a case?
- Why do I want this group to learn that specifically?
- How does using a case study fit into and around the other activities I am planning?
- How might it help the group to work with a case study at this point?

You could decide you want to use a case to simply vary your activities in a cost-effective manner, or you might want to push the group to develop deeper insights together. But you need to be clear about your purpose because this will help you find the right case study for the group.

A case study can work very well when a group doesn't really know each other and is learning to work together. When everyone does know each other, you can expect robust conversation when people take opposing points of view – and that can be really stimulating and energising for everyone.

Working with a case study means using brilliant facilitation skills to shut some participants down, draw out lessons and invite others in. We don't recommend using a case study if it's your first time on your feet in front of a larger group of people.

Using great cases

You have two options for using great cases. You can either use one that's been developed by others, or you can develop one yourself. Naturally, there are pros and cons to both.

Working with others' case studies

The big benefit of working with others' case studies is that they save you a huge amount of time and effort. All you need to do is hunt for something that suits your purpose.

Here's where you can start to find case studies that will support you if you are running workshops focused on business needs:

- **Darden:** `http://store.darden.virginia.edu`
- **The Case Centre:** `www.thecasecentre.org/`
- **Harvard:** `http://hbsp.harvard.edu/product/cases`
- **IESE:** `www.iesep.com/en`
- **Indian School of Management:** `www.isb.edu/faculty-research/research/case-simulation-pedagogy`
- **INSEAD:** `www.insead.edu/facultyresearch/research/search_cases.cfm`
- **Ivey:** `www.iveycases.com`
- **Asia Case Research Centre, University of Hong Kong:** `www.acrc.hku.hk/case/case_topicindex.asp`

To find a suitable case study, go to each website (Harvard is a great place to start) and locate case studies. Search for your subject, and you'll get all the case studies with that word in it. Each case study will have a brief synopsis of what it's about. If you want to read the whole case, you'll need to buy it, which generally costs between $5 to $10.

Developing your own case study

We'll be really upfront with this: It's a huge amount of work to generate a case study. What you have to do is

- Find a common or everyday problem that is applicable to the group you'll be working with.
- Look for a theoretical framework for selecting the case and debriefing it to participants.
- Collect evidence to build out your case.

You do this by

- **Interviewing people:** This will help you understand how people actually behave in the type of situation you are interested in. You should ask about real responses and actions, the emotions experienced and the consequences. That way, you'll get insights into what really goes on in a scenario you want to use, and you'll be able to build complexity into it.

- **Observing interactions:** Ideally, you should at a minimum watch and write up helpful and relevant interactions. If you can, video these interactions, too; it's amazing what you'll pick up the second or third time of viewing. Videoing it will enable you to add rich detail that will make the case feel as realistic and factual as possible. This extra work will mean that participants will be more likely to engage with the case because it's so realistic.
- **Getting hold of documents and data:** These will help you get to another whole level of understanding in building your case study. You'll get insights into mistakes, speed of response and stakeholder reaction, too. Even better, you'll be able to amend and use some of this information to build your case study . . . disguised of course.

The biggest advantage of writing your own case study is obvious: It's much more relevant to your audience.

Just don't do what we've seen on several occasions and develop a fantasy or fictional case study. Good case studies need to be clearly related to work. Those that are set in a galaxy far, far away or on pirate ships (yes, we've seen both) just turn a lot of people off at best and make them difficult at worst. Stick to business schools' stuff instead.

Managing everyone's preparation

Once you've found or developed your case study, you need to work it through so you've thought in depth about the situation and gone through the participants' learning experience, too. That should take you two to three hours.

Like them, you'll need to

- Read the case.
- Reflect on the case by:
  - Articulating the main issues and the subordinate ones
  - Working out the goals the central character and their organisation both have
  - Identifying the constraints
  - Thinking through alternatives

- Selecting the best options
- Thinking about your top five actions

Doing this will enable you to answer the questions you set your participants as they prepare to work with the case in your session. And you need to set participants questions because they become fully invested in their positions, so you get more interesting discussions.

The questions that are useful for debriefing most case studies are often broad and generic. They include

- What are the issues at play in this situation?
- What's the context this is happening in?
- What key factors need to be taken into consideration?
- What alternatives are there?
- What would you do or recommend?
- How does this apply to you?

It's useful to think the answers through with someone else to check you haven't missed anything. You need to do this before you work with the group so that you can push them towards the insights that the case study offers.

Then you'll be ready to work with the group.

Working with the group

To make sure that the participants get maximum value from the case and to deal with anyone who hasn't prepared the answers to your questions in enough detail, we like running the following process:

1. **Divide the group into sub-teams of four to five people and give them 30 to 45 minutes to work together in break-out rooms.**
2. **Get the sub-teams to think through the answers to the five or so questions you set them.**

   Explain that they have to achieve consensus as a group and come up with group answers.

3. **Give each sub-team one specific question to present back into the room in plenary.**

   Each sub-team will need to select a presenter from amongst their group to speak on their behalf.

4. **Facilitate conversation in plenary when each sub-team is presenting back by**

   - Asking challenging questions and being a bit provocative if you need to be.
   - Drawing out opposing views and looking for additional opinions, so you lead the whole group towards important insights.
   - Noticing what's going on right around the room; if people are making notes and actively contributing they are engaged with you.
   - Getting people to stand or do a show of hands if they greatly agree or disagree with a particular position.

5. **Make sure you capture key insights on a white board or flip chart and that you are clear about the major learning points that the case presents.**

If you want to turn this into a competition, you can. Just allocate points for the best presentation, comment, insight and challenge.

A case often has multiple answers depending on how the problem is defined, the perspective a reader takes and the assumptions they are making. You will need to check all those when you are facilitating your plenary discussion.

You should also be aware that there are always some people who will feel that they don't have enough information and that what they would do 'would depend.' In other words, they won't commit. The point to make then is that real life involves making important decisions in a short time when often there is little or no information. Welcome to the world of management and leadership.

Your debrief shouldn't take much longer than 60 to 90 minutes or it will be too long.

For more tips on working with groups, see the Skills, Behaviours and Competences article at `www.dummies.com/go/rungreatmeetingsworkshops`.

If you want to add extra piquancy, introduce role play into your session. You'll have plenty of opportunity for that if you are using a good case study.

Working with Role Play

It's weird. Kids love pretend-play just as much as adults profess to hate it. What is it that happens in between? There's nothing like role play to accelerate learning a skill.

Funnily enough, role play is entirely accepted in some industries. After all, you'd never stay on a plane if the pilot announced, 'Ladies and gentlemen, welcome aboard and relax. Just to mention I've only flown this kind of aircraft a couple of times before, and I've never practiced in a simulator. But don't worry about the upcoming storm.' You'd be correct to assume that all pilots, all medics and all artists have countless hours of practice. Every day.

Carry this concept over to managers and leaders, and they kick up about simulation, learning and rehearsal – which is what any role play is all about. Though they may not be working in life or death situations, they often have others' well-being and large sums of money in their hands. And they are often doing cutting edge work.

The simple truth is this: Serious professionals practice and rehearse. That's how you get good at something. And that's the point of a role play. You do nothing in life brilliantly the first time, whether it's using a new phone, driving a car, comforting a newborn or leading a team. You try, experiment and learn what works best for you.

But you can take a shortcut through this process by doing role plays.

The purpose of a role play is to provide a safe environment for learning or developing an interpersonal skill, such as interviewing, negotiating, presenting or selling. The idea is that participants can make mistakes and learn without damaging real relationships.

So why do people dislike role play? They feel embarrassed by

- Scenarios that provoke anxiety in the first place
- The possibility of failure in front of their peers
- The fear of speaking let alone performing in public

To counter this, you have to

- Believe that it is the right thing to do.
- Call it what you will.
- Develop realistic and appropriate role plays.
- Set your role plays up for success on the day.
- Understand your role-play options.

Believing that it's the right thing to do

Fifty per cent of whether any role play works or fails is rooted in how you feel about it. If you hate them or are unsure about your scenario, the group will sense that and push back. But if you feel confident that this is the best way for the group to learn and that what it does is appropriate to everyone's needs, the group will stay with you and go for it.

By the way, individuals know that role play is helpful because it focuses on them in an individually centred way and is therefore one of the quickest ways to learn. For example, research at Idaho University showed that out of 32 methods of learning, adult learners ranked role play among their least favorite. Yet when those same people were asked which of those 32 methods resulted in the best learning, role play was among the top five.

And this is backed up by our experience, which is that when you ask groups, 'How would you best like to learn or improve a skill?' the answer is always 'with role plays.' It's also the part that always gets the best evaluations. You can't learn except by doing, which is the opportunity that role play provides.

Calling it what you will

To counter any negative reaction to the phrase role play, simply call it something else. Here are a few options:

- Simulation
- Real play
- Skills practise
- Skills building
- Development practise
- Scenario implementation
- Learning scenario

As Juliet said about Romeo, 'That which we call a rose by any other name would smell as sweet.' It's the same for role play.

Developing realistic and appropriate role plays

Unlike a case study where we don't recommend you develop your own unless you absolutely have to, you should always write context specific role plays. That's because generic role plays just don't work.

To get a role play absolutely right, it needs to

- Have enough detail, so it's **recognisably rooted in the organisation** you are working within. That will help with buy-in.
- Offer exactly the right level of challenge for the group, so it **tests basic and more advanced learners.** That will help with engagement.
- Be positioned, so you can **draw out the frameworks and tools** you are teaching. That will help participants to see the utility of the role play.
- **Be complicated enough to learn from** but not so complicated that it takes a long time to assimilate what's happening. That will maintain momentum.

To write a good role play takes a bit of time. You need to research the background, get into the skin of your characters to make them and their challenges real for participants, write both sides of the scenario (there are always two sides), test the scripts out and then get them signed off. If you just bang something out, you should be prepared for your role play not to work too well the first time out.

A good scenario

- **Explains the central characters and their different motivations.** Each character should have their own opinion about what is happening along with different motivations and goals. For example, you have a buyer and a seller, a customer and customer service desk, a boss and an employee.
- **Puts up a challenge** that both the central characters have to deal with. This is a sale, negotiation, performance review or conflict situation and is clearly framed as such within the context of the workshop.
- **Offers scope for bad to good interactions.** There's enough information to send someone down a blind alley if they choose to go there. One of the points of a role play is to learn what relevant information is and what not to deal with because it will get in the way of the main issue.
- **Is framed as a dialogue,** which ideally needs moving towards resolution. You need to flesh out a scenario that will be supported and move faster when participants use the frameworks, tools and techniques that they are there to learn.

We recommend you have a dry run or two before you go live with your role play. There are always a couple of tweaks or tricky issues that you want to sort out or find answers to when you are not in front of a group. And you'll also want to work out what you'd like to direct participants' attention to as the role play progresses. You can do this much better when you've practiced a few times.

Then you're ready to use your role play for real.

Setting the role play up for success

A good role play is well set up so everyone knows why they are doing it and what the process is.

As you introduce your role play, you'll need to explain the benefits to your participants. Role plays mean that participants

- **Practise learning** in a safe environment.
- **Get a hands-on experience** to turn something theoretical into something practical.
- **Increase their confidence** in difficult situations.
- **Build self-awareness** of their skill level, their strengths and their weaknesses.
- **Embed and rehearse feedback skills,** as they both give and receive it.
- **Develop a practice and culture of personal development,** which is how they build a learning organisation.

Once you've covered these with the group, then you can move into explaining the process.

Managing and explaining the process

Generally, there are four stages to every role play:

- **Instructions:** You clarify your ground rules, what will happen, with whom and when.
- **Preparation:** Your participants read the role play and get ready.
- **Implementation:** Everyone works to try the scenario out and use their recent learning.
- **Debriefing:** Participants reflect on what happened.

Instructions

The first thing you need to sort out are your role-play ground rules. Table 9-1 lists some useful ones you might like to think about and discuss with the group before you begin:

Table 9-1 Ground Rules for Role Play

Don't	*Do*
Make it ridiculous or spoil the learning on purpose	Try the frameworks, tools and techniques you are there to learn
Go overboard on being difficult; you're not a diva	Be yourself
Say something deeply unrealistic like 'you're sacked' or 'I'm dead'	Stop or take a timeout if you need to
Use wishy-washy comments like 'It was fine' as that's unhelpful	Give evidence-based, specific and actionable feedback
Get defensive when you receive feedback	Listen to peer feedback and reflect on it

You then need to worry about who is doing what, where and when.

The easiest thing is to write up this key information in as many places as possible because if participants can misunderstand, they will. So put them on a slide, a flip chart and at the top of the role-play scenarios, too. Then encourage participants to take a photo of what they are supposed to be doing. That way, if they move to a breakout room, they know what's happening and when. Make sure you walk through your key information at least twice and even then check that everyone understands.

The main items you need to be clear about are general and specific timings and locations. Table 9-2 provides an example.

Table 9-2 Sample Information to Clarify Role Plays

Action	*Timing*	*Who*	*Where*
Preparation time	20 minutes	Grouped by	
	14.00 – 14.20	Managers (Rosie, Jim, Fadi)	Room A
		Employees (Pierre, Raj, Tom)	Room B
		Observers (Ahmed, Mariam, Abiye)	Room C
Role play in action	30 minutes	Role play (10 minutes)	
	14.20 – 14.50	Feedback:	
		Self (3 minutes)	
		Person B (5 minutes)	
		Observer (12 minutes)	
		Group 1: Rosie, Ahmed, Pierre	Room A
		Group 2: Jim, Mariam, Raj	Room B
		Group 3: Fadi, Abiye, Tom	Room C
Feedback in plenary	20 minutes	All groups	Plenary
	14.50 – 15.10		(A 207)

Preparation

If you're working with a two-sided role play, you'll ideally need four-person groups, two to role play and two to debrief. For example:

- The manager
- The employee
- Observers (one to observe the manager, and one to observe the employee)

We like to get all the relevant groups preparing together. For example, all the managers and employees work together, while all the observers get ready by reading both sides of the situation.

Observers have a different role, and you will need to brief them to

- **Write down the specifics** of what was said, in particular what hindered or helped the conversation.
- **Notice body language** and reactions, including facial expressions, pauses and pace of the conversation.
- Identify where and when participants used or didn't use their **new tools and frameworks.**
- Focus on what role players should **keep** doing and what they should **start** doing in a respectful, constructive and evidence-based manner.

You can always give them an observer sheet so that this makes the job easier and they remember what they need to look out for. You can find a sample worksheet for observers by going to `www.dummies.com/go/rungreatmeetingsworkshops`.

Before you let your observers loose on their peers, test them to make sure that they are up to the job. Demonstrate a few lousy behaviours and ask them to note down what they observe and then check that this is what you're looking for in terms of being accurate, evidence-based and actionable. Then you can be confident that the first set of observers can give clear and constructive commentary to their peers.

By the way, this is crucial to the success of your role play because flabby input afterwards will set you up for falling at the last fence. Participants have to get real value and insights from their peers or the whole activity will be a waste of their time. Role players must understand what they did well and what they could do better in future if they are to leave the whole session knowing what to keep on doing and what to change for the better.

That's why we talk about giving feedforward rather than giving feedback; the emphasis is on what a participant can do to make things better in the future rather than what they did that was unhelpful as they worked through their scenario. Unless they are a rhinoceros, they'll be completely aware of their mis-steps anyway.

Depending on the complexity of your role play and the length of your workshop, preparation can take anything from 5 to 60 minutes. Once everyone's ready, and participants will always want more time to prepare, then move into different areas. That way, they won't be distracted by what's happening at a table next door.

Ideally, you or another facilitator will be able to supervise every group so that everyone gets observed and given feed-forward by an expert practitioner.

Implementation

Just before everyone goes to their breakout areas, make sure one final time that they understand the process. Now's the time that you should make sure each group appoints a timekeeper.

If you are being an observer, go with the group and explain your role. Your job is to pick up on the stuff that others find hard to see and that *isn't* the body language. It's the structure or arc of the conversation, the use of learning and any hijacks that happen. Write down all the questions that are asked and the answers that are given, watching out for the relationship between both parties.

The reason you write everything down is that playing back people's precise words helps them learn – and they can't argue with what they said if you quote it verbatim. If you can only say, 'You said something like. . . ,' they can argue, quite rightly, that they didn't.

We like to use two columns to keep notes in. One column takes up three-fourths of the page, and in that, we record the conversation using initials to denote the speakers. In the other column, we note down happy or sad faces depending on what was said, the learning as it's used and unhelpful behaviours (for example, overtalking or repetition of comments). These signal something hasn't been properly dealt with, and there wasn't real listening.

As you observe

- **Ask yourself** how each statement moves the conversation into a helpful and constructive place, making very brief notes about your perceptions in the right-hand column.
- **Interrupt the role play** if you see a ginormous rabbit hole appearing. Simply call a timeout and ask participants what's going on and what they would like to do about it. Then back-track to restart the conversation.

- **Pay attention to time** and signal when it's nearly up so both sides can end the conversation, even if the situation isn't resolved.

Debrief

Once a conversation has ended, get the main role player to reflect on these questions:

- What did you like about what you did that you should **keep** doing?
- What would you like to have done differently and that you should **start** doing?

At this point, don't give your opinion. Save what you have to say until everyone else has finished, as it's their learning not yours.

Then get the secondary character to give their opinion on

- What did he or she like about what just took place and that either party should **keep** doing?
- What would he or she have liked to be different and that either of party should **start** doing?
- How he or she **felt** as the situation unfolded?

Thirdly, the observer should talk about what he saw in terms of what both parties should keep doing and what both parties should start doing. As he was outside the conversation, he should be most specific in terms of frameworks, tools, words, voice and body language used. All this time, you simply facilitate the conversation.

Finally, it's your turn. You only add what others have missed; if they've said it all, just move on.

Note that the role play debrief always takes at least twice as long as the role play itself if it's being properly done. So leave enough time for that to happen.

Once all the role plays have been done and everyone has been person A, person B and the observer (you may need several role plays), you need to facilitate an overall debrief. Useful questions to ask here are

The power of right role play

So this participant gets up, looking very glum, and quietly leaves the room at the end of a role-play debrief. His hands are in his pockets and his eyes downcast. He's not clutching his phone, so it can't be an urgent call he needs to take or make. I (Jess) wonder what's happening, but with a roomful of people, there's nothing I can immediately do. And we're not due to have lunch for another hour.

He comes to find me when I'm at the buffet.

This time, he's elated and full of energy. He says, 'I had an epiphany as we were doing the role play, and during the debrief, I realised I had to do something about it. I had been managing a team member exactly as I shouldn't have been; the parallels with the role play were uncanny. I had to leave the room because I needed to think about what to do. I knew I needed to call this guy to apologise, get his input and use the framework you shared with us. I had the best conversation I ever had, feel 100 per cent positive about his actions and that we're at a whole new level in our relationship. If it's okay with you, I'd really like to tell the group.'

- What happened in each group?
- What did you experience in the different roles?
- What was difficult, and what was easy?
- What are your main takeaways?
- How are you going to use this?

Make sure that everyone captures two or three concrete things that they can do and check if they want any more clarification before you summarise and move on.

Understanding your role play options

Ideally, you want your participants to all do a role play so that everyone rotates through person A, person B and gets to observe. Then after that, you repeat the process to further develop everyone's skills.

Of course, this would get to feel far too same-y. Your options are then

- **Do the second role play by Skype or phone** to see how to use the skills remotely. If you can't do this, get people to sit back-to-back instead.
- **Hot-seat the scenario at the front of the room.** Hot-seating means getting your participants to do a short part of the role play and then swapping them over after a few minutes. The advantage is that you get more people involved in one scenario. You can then either debrief the contribution an individual made or carry on to the end and do it all at the same time. In our experience, everyone gets more out of it if you do the former, and it's easier to get participants to repeat and improve what they did if they want to.
- **Work with actors.** Getting actors to come for part of your workshop makes the whole thing much more realistic. Properly briefed, your actors should respond positively to what's good and negatively to what isn't. Most participants get a huge amount out of working with actors and love it when they can then rehearse real situations. Any actor worth his or her salt only needs a short briefing session to do a fantastic improvisation from which participants learn lots.

Reinforcing the standard

If your participants are not used to giving each constructive and detailed feedforward, their role plays may not be as useful as they could be.

When you don't have the resources to spend time with each group, bring everyone together at the end of each rotation and check that the new observers can give decent and useful input. That way, you'll also get to see who the weakest observer is, and you can stay with them. Not only will you help them improve their feedforward skills, you'll also make sure the group gets value from the exercise. And it's always better to be safe than sorry.

Of course, if you want to really give superb feedforward what you need to do is video the role play and then review the footage.

Using Video

Working with video footage of any role play is one of the most powerful ways to reinforce learning and build self-awareness. Video provides participants with a lot of complex information and personal insight.

Although lots of people say that they hate seeing themselves on camera, they are often intrigued at the same time. It's your job when using video to get participants to

- Reflect on their personal performance.
- Think about their interactions with others.

Reflecting on personal performance

If you are running a workshop where participants are only focusing on their personal performance (for example, a presentation skills workshop), then the debriefing will focus on what the individual said and how they said it.

What was said

You need to use your footage to draw a participant's attention to

- What information was provided and how it was structured: This includes
    - Starting and ending
    - Order of material
    - Clarity when moving between subjects
    - Emotional connection with the subject and audience
    - Explanations and question handling

- How the information was presented: This includes
  - Use of frameworks or tools they have been learning
  - Fillers (for example, um, er, sort of, basically or like)
  - Long rambling sentences that circle around a point
  - Pace at which someone speaks (Most people are too fast to allow themselves time to think)
  - Gesture, posture and body language

Notice that gesture, posture and body language comes last as it's the easiest stuff to recognise.

Observing personal performance

If you are videoing an interaction between two people and debriefing that (for example, interviewing skills, coaching, negotiation or conflict management), you'll need to get your main role player to watch and listen to

- How he or she framed the whole conversation
- How he or she created rapport
- What questions he or she asked
- How well he or she listened to the answers given and built on them or probed for more information
- How well he or she noticed what was going on for the other person
- How the relationship developed and what is likely to happen next
- How he or she concluded the conversation

Doing this will add huge value to your footage review.

Reviewing footage

We prefer to debrief a conversation sentence by sentence. When you go forensic on an interaction, you can really see what works and what doesn't. It's in this detailed analysis that a participant really learns from the video, and it becomes almost impossible to reject the hard evidence you place in front of them. They may get defensive or say things like, 'I never usually do that' (and we wish we had $10 for everyone who said that), but the fact is they did, and you have it on tape.

If you don't have time to do a detailed review in your workshop, you can always arrange to do it afterwards either face to face or remotely. (For more on remote workshops, see Chapter 12.)

Here is a list of things you need to do when you debrief video:

- Stop the video after 1 to 2 minutes and invite your participant to focus on a couple of concrete things that she likes about herself and her performance. Focusing on the positive will take her away from what she dislikes.
- Coach improvements as far as possible. For example, instead of saying, 'Stop wringing your hands,' say 'How could you use your hands to better effect next time?'
- Stop the video and invite your participant to try a small section with you again, so that she experiences the difference. Ask her to comment on how she feels. Point out that if it feels unusual, it's simply because she isn't used to it.
- Focus on what is actionable and leave everything else. For example, if your participant has imperfect English, she will be aware of this. You don't need to make a judgement about it. It's much more important that she can be understood than that she is grammatically correct.
- Pay attention to the tone of voice you use. Warmth and empathy can greatly reduce defensiveness.

Getting the right technology

We generally use an HD camera so that you capture all the details of an interaction. They are simple to use, and it's quick to transfer footage to your laptop so you can be ready to review any role play within minutes.

Make sure you have your tripod, enough spare batteries and carry an extension cable so you never run out of power. You look like a complete numpty when you do, and it will only throw you into a spin.

If you don't want to invest in a camera, tablets and phones are so good that it's often just as easy to use them instead. Then all you need to buy is a phone tripod. The only issue with phones and tablets are that sometimes they can take longer to download than a camera, especially if you have four lots of 15-minute videos.

Experiment with what you have to see what works best for you. We use cameras as the main resource and phones as a backup.

The main thing is to know how your camera works, how you transfer files and how you open them to review footage. You don't want to learn any of this in front of a group, so have a few practice sessions. Then you'll look slick and polished even if you don't feel it.

Having the right software

Here's a horrible nightmare: You've got all that lovely footage and then can't make it play on your laptop. Or anyone's laptop. Don't panic and do download VLC, which is an open-source program that supports virtually all video formats. This means your Plan B will always work and your Plan C, too, which is borrowing someone else's phone.

You don't want to be distracted by your hardware or your software. Your aim is to be 100 per cent focused on participants and their needs.

This way, you will be.

Chapter 10

Running Focus Groups

In This Chapter

- Understanding what focus groups are and how to use them
- Getting ready to run one
- Doing it right
- Analysing your data

Focus groups are a simply fantastic way of getting lots of data because they are simply mass interviews. So when you run them (and you usually run a series), you'll get copious material that should provide you with loads of actionable insights. To achieve that, you need solid end-to-end planning and robust execution.

Then you'll get the results you want, which are clear understanding and practical actions emerging out of all your useful data. This chapter covers everything you need know about how to plan for, manage, facilitate and write up a focus group.

Knowing When to Use a Focus Group

You run a focus group because you want information that will lead to action, and that information is best gathered by bringing together a group of people to share their thoughts, feelings, perceptions and opinions about a specific issue. The point of a focus group is to talk, answer questions, exchange stories and comment on shared experiences and points of view.

The context in which you can use focus groups varies. You can use them to plan, to evaluate ideas, products or services, to investigate the status quo, to identify problems, to develop strategic plans or to work on vision or mission statements.

The aim of any focus group is to

- Explore what people think and why
- Collect input
- Generate data that leads to recommendations
- Implement efficient and effective actions

Thinking About What You Want to Achieve

Most people make the mistake of running far too many focus groups. Before you commit to the time and expense of running ten sessions, think 'Could we achieve the same result with six to eight instead?'

If you are planning to run focus groups, just be aware that the bulk of the work comes not in preparing or running the sessions; it comes afterwards when you collate the data and report back.

Here are the stages of a focus group:

1. **Preparing for the focus group.**

   This stage includes writing your purpose statement, finding your participants, writing a script and managing logistics.

2. **Running your sessions.**

   This stage involves answering the questions, sticking to the script, working with participants and managing the information generated to prepare for analysis.

3. **Reporting back.**

   This means transcribing audio, video or writing up notes, analysing your data, extracting themes or actions, consolidating everything and reporting back to your sponsor.

The rest of this chapter moves through all these steps.

Side effects of a focus group

There are a couple of interesting side effects when you run a focus group:

- When people discuss a topic of common interest, they bond.
- When you run a focus group inside an organisation, you also generate a sense of progress.

Focus groups signal that change of some sort is underway, which is why follow-up and actions are so important. Don't run a focus group if nothing's likely to happen as a result. You simply set up expectations that then aren't met.

Characteristics of a focus group

So what characterises a focus group?

Typically, a focus group

- **Has a sponsor** who is interested in the answers to the issue or topic under discussion
- Involves participants who have **an understanding, experience or interest** in what's going to be discussed
- Is designed **to air and share ideas** in a short space of time
- Lasts between **1.5 and 2** hours
- Is generally **run more than once** to generate enough useful data
- Leads to output that is **actionable and specific** to the topic under discussion
- Involves **no fewer than 5 people and no more than 12** so that there's enough substance generated and everyone gets heard
- Has a clear, outcomes-oriented purpose statement

If what you're doing doesn't have these characteristics, you're probably running a discussion group instead – in which case, some of this chapter will apply along with some of the material you'll find in chapters dealing with meetings (for example, Chapters 2, 4 and 5).

Preparing for Your Focus Groups

You'll need to plan your focus group so you know what happens by when and also how much it's going to cost you. You'll want to make a budget estimate as you start. You'll also need to

- Define a clear purpose statement.
- Build your timeline.
- Get the right people in the room.
- Generate the right questions.
- Develop your script.
- Select a location.
- Prepare your materials.

And this is just the work that has to happen beforehand.

Defining a clear purpose statement

You need a clear and specific purpose statement to develop the right questions and get the best information from the group.

Something broad or general like 'finding out what people think about *x*' makes it harder to consult with your sponsor, identify who you should invite, develop good questions or get useful results.

Here are some examples of clear purpose statements:

- To discover, clarify and record themes regarding employee perception of and reaction to our new time bank. To realign its implementation based on feedback.
- To consult with parents and teachers to investigate responses to our school's proposed extended operational hours. To review and decide on go or no-go.

- To understand why our organisation does not attract more graduates from the top-tier universities. Based on the information and opinions of the focus groups, develop strategies to address this issue.

Once you have crafted a good purpose statement, ask yourself 'Why do we want to know that?' Your answer will often lead to a more refined and specific purpose statement.

The reason you want to invest time in nailing your purpose statement is that when it's really clear, it's really easy to design the rest of the process.

Building your timeline

Table 10-1 gives you a rough timeline to help you manage everything you need to do in advance of running your focus group.

Table 10-1 A Focus Group Timeline

Activity	*Weeks Before the Focus Group*
Develop your purpose statement	6–8 weeks
Identify potential participants	6–8 weeks
Invite and chase up your participants	6–8 weeks
Develop and test your questions	5–6 weeks
Write your script	4–5 weeks
Book the venue	5 weeks
Write and send the invitation	4 weeks
Follow up the invitation with a phone call	3–4 weeks
Arrange logistics (the room, seating, flip chart, audio visual, coffee and so on)	2–3 weeks
Remind your participants they are coming	1 week
Check in with your participants one more time to ensure they'll attend	2 days

Getting the right people in the room

Obviously, you want to ensure that you get people together who have something to say on the topic in hand. And you've two main ways of doing this:

- Random selection
- Specific selection

Random selection

Random selection means inviting a cross-selection of anyone in your target group. First you identify everyone who could come, and then you select them.

You can ask the first ten on the list and then go to the next ten depending on who replies. You can pull their names out of a hat or use a random generator. There are several apps that help; you simply stuff a list of names into them, and they generate your list.

Specific selection

Specific selection involves inviting people who have expressed an interest, belong to the same group you want to talk to, have an expertise in the subject or are *key influencers.* These are important people who have a big impact on others. You just need to make sure that everyone who comes is willing to talk. Most importantly, as far as you are able, check that there are no conflicts of interest between participants.

In either case, remember that you are inviting people. Compulsory attendance makes people cross, so make it clear that they should come because they want to.

You should expect a dropout rate of anything between 10 to 40 per cent, depending on whether you're running an internal or external focus group.

- *Internal focus groups* happen in-house, and people are more likely to turn up.
- *External ones* bring people together who have no previous connection with each other.

People who are invited to an external focus group are more likely to cancel at the last minute or not to show up. Plan your invitations accordingly.

Generating the right questions

Crafting the right questions and putting them in the right order are the most critical steps in preparing for a focus group.

In this section, we use the scenario of running a series of focus groups to find out how to attract graduates of top-tier universities.

The questions

Your main aim is to get people talking: Just remember that general questions generate general answers, while specific questions generate specific answers.

Think about the differences between these two questions:

- What should we do about our graduate recruitment policy?
- What are the three most important things we could do to recruit high-calibre graduates from the best universities?

What you want is to drill down through the detail so that you uncover the effective actions that can be implemented afterwards.

Because a focus group lasts a maximum of two hours, you don't have time for many questions. Realistically, you'll probably get through four or five questions, so generating six will mean you have a back-up in case you get a quiet group.

This process will help you get to your questions:

1. **Think through what you would like to know as a result of these focus groups.**
2. **Turn those statements into questions.**
3. **Review your questions by checking that they align with your purpose statement.**

4. **Test your questions out on a couple of interested people to check that they are clear and answerable.**
5. **Leave everything for a few days.**
6. **Do a review to see that your questions really do the job by answering them yourself.**
7. **Answer them yourself.**

And here's what you need to know about the wording of your questions because there are only five types of questions you need to bear in mind for the design of your focus group.

If we continue with the scenario for attracting high-calibre graduates, here's how those five questions work:

- **Starting questions** are easy to answer, put everyone at ease and help the group get going. For example: 'Tell me your name, your job and which college you graduated from.'
- **Introductory questions** get the group thinking about the topic under discussion. For example: 'How was it you heard about us when you were at college?'
- **Transition questions** serve to focus the conversation more. For example: 'What made you decide to apply for a graduate job here?'
- **Key questions** zoom in on the meat of the meeting. For example: 'What should we do to get greater numbers of high-calibre graduates to apply to us?' or 'What messages and channels could we use to attract high-calibre graduates?'
- **Ending questions** signal that the focus group is coming to a close. For example: 'When you think of what we've talked about today, what have we missed?'

You can see from this example that the questions flow in a logical manner and have a natural start, build and end that makes writing a script easy. They also lead to a natural order.

The order

The sequence of your questions matters; you can see from the list in the preceding section that you start with more general ones and then move to more specific questions.

You don't want to ask anything too probing or tough early on; your participants need time to warm up and to work as a group, and then they'll be comfortable sharing more negative information.

Once you've thought about the order, you can then start to develop your script.

Developing a script

You need to write a script or guide for a whole bunch of reasons:

- If you're running multiple focus groups, you need to run them all in the same way so you **generate reliable and consolidated information**.
- If you're going to work with someone else or leave time between focus groups, then a script is a must because it will **keep you or anyone else on track**.
- If you're working for a sponsor, you'll need to show her your script so that they know what questions you'll ask and what activities you plan to generate useful information. You need to **get sponsor input and sign-off,** so you don't generate any nasty surprises when it's too late to deal with them.
- If you write a script, you **internalise what you're going to do,** so you're better prepared for leading the discussion.
- If you have a script, you'll **never panic about what you do** next, and you'll always have a reference for what you did.

Writing a script: High level

There are three main parts to writing a script:

- **Your start** consists of your welcome, the purpose, an overview of your agenda, introductions and ground rules.
- **Your questions and activities** include reviewing information and products, completing tasks or reflecting as individuals, pairs, trios or as a group.
- **Your close** should include thanks, how to give further input, confirmation of confidentiality, results and data use.

When you are writing a script, start by writing the purpose statement at the top. Then you can regularly check that what you do is aligned with it.

Writing a script: The detail

When you are new to running focus groups and you want to ensure each one in a series is as standardised as possible, here's how you could write the start of your focus group on 'What should we do to get greater numbers of high-calibre graduates to apply to us?'

> Good afternoon, everyone, and thank you for taking the time to be here today to talk about how we attract calibre graduates. My name is Jane Smith, and I'm going to be your facilitator for this morning's focus group. Tim is here helping me capture all your valuable information, and he'll be supporting the write-up and analysis, which we'll let you have in about eight weeks.
>
> The purpose of getting together is to find out what we can do to make sure we hire more people like you, which is why we specially wanted your help and input.
>
> We're going to ask you a series of question to which there are no right or wrong, good or bad answers. We just want information so that we can invest wisely in hiring the best people. I'm sure you'll have different ideas, so please bring them to the table. We're also interested if you agree, disagree and have examples and stories to share. We'll be doing some paired work, some brainstorming and some general conversation.
>
> My role is to ask the questions, listen to your answers and make sure you all get heard, that I understand you, and that everyone gives equal input.
>
> We're going to record what you say as well as keep any flip charts you generate. What we want is to collect general themes and specific ideas. Having said that, what you say here is confidential, and we'd like your agreement that what's said in the room stays in the room after the session. In the same vein, no one's name will be associated with specific comments when we do the write-up. To help that write-up, Tim and I will be taking notes. You've got name badges to help all of us during the session, but we won't attach your names to any statements you make.

Can we agree to a few more ground rules for us as we work together? I'd like to suggest that we

- Turn off phones
- Allow everyone talking time
- Respect each other's opinions
- Accept that differences will lead to interesting input
- Understand that in the interests of time, we will have to park some issues

I'd like to start by asking all of you to introduce yourselves by saying who you are, what your job role is and which college you went to.

You can see from the introduction that you have covered everything you need to say for the start of your focus group.

Writing a script: Things to do

As you write your script, it's useful to

- **Add approximate timings,** so you know how long things take. Make sure you allow for slippage.
- **Highlight your most important questions,** so you can see them when you look down at your script.
- **Write down examples of probing questions** that will help you dig for more information. For example:
  - Can you tell me more about that?
  - Please can you explain that in more detail?
  - I'd love an example of what you mean.
  - What specifically is . . . ?
  - Why do you think that is the case?
  - I'm not clear about. . . .
  - What else matters in this?

Once your script is ship-shape, you'll need to rehearse what you say. You'll also need to have thought well in advance about how you want to record information.

Recording information

If you are going to record information, you'll need to think about your options. As always there are pros and cons for each possibility:

- **Audio tape:** You have the sound only. You'll need to ensure your microphones are powerful enough to capture what people say, especially if you have a larger group. The pros of audio is that it's simple to manage.
- **Video tape:** You capture everything. This means that the write-up can be more complex as you can see everyone's body language, and this helps you interpret their responses. Another bonus is that it allows you to add short video clips to your write-up. (For more about using video, see Chapter 9.) There's great technology to blur faces and keep confidentiality; for example, Movie Maker, Adobe or Camtasia.
- **Scribe:** Someone writes everything down. The disadvantage is you can easily miss comments, especially when the conversation is speedy. The advantage of scribing is that straightaway you have a transcript.
- **Flip chart:** You may not capture the nuances of how things were said, and if you ask participants to write, they tend to sanitise and shorten what they say. You might like to get support by asking someone to write for you. This can be really helpful if you're planning to run a lot of focus groups because then you'll have a large amount of data to assess, analyse and report on. Of course, the pros with this are that it's speedy, and you won't have a big transcription job to deal with.

Just think through which approach will best serve your need – and your budget. And make sure you test it out a couple of times before you use it, so you're not fumbling with technology in front of your participants.

Preparing your kit

In addition to the materials listed in Chapter 5, you'll also need to make sure you have

- A list of participants, so you know who turns up
- Name badges for everyone

- Two means of recording information (in case one breaks down
- Spare batteries (if your recorder uses them)
- An extension cable, so you can plug your recorder in near the group.

Now you're ready to roll.

Running a Focus Group

After you open up the focus group, you transition to the heart of what you are there to find out. As you work through the content, you'll need to

- Guide the discussion with general questions, followed by specific questions to clarify thinking.
- Keep everyone on track.
- Recognise when the group needs to move on to the next question.
- Discourage more vocal participants and encourage the shy ones.
- Explain what will happen next and by when.
- Thank everyone for their time.

Working with observers

A couple of observers are fine as long as they don't prevent participants from speaking their mind. You need to agree with them what their role is before the focus group starts. If they start to join in, remind them of their role; observers are not participants!

At the end of the focus group, do ask the observers for their insights. They may have useful ideas to share because they will have had a different perspective to you.

Pausing

One of the key skills that's particularly pertinent to focus groups is doing a powerful and pregnant pause. Saying nothing often leads to participant elaboration and elucidation and gives you a golden nugget. So bite your lip, raise a quizzical eyebrow and see what happens.

When you're new to running focus groups, pausing will feel really awkward, if not painful. But five-second pauses are what you should be aiming to do.

And, of course, you'll be using all the other skills outlined in Chapters 2 and 3.

Checking your technology

Your technology can be the most stressful part of the focus group. Just before you start your session, test it to make sure it works. Then do that again at the end of your session to see that you successfully recorded everything.

If it didn't record, don't panic. Just try to reconstruct what was said as soon as you can. Ideally, you should get in touch with a couple of participants to check out your impressions and perceptions.

If the recording was fine, still make a few notes about

- What you thought and any insights or surprises you had
- How the content worked for this particular group
- What you'd like to keep on doing and start doing the next time you run your focus group

If you do this after every session, you'll glean some interesting insights about the different groups you work with.

How clear purpose statements and parking lots can help

Having a clear purpose statement makes it easy to spot a hijack attempt and then deal with it. I (Julia) was running a series of focus groups for a consulting business. The purpose was 'to consider what we need to make it easier for everyone across the organisation to contribute their best at work.'

The focus group kicked off well, and everyone started sharing ideas. But about a third of the way through, a participant called Mike started to talk about how important it was to him to listen to music in the office. After a few minutes, everyone else started to look uncomfortable and get irritated, but Mike just kept going.

To deal with him, we just went back to the purpose statement and asked Mike to agree that this issue was not relevant across the organisation, even if it was pertinent to him. Then we parked the issue and kept it visible on a flip chart.

What made this easy to manage was the critical phrase in the purpose statement 'across the organisation.' Mike was on a soap box about an issue that mattered only to him, but he needed to feel heard, and we needed to move on. The clarity of the purpose statement and the help of a parking lot made both happen.

Writing It All Up

Preparing for and writing up your material is a huge piece of work. That's because focus groups generate tons of detailed material, and wading through it all takes time. In fact, it always takes more time than you think.

To get going, the first thing you need to do is pull together everything you've generated.

Transcribing your material or writing up your notes

If you have to transcribe the recordings, set aside the time to do this as soon as possible. It's much harder if you put it off because then you're guaranteed to have forgotten who was who and what they meant.

By the way, this is particularly important if you've decided to use notes to record your information. It's all too easy to be bamboozled by your own shorthand a few weeks later.

As you write up or transcribe your notes, make sure you have a system for numbering your focus groups and then identifying the questions and answers that apply to each of them. Otherwise, you'll get yourself in a terrific muddle.

Having written it all up, you'll be ready to sort your data properly, so you can analyse it fully.

Sorting and then analysing your data

You'll only be able to analyse the data when you have sorted, managed and interpreted it all. Sounds daunting, but if you keep it simple, it's more time consuming than baffling. So here's a really simple way of doing it:

1. **Get your typed up or transcribed notes** and edit out all the non-essential words for the answers you were given by your participants.
2. **Create a spreadsheet with three columns for codes, participants and responses.**
3. **Allocate numbers to the participants so they are anonymous, leave the codes blank and just enter all responses.**
4. **Look through all the responses you get, try to thoughtfully identify different categories and then code each one.**

   Figure 10-1 gives you an example of how to go through this process.
5. **Use the spreadsheet sort function to group entries by category.**
6. **Review the categories for consistency or merge them if you have too many.**

Who influenced you most as a leader?			
Category	**Participant**	**Responses**	**Codes**
A	1	'Mother and father'	A = Family
B	2	'Gandhi'	B = Politicians
A	3	'My parents'	C = Teachers
B	4	'Bill Clinton'	D = Bosses
C	5	'My English teacher'	
D	6	'Boss'	
A	7	'My older step brothers'	
D	8	'Boss'	
B	9	'Barack Obama'	
D	10	'First boss'	

Figure 10-1: An example of how to categorise and code your data.

7. **Capture your insights.**

   For example, your insight could be that participants' leadership role models appear to belong to four different and discrete groups. These include real and assumed attributes.

8. **Repeat this process for every question you asked and all the focus groups you ran.**

9. **Extract your main words and then put them into a word cloud to use in your report.**

`www.wordle.com` will provide you with a free tool to use that will bring your data to life visually by popping it into a word cloud. You can see an example of the output in Chapter 1. If you want to go for a more sophisticated tool, you can use software specifically designed for qualitative data analysis. This is called CAQ-DAS.

Interpreting your data

Once you have analysed your data and found your categories, it should be pretty easy to identify themes, especially if you've been running a series of focus groups. That's because you'll have heard the same things, and you'll probably start to see how they link together.

Now you're ready to look for

- Trends
- Patterns
- Links
- Issues
- Problems
- Contradictions

Once you've made some rough notes and thought about your conclusions, you can then mull over what your recommendations will be. Just bear in mind that there are never 25 good reasons for doing anything.

Now you're ready to write it all up.

Writing up your report

Once you've done your data analysis, you'll have a list of key themes and insights. You want to make sure that you have summaries for each main point along with a few examples of participants' actual comments.

Don't write long reports because no one will read them. Less is always more when it comes to reports.

Here's what your report should cover:

- **Cover page:** Include the title, date, sponsor and names of anyone who led the focus groups.
- **Executive summary:** Explain what you wanted to accomplish, your key findings and your recommendations. Remember that some people will only read this section, so make it punchy and clear.

  You generally write the summary after you've written the report.

- **Introduction:** Describe why you ran the focus groups and lay out the purpose. Include any background information that will help set the context of the work. This might be competitor or public information that helps clarify the issue and explain its importance.
- **How you went about it:** Write about what you did, including the number of focus groups, date, time and location of each, number of participants, recruitment process and whether you had observers. List the questions you used and how you recorded the information.
- **What you found out:** Summarise the results overall and then flesh them out for anyone who might want more information. List the key points for each question and include two or three salient comments from your participants.
- **What you recommend:** Finish the report with a strong conclusion. Explain what you learned from the focus groups and make concrete recommendations.

Before you send it off, get a colleague to read it one last time. There's nothing more annoying than sending it off with a couple of typos or mistakes because no one gave it a final check.

Putting it all into action

Now's the time when the organisation should start to think about how to implement your findings.

The greatest failure of focus groups lies in two areas:

- Reporting back to participants
- Applying the results

If you've gone to all the effort to put focus groups together, don't squander it. Let everyone have a one-pager or your executive summary and encourage your sponsor to implement the recommendations. That way, people will see that their input results in output, so they'll be ready to get involved again.

You can build terrific goodwill when you run focus groups, or you can make people even more jaded and cynical. The latter is never an outcome you want your name to be attached to.

Recognising the disadvantages of focus groups

Before you rush off and decide that focus groups are going to be the next best thing, you should be aware of some of their disadvantages:

- Group dynamics can interfere with or skew the results.
- Real reasons remain hidden because participants worry about lack of confidentiality or anonymity.
- The facilitator's opinion can affect results because if he or she is biased, the results will be, too.
- The results are so obvious that running them is a pointless or political task.

If you are worried about any of these, think twice before you get involved. You'll save yourself a lot of time and effort, and an organisation will save a lot of cash in the process.

If, on the other hand, you want good strong qualitative data, running focus groups can be a brilliant and enriching way to get it.

Chapter 11

Taking It to the Next Level

In This Chapter

- Leading brainstorming sessions
- Using group processes efficiently and effectively
- Working with Appreciative Inquiry
- Recognising when you are in a parallel process

Once you start to lead groups either in meetings or in workshops, you'll need additional tools to help you. After all, the main point of group work is to bring everyone together to solve common and complex issues. And that doesn't happen just because you want it to. You need process and planning. This chapter walks you through some tried-and-tested group processes that help get things done.

Brainstorming: Best Practise

If you want a group to come up with ideas together, you'll probably think, 'I need a brainstorming session.'

The practise of getting people to think aloud as they generate ideas started in the '50s, and it came out of the advertising industry. Back then, typical rules were developed, most of which are used today:

- **Freewheeling works best:** Just say whatever comes into your mind.
- **Deferring judgements:** It's all about idea generation, not critiquing others' work.
- **Building on what's offered:** This means taking an idea and extending it.
- **Writing down lots of thoughts:** Think quantity not quality.

But why brainstorm in the first place? Well, there are a couple of assumptions behind the practise of brainstorming:

- There are no lone geniuses who can solve problems in isolation because work problems are so specialised and generally involve a process which many people have to contribute to.
- The perception that brainstorming is an energising, motivating and involving process.

This all sounds great in theory. Actually, there are considerable problems with brainstorming as research and practise show.

Recognising problems with brainstorming

Here are a few problems with brainstorming:

- **Vocal people tend to dominate,** which means that quieter people find it hard to get heard. Vocal people then reduce their ideas; they may be vocal, but they aren't insensitive and frequently feel that they can't offer up ten ideas if other group members are sitting back saying nothing . . . which leads to the next problem.
- **Some people do nothing,** letting others carry the can for them. Of course, these shirkers then irritate the workers.
- **Anxious or new group members don't speak up** as they lack confidence or worry that their idea may not be good, relevant or fresh.
- **Only one person can talk at a time,** so others forget their good ideas while someone else is speaking.
- **Lazy thinking** means that groups easily follow the same line of thought and don't come up with any new ideas.
- **It's hard to challenge group direction** if you are the only dissenting voice. Check out Asch's experiments on YouTube to see this in action.

Finally, there are three killer facts you need to be aware of when it comes to brainstorming.

- Research over 20 years has consistently shown that brainstorming in groups is much less productive than getting individuals to work alone on a problem and then come together.
- Dissent and disagreement means that ideas get improved, refined and built on. So constructive criticism is a *good* thing when it comes to idea generation.
- People come up with much better ideas once they have slept on a problem. So brainstorming works best as an iterative process, not a one-off event.

Brainstorming effectively

When a group of people work in a structured process towards finding an answer to a problem, they will always do better than an individual working alone. (Just run the NASA lunar survival exercise with a bunch of friends if you don't believe us; you can find it online.) The key point to getting brainstorming right is structure and process.

The best brainstorming, which produces the most ideas in the shortest space of time, involves

- **Thinking through thoughts,** solutions and ideas alone and writing them down without talking.
- **Getting everyone to present their thoughts** to the group and to clarify what they mean as they present.
- **Clustering those ideas** as you go, so categories or groups of thoughts start to become self-evident.
- **Discussing, probing and challenging the best ideas** once they have been identified so that they can be refined, built on and improved.
- **Finding the best five to ten ideas** with a voting system.
- **Prioritising the top ideas** by using a priority matrix.
- **Checking in** to see how the group feels about their output before they start working on concrete actions.
- **Action planning,** which involves deciding what happens, when and who's involved.

So you can do this really well, the following sections give you some more detail about each step.

Of course, the first thing you need to do is set up the activity and explain the objective and all the steps you'll be going through. Then everyone will feel secure in the process; if you run a magical mystery tour, you run the risk of irritating your participants. So explain what you'll do and for how long you'll do it as your very first step. Then walk through the following actions.

Thinking through thoughts

Before you get going, you need to know how many people will be doing this brainstorm. With 3 to 11 people, you can run the process next described. With 12 or more people, you'll need to break them into groups of 4 or 5, find the best ideas in breakout groups and then present back in a plenary session. Otherwise, your participants will get very bored as they have listen to every idea no matter how good – or bad.

If you are running a brainstorm with more than three people in a room, the simplest and cheapest way of doing it is to give everyone a bunch of sticky notes and a marker pen. Ask them to write down all their ideas on a sticky note, using one idea per sticky.

Pay attention at this point. No matter how clear you are in your instructions, some people will always write all their ideas in tiny writing on one sticky note. So model what you want as you explain the process, write your instructions on a flip chart and have a bunch of marker pens ready. Then everyone will be able to see and read the ideas once you share them.

You can either give people an allocated amount of time (for example, between five to ten minutes) or simply watch what happens. You'll know that they have run out of steam because they'll start to fidget, check their phones or chat to each other.

Getting everyone to present their thoughts

You'll need a section of wall, pin-board or pin-board paper to complete this part of the activity. That's because flip chart paper just isn't big enough. Make sure you have a good space, especially if you are working with a larger group. (You can hire or buy light, cheap, collapsible pin-boards, paper and lots of other facilitation materials from PinPoint UK who ship anywhere in the world.)

Write the title or objective of your brainstorm so everyone can see it and then invite everyone to present all their ideas. If you have a group of eight participants, you might want to ask them to present their top five ideas only. As each person presents, tell the group that they can ask questions for clarification only. Right now, you're aiming to put everything on the table.

Clustering as you go

Getting everyone to cluster ideas means that the group

- Remains involved in the whole process.
- Starts joining one idea to another, which is how better ideas emerge.
- Thinks not only about the idea but what that idea implies.

Make sure that it's not you who does the clustering but the group who comes up with what goes together and what clusters should be called. That way, the group owns the output. Wait until all the ideas have been presented before you give that cluster a name so that you don't waste time moving sticky notes around too much. And if you've taken part in the brainstorm because perhaps you're the boss, make sure you present your ideas last, or everyone will just follow what you do.

Discussing, probing and challenging ideas

Now's the time to discuss, challenge, add to or subtract from what you have on the table. This is when better ideas emerge, when you combine one idea with another, ask 'What if . . . ?' or 'How about . . . ?' and see what else you can spark amongst the group. If the group is shy in speaking up, get them to do this activity in twos or threes.

By the end of this process, you should have added some new ideas and removed ones that everyone thinks won't work. This can often take 20 to 30 minutes but don't shortchange the activity because this is often when the best ideas are born.

Finding the best five to ten ideas

If you've asked people to present their top five ideas only, get them to look through what they left out and see if they have one or two more ideas that they strongly feel should still be in the mix. That way, you'll respect everyone's work, make sure that anyone with an axe to grind gets heard (which is often all they want) and you'll keep anything useful.

Now you can vote on what the group should take forward. To vote, either give everyone three stickers, check marks or asterisks. Ask them to come up and place the stickers, checks or asterisks next to their favorite ideas. The only rule is that you can't vote for your own idea!

Participants can allocate their votes

- Using them all for one idea if they love it
- Sharing them equally between three ideas
- Using two votes for one and one for another

The choice is up to them. Again, if you are taking part in this activity, make sure you go last so you don't influence anyone unduly.

After you have your top ideas, you need to prioritise them.

Prioritising what you've got

The easiest way of doing this is with the priority matrix (see Figure 11-1). Make sure you have taken a few photos of the brainstorm and the votes so that anyone who couldn't be there can see what the process was and so you have a clear audit trail; you never know when you might need it.

Before you place items on the matrix, you'll need to explain it as follows:

- *Quick wins* are what everyone's looking for. They'll be easy to do and have a high impact. There tend to be not too many of them around because this low-hanging fruit has often been plucked.
- *Quality investments* take longer. They require more effort, but long term payback will be high. These need special attention.

- *Questionable items* are easy but have low impact, so they won't be worth the time. These actions often get taken because of pressure and the need 'to do something.' Agree to eliminate them.
- *Quit items* won't give anyone a return, so, like the questionable items, simply ignore anything that falls into this quadrant.

Effect \ Ease of implementation	Difficult	Easy
High	Quality Investments	Quick Wins
Low	Quit	Questionable

Figure 11-1: The priority matrix.

Invite group members to try to achieve consensus as they sort the items out. That way, everyone will buy into the action-planning session. (For more on consensus, see Chapter 5.)

To sort each item out:

1. **Draw the matrix up – preferably before the session starts.**
2. **Take each priority item, starting with those with the most votes off the pin-board or wall.**
3. **Ask the group in which quadrant it belongs.**

   Job done.

By the way, if you are running a very large group brainstorm – for example, between 50 to 100 people – you can use this sorting technique before you share ideas in plenary with everyone. You simply ask each breakout group to talk about its one quick win and two quality investments in not more than five to ten minutes.

Then you're ready to check in with the group to see how everyone feels about what they have done and what they still have to do.

Checking in

Get everyone to reflect on the work that they have done so far by asking

- On a scale of 1-10 how happy are we with what we have? And why?
- How energised are we about taking these actions forward, 1-10?
- What do we want to do next?

You can share these reflections by asking everyone to stand as you call out numbers, complete a grid on a flip chart or do a human bar chart.

To create a *human bar chart,* or a bar chart using people, you need some space and some masking tape. Before your meeting, stick between 10 to 15 feet of masking tape on the ground and mark numbers 1 to 10 on it in equal distances. Explain that you will ask your participants to stand on the line to identify first how happy they are and second how energised they feel. Then get them to do it.

Creating a human bar chart will help everyone see how everyone feels about the work they have done and what they have to take forward.

Then you can debrief the reasons why everyone feels the way they do before you get into the action planning.

Of course, you can repeat the human bar chart after the action planning, if you like – or leave it until then. We recommend doing it now because it helps galvanise everyone around the developing embryonic project plans that turn words into deeds.

Action planning

Here's something you need to remember: Just because someone has an idea doesn't mean that he necessarily wants to own it or make it happen. Sometimes the best ideas come from people who are one step away or more removed from an issue; they see it more clearly and can be more innovative precisely because they aren't aware of all the constraints. On the other hand, they may be itching to make it happen; so check first before you make any assumptions.

The easiest way to action plan is to look at the quick wins and quality investments and to ask who is keen to work on which ideas. If no one comes forward to work on an idea that's a quality investment, you should challenge the group to dump the idea as it's never going to happen.

You need to set up your action planning, so it runs as smoothly as possible. In our experience, this can feel quite unstructured, so you need to give it that sense of structure by being planned and organised about the process.

Running a multiple action planning session

To run a multiple action planning session:

- Invite everyone to **get into sub-groups** to action plan around the ideas that most appeal to them. Each sub-group should have two to four people working on one issue.
- Make sure you have booked enough **breakout space** and have a **flip chart or pin-board** available for each sub-group. Even if you are working with a team of eight people, not everyone should do everything, or it will take far too long.

- Give everyone **enough time** – for example, not less than 40 minutes – to come up with the next steps for making their one to two ideas happen. They should think about
  - What's the outcome (if it's not clear already)?
  - What resources will be needed?
  - What has to happen?
  - Who needs to be involved?
  - What are the next steps?
  - What does a rough time-line look like?
- Explain that sub-groups will be **self-directed** (unless you are working with several colleagues) but that you will be circulating to see how they are doing and checking in with them as they work.
- Invite them to actively find and **get help from others** in different sub-groups as they need it; doing this will make the activity feel energetic and dynamic.
- Tell the sub-groups that you will want someone to **present their output** once the breakout activity has finished, so they should come back ready to talk their work through.

It may be that some sub-groups will need help from people who aren't present, especially if there are financial implications. To check if this is the case, encourage breakout groups to do a RACI analysis (see 'Common Group Tools,' later in the chapter).

Circulating during action planning

As sub-groups are working, make sure you know where they are located and that they are actually following the process. The danger is that without you there, they go off on a tangent. Now that tangent might be valuable, but it might not, so make sure that you check in regularly to see what's going on.

If a sub-group is heavily involved or working around a flip chart, don't interrupt; a few seconds listening will tell you that they are on track. If they are having a heated discussion, do exactly the same; just listen to the conversation before deciding to intervene.

Once there is ten minutes to go to the end of the activity, do a quick time check to see that the sub-groups will be ready to reconvene so that you stay on time. If you can, plan a break before they all come back, so any group who needs more time has it without upsetting the flow of the whole day.

Presenting back

Explain that presenting shouldn't take more than ten minutes per group, including questions. If you have a large number of groups, you might want to make this even shorter.

After each presentation, allow enough time to challenge, refine and clarify ideas and actions so that the next steps get perfected.

You'll need to prevent people going down detailed and distracting rabbit holes, so leading this activity can be quite a difficult balancing act. If a conversation appears to you to be off-tracking, ask the group whether that's the case and check how useful it is right now. If it's worthwhile, continue with it if it's not, agree to draw it to an end.

If you prefer, you can run the sharing of ideas as a marketplace session. Everyone has an allocated space, and the whole group moves around as many times as you have groups.

Nailing the last hurrah

Once everything has been presented back, questioned and hopefully agreed, two remaining actions are immensely important:

- **Making sure that everything is written up.** Be clear about who will capture all the actions, owners and timelines, who will collate everything and by when all of that will happen. This is hugely important for maintaining a sense of momentum.
- **Deciding what the next steps are** as a group before everyone leaves the room. This is so often overlooked, and it's a main reason why projects that start with a bang end with such a whimper.

Managing large group brainstorming

The only way you can effectively manage really large groups of people brainstorming is with technology. That means a skilled facilitator at the front with access to reliable wifi for the group.

There are three really simple, free and useful technologies you can try.

All our ideas

This simply fantastic free tool at `www.allourideas.org` allows you to generate ideas and prioritise them at the same time. It's easy to use. All you do is start with a question, add a few ideas and let everyone have a link.

The advantage is you can use this in real time or leave it open so that if your participants are in different time zones and locations, they can jump onto it whenever suits them.

Participants add their own ideas and select between them as they go, which is how you brainstorm and prioritise simultaneously. All you have to do is decide when the session is going to end and then show everyone the results. Each time you hit refresh at the front of the room, everyone can see new ideas and how they have been prioritised.

Yammer

This tool allows everyone to post ideas in a closed Twitter-esque environment.

Although it's fantastic for capturing ideas and asking about them (you can add external links, documents or questions and use tags to find ideas), it doesn't allow you to sort and prioritise in real-time. What it does provoke is active conversation and ideas between lots of people.

Google spreadsheet

A Google spreadsheet is a great way of capturing a lot of ideas in one document.

To prevent frustration and accidental overwriting of cells do these two things:

- Create a document that everyone can see without needing to scroll across a page.
- Make it really clear about who can write where.

All you need to do is open up the document, so everyone can type into it at the same time. Up to 50 people can edit a Google spreadsheet simultaneously, and then all the output is available in one place. And you only need a Google account to make it happen.

Managing small group brainstorming

If you are working collaboratively with two or three other people, you won't want to go through a paper or tech process, but you'll still want to generate ideas effectively.

One effective solution is to use mind-mapping software. The advantage is that you then capture, sort and retain all your ideas as you work, combining the thinking and writing process.

Here are a few of our favorite software options:

- **Freemind** is a free powerful mind-mapping tool that offers complex diagrams, loads of branches, graphics and icons to differentiate notes and connect them. You can embed links and multimedia in your mind maps and export them as HTML, PNG or PDFs, amongst others. It's not beautiful, but it is free.
- **Mindjet** is mind-mapping software with a whole bunch of tools that help you brainstorm and then manage actions and projects. Best of all, it integrates with tools like Office and Entourage, so you can export your mind maps as you need them. This commercial software ranges in price from $129 to $349 for different levels of access.

- **XMind** is an easy, open source way of organising your ideas and thoughts in a load of different styles, diagrams and designs. You can use simple mind maps or more complicated fishbone, tree and logic charts if you prefer. Like Mindjet, you can add images, icons, links and multimedia. If you want to turn your work into a project, you can use XMind's Gantt view to manage project tasks. XMind pricing ranges from free to $79 per year, and there's a Plus and Pro offering for organisations.

Brainstorming alone

If you prefer getting everyone to brainstorm before the meeting or workshop, here are three brilliant tablet or smart phone apps for you to use:

- **iThoughts** is simple to use and it keeps track of any changes so you can revert back to a previous mind map if you need to. You can format your work easily, and it's compatible with lots of other desktop map tools.
- **Popplet** has a really easy interface for capturing ideas, sorting them visually and collaborating with others in real-time. There's a lite and full version, which you can share with other users and export mindmaps as PDFs or JPEGs. It's not available on Android yet but Mindjet is a possible alternative.
- **Blitz** is a great little tool with prompts to get you to think up nine new ideas in two minutes. You can then prioritise, edit, share or print what you've come up with.

Of course, the point of a brainstorm is to generate ideas. The most important thing is getting together in a meeting or workshop to decide what to do with those ideas.

Having tackled brainstorming alone, in small and large groups, you'll now be able to use it as part of another process, if you need to. The next section explains what some of those processes are, when you use them and how.

Working with Some Common Group Tools

This section covers when and how to use some of the easiest and most practical tools when you want to get a group from A to B. Table 11-1 shows the name of the analysis and when to use each of them.

Table 11-1 Tools and Their Purpose

Tool	*Use This When You Want To . . .*
3Ws	Do a gap analysis and work out how to bridge it
SWOT analysis	Evaluate a project, decision or venture
RACI analysis	Clarify roles and responsibilities
Force field analysis	Make and then communicate a go-no go decision
Fishbone or Ishikawa	Work out the root causes of a problem
Decision trees	Decide between available options

Here's how you work with each tool.

3Ws

This is an easy technique with three simple stages. The objective is to complete a gap analysis by focusing on

- Where are we going?
- Where are we now?
- What do we need to do next?

The benefits of this tool are that it's very simple yet effective. Because it's so straightforward, it's something you can deliver when you have no time to prepare and need to think on your feet.

To use the 3Ws:

1. **Explain the whole process to the group.**
2. **Get the group to answer each of the Ws by working through the questions listed in Table 11-2.**

Table 11-2 3Ws and Questions to Ask

Stage of the Process	*Useful Questions to Flesh Out Each Stage*
Where are we going?	What are we trying to achieve?
	What is our main objective? Why?
	Who are we doing this for?
	What involvement do key stakeholders need?
	What will our success measures be?
	What can we conclude from all this?
Where are we now?	What's going on right now?
	Why? What are the factors contributing to our current situation?
	What have we done so far?
	What happened (facts)?
	Why?
	What have we learned?
	What can we conclude from all this?
What do we need to do next?	How will we tackle this?
	What are our options?
	What do we want to do?
	What is our plan?
	What can we conclude from our analysis?

3. **Summarise as you work through each section and signpost clearly when you have completed one and are moving on to the next part.**
4. **Make sure you get agreement from the group so you check everyone is with you as you proceed.**

Doing this thoroughly will take at least two to three hours and possibly longer depending on the complexity of the issue you want to deal with.

SWOT Analysis

A SWOT analysis (see Figure 11-2) is really helpful when you want to understand the full implications, benefits and risks of a new venture. This could run from making a fairly simple decision about employing someone, all the way to evaluating potential partnerships, suppliers, projects and business ideas. SWOT stands for Strengths, Weaknesses, Opportunities and Threats and involves thinking through each area in turn.

	Helpful	Harmful
Internal Factors	Strengths	Weaknesses
External Factors	Opportunities	Threats

Figure 11-2: A SWOT analysis and its quadrants.

Strengths and weaknesses are often internal to your organisation, and they are easily identified as they are present in the current environment. Opportunities and threats generally relate to external factors and are future-oriented.

We like using pin-boards, so you have enough room to write relevant details in each quadrant. Alternatively, you need a very large sheet of paper; consider sticking four pieces of flip chart together, one for each quadrant, and then write the name of the project or idea on it, so what you are doing is always front of mind.

If you are going to be doing lots of group work in the same rooms, think about getting IdeaPaint and create a wall that acts as a reusable white board.

As you lead the evaluation, answer the following questions, adapting them where you need to. If you start with strengths, you'll set off with a bang as talking about what's positive is always motivating and energising.

Strengths:

- What advantages do we have in this situation?
- What do we do better than anyone else?
- What do our clients or competitors say about us?
- What resources do we have in terms of people and cash?
- What capability have we built to support this?
- What do our competitors/clients/customers see as our strengths?

Weaknesses:

- What are the inherent disadvantages?
- What are the gaps in terms of people or cash?
- How are our customers/clients, the market and economy doing?
- What are the blockers?
- What challenges are presented by our processes or infrastructure?
- What factors currently lose us sales?

Opportunities:

- What good opportunities can we see coming?
- What interesting trends have we noticed?
- What are our customers/clients and the market telling us that's missing?
- What changes are happening that we are well placed to take advantage of?
- What's the business case for taking this course of action?

Threats:

- What obstacles do we face?
- Have we got real commitment from customers/clients?
- What is the competition doing?
- How will doing this distract us from core activities?
- How robust are our plans and budgets?
- What reputational risks are there?
- Could any of the weaknesses seriously threaten our business?

To do a SWOT analysis:

1. **Explain the whole process to the group.**
2. **Get the group to work through each quadrant answering the questions listed previously to check you have thought everything through.**
3. **Prioritise all the items you have listed by significance.**

   Rank order them with the most important first and least important last.
4. **Work out what you need to do about the top three or four most important items.**

   Plan a brainstorm around minimising weaknesses or threats and maximising the strengths and opportunities.

Make sure you leave enough time to work through this properly. It can often take three to four hours to do a detailed SWOT analysis, especially if the consequences are opaque.

RACI analysis

RACI stands for

- **Responsible:** Someone who does part of or all of the work.
- **Accountable:** The buck stops with this person, so he or she tends to have the final say.
- **Consulted:** Someone who needs to contribute to and give feedback to the task or project,
- **Informed:** The person that needs to know about decisions and actions.

A RACI analysis is useful for when you are

- Analysing work
- Allocating tasks
- Creating a project plan
- Resolving interpersonal role-base conflict
- Going through a reorganisation

The benefit of doing a RACI analysis (see Figure 11-3) is that it leaves no room for ambiguity about who does what.

	Programme Manager	Programme Team	Sponsor	Client	Board
Activity 1	R		C	C	IC
Activity 2	A	R	I	C	I
Activity 3		RA	C	C	I
Activity 4	RA		C	C	I

Figure 11-3: A sample completed RACI chart.

To do a RACI chart:

1. **Explain the whole process to the group.**
2. **List all the stakeholders involved in what you are trying to do along the top of a page.**
3. **List all the tasks in order of priority or time down the left.**
4. **Get your group to decide who is to be Responsible, Accountable, Consulted or Informed.**
5. **Check that everyone agrees.**
6. **Review your matrix.**

   You should find you have a good spread; if you don't, consider what to do using Table 11-3.

Table 11-3 Checking Your RACI Chart

Too Many	*None*
Rs: How will they co-ordinate the work?	**Rs:** Who'll do the job?
As: Are there too many fingers in the pie?	**As:** Why? Who actually owns stuff?
Cs: How slow will this project be?	**Cs:** What difference might a sponsor or mentor make?
Is: Who's managing all the communications? What does this imply?	**Is:** Why is this happening in a vacuum? Who needs to know?

Be careful when you are using a RACI chart; you need to work appropriately with it. You don't need to do it with a group to work out who opens the mail!

Force field analysis

Force field analysis is a decision-making tool that is widely used to manage change. Its main purpose is to help you analyse the forces for and against what you're about to do.

The benefit of using it is twofold: You make a decision and, in going through the process, get all the information you need to communicate your decision effectively. If you decide to go ahead, you then can work out how to increase your chances of success. And you do that by working out how to maximise the forces that support change and minimise those against it.

Again, you need a large sheet of paper, a wall or pin-board. Before the session, draw up the diagram with nothing in it except a statement of the problem and the headings underlined as in Figure 11-4.

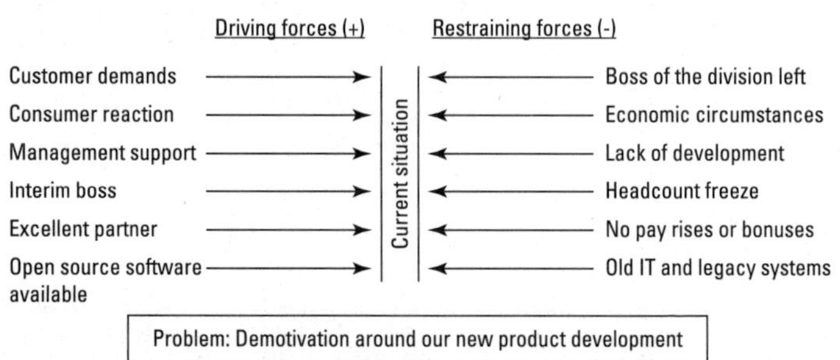

Figure 11-4: Sample force field analysis.

To do a force field analysis:

1. **Explain the whole process to the group.**
2. **Describe the current situation as it is now and the desired situation as the vision for the future.**
3. **Identify what will happen if there is no action taken.**
4. **List all the driving and restraining forces for the change.**

   Here are a few for the group to consider:

   • Available resources
   • Costs
   • Time
   • Vested interests
   • Politics
   • Leadership
   • Support

- Structures
- Attitudes
- Beliefs
- Assumptions
- Regulators
- People
- Norms
- Behaviours
- Culture
- Values
- Expectations

5. **Discuss the key driving and restraining forces with the group and check none have been left out.**
6. **Determine each force's strength by giving it a score of 1 to 10, where 1 is very weak and 10 is very strong.**
7. **Add up the numbers and evaluate what you have.**

   If one number vastly outweighs another, your decision is pretty clear. If it's a no-go, end here; if it's go, complete the remaining steps.
8. **Explore the restraining forces and the best way to minimise them (brainstorm and discuss).**
9. **Explore the driving forces and the best way of maximising them (brainstorm and discuss).**
10. **Create an action plan.**

This process can easily take half a day or more to implement, depending on the complexity of the decision that needs making.

Ishikawa or fishbone diagram

The fishbone method diagram explores all the things that cause a serious problem before starting to think about a solution. That way, you know you have taken everything into consideration, so you don't start to try and fix the wrong thing.

Ishikawa, the developer of the technique, describes the process as one in which 'You write down your problem on the head of the fish and then let it cook overnight' meaning that ideally, you use the technique over a couple of sessions to check you capture everything.

The benefits of the fishbone diagram are that you can

- Review and reflect on all parts of a problem before making a decision.
- See the relationships and relative importance of items.
- Start to find a logical sequence for solving a problem.

You can either cluster similar items as you brainstorm them or start with a framework that you believe is relevant to the situation. Figure 11-5 shows an example of a specific framework designed for weak sales of a new product.

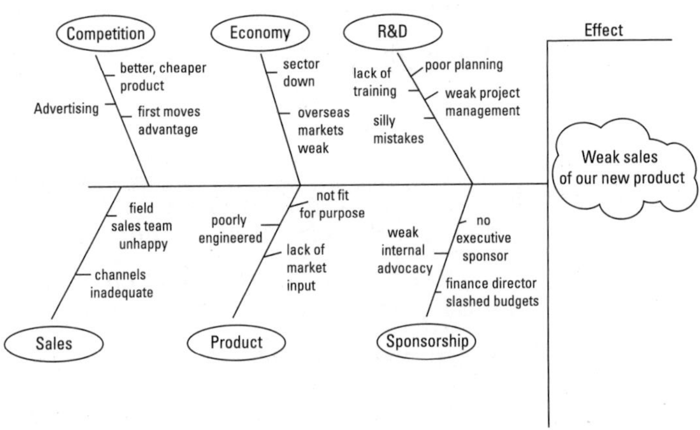

Figure 11-5: Sample Ishikawa to examine weak sales of a new product.

To do an Ishikawa analysis:

1. **Explain the whole process to the group.**

   This should include what you will do and how long it might take.

2. **Write the problem on the diagram at the head of the fish and make sure everyone agrees with it.**

   Everyone needs to work towards solving the same issue, so you have to be 100 per cent clear about what that is.

3. **Brainstorm the major categories of the causes of the problem.**

   They are the items you see in circles at the end of each bone. If that's hard, try some generic headings. These could include for example people, product, process, environment, economy, training, competitors, measurement, sponsors and stakeholders.

4. **Delve into the details once you have listed all the headings.** You can do that by asking, 'Why does that happen?' Then create mini fish bones leading off the main one. That way, you check you are getting to the root cause of a problem. Don't worry if some ideas appear in two places: it simply shows you how important they are.

5. **Make sure you focus on the areas where there are fewer ideas as these can be critical.** These areas might give you important insights about what really is going wrong.

6. **Allow enough time to review and reflect on your analysis because new ideas are bound to emerge.**

   Consider leaving the analysis and coming back to it the following day so that you can be sure to have captured everything.

7. **Start to solve the issues only when you are sure you have fully identified all the causes and have agreed what to prioritise.**

   You can use the priority matrix (see Figure 11-1) to help you. Depending on the complexity and importance of the problems you identify, you may need to further investigate the most likely causes. This could involve a task force, interviews, observations, focus groups, surveys or whatever is the most relevant to getting the problem fixed.

There are several useful fishbone frameworks to work through. For example:

- McKinsey's **7S framework** helps check alignment of a team, division or organisation (Strategy, Structure, Systems, Shared values, Skills, Style and Staff).
- Marketing works with **4Ps** (Product, Place, Price and Promotion).
- The service industry uses **4Ss** (Surroundings, Suppliers, Skills and Systems) or a more detailed option, **7Ps**: Procedures, Policies, Place, Product/Service, People, Processes, Price and Promotion.

Although the analysis is important, it's much more important to do things to fix issues. That's when a decision tree can help you.

Decision trees

A *decision tree* is a kind of flowchart to help you determine what you want to do. It's an excellent tool for helping you choose between several courses of action because it gives you a really clear way of visualising options and calculating outcomes. Best of all, a decision tree guides you to a logical and informed decision based on the likelihood of achieving the results you hope to get.

First of all, a decision tree, uses a formal notation:

- A square represents a decision.
- A circle represents an uncertain event.

To use a decision tree:

1. **Explain the whole process to the group.**

   Outline what they will do and how long you think it will take.

2. **Write down all the options that are available to you to make your decision.**

   You can prepare the group in advance by telling them to arrive having thought about what these are.

3. **Prioritise the options to identify your top three to four.**

4. **Draw a box on the left hand-side of the page or place where you are creating your decision tree.**

   This represents the decision you want to make.

5. **List your top three to four options connecting out from the box.**

   Don't list too many or the process will take too long.

6. **Create at least two (but no more than four) lines that represent the outcomes of each specific decision.**

   At least one line will represent success and the other failure. Repeat this for the other two options you listed under step 3.

7. **Work out the likelihood of success for each outcome in percentage terms.**

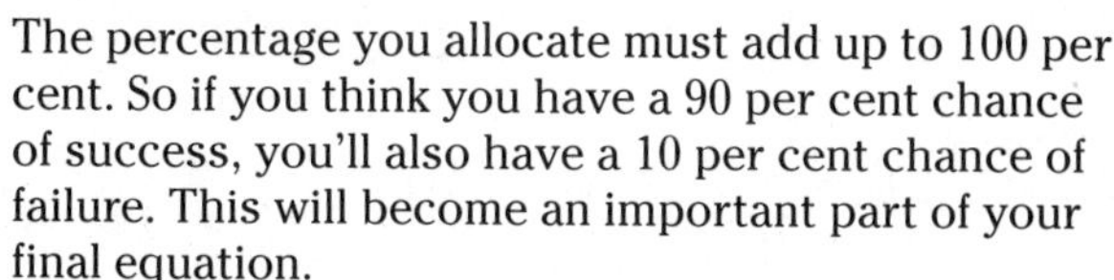

   The percentage you allocate must add up to 100 per cent. So if you think you have a 90 per cent chance of success, you'll also have a 10 per cent chance of failure. This will become an important part of your final equation.

8. **Based on your options, do a calculation.**

   Work out the cost and the profit of your decision. Then you are ready to take it.

The decision tree in Figure 11-6 illustrates a process to work out whether a team should go with product A, product B or neither.

In the preceding example, you can see that the likelihood of success with product A is only 50 per cent, while product B's chance of success is 80 per cent. Now you need to work out the expected value to be really sure you're doing the right thing. So you turn 50 per cent into 0.5, 80 per cent into 0.80 and 20 per cent into 0.2 taking the net profit and possible loss into account like this:

Product A: 0.5 x $900,000 + 0.5 x (–$100,000) = $400,000

Product B: 0.8 x $350,000 + 0.2 x (–$10,000) = $278,000

Your full decision tree analysis shows that product B is the more attractive proposition, so it's the one you should develop.

But what happens if you need a radical shake up? If that's the case, you might like to think about using Appreciative Inquiry.

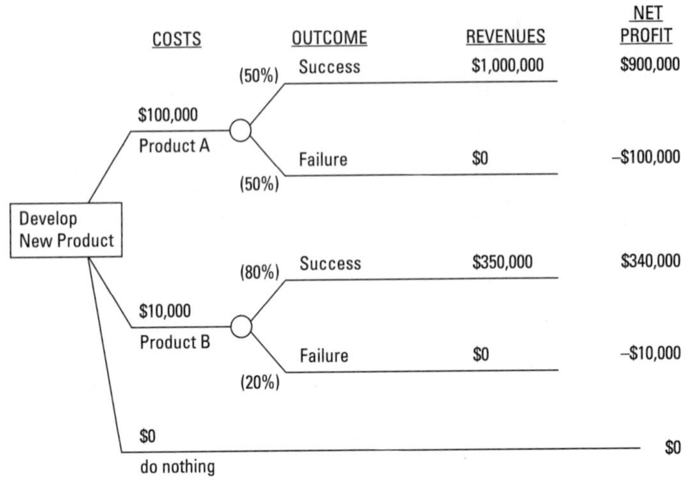

Figure 11-6: Sample decision tree: Whether to develop a new product.

Using Appreciative Inquiry

Appreciative Inquiry is a fantastic technique developed by David Cooperrider and Suresh Srivastva in the '80s at Case Western University. The heart of the methodology is to solve problems by looking at what's going right instead of looking at what's going wrong. Examining what's broken is the conventional way of trying to resolve a problem, and it's really well illustrated by questions like 'What's wrong?' or 'What needs fixing here?'

The thing about a deficit-focused approach to problem-solving is that it can be very de-energising. And when something is de-energising, individuals and groups simply don't follow up.

A more positively framed approach is to look at the things that are working and then build on them. That's what Appreciative Inquiry is all about: positives, strengths and what works.

The first step of the Appreciative Inquiry process is to identify and describe the problem you're trying to solve. From there you go on to look at the issue in four phases: Discovery, Dream, Design and Deliver. This approach is described in the five steps that follow.

Appreciative Inquiry is often explained using four Ds:

- Discovery
- Dream
- Design
- Deliver/Destiny

We like to put a fifth D, Define, which helps clarify the first step.

Step 1: Define phase

Before you can analyse a situation, you need to define what it is you are looking at. Making this positive will help frame the entire process. For example, if you want to 'stop top talent leaving,' you could frame this as 'ensuring top talent stays committed to this organisation.'

This subtle change in wording can have a big impact on what you then decide to focus on.

When framing your question, make sure you keep it broad because otherwise your solutions won't be as wide as they could be.

Step 2: Discovery phase

Here you need to look for the best of what has happened in the past, as well as what is currently working well.

Try to involve as many stakeholders as sensibly possible and get them to explain what they find most valuable (or appreciated) in this context and invite them to focus on what works particularly well.

Using the example from Step 1, you could talk to people who have left and talk to people who stayed in their jobs, focusing on getting to the core of what they like(d) about the job, as well as what they enjoy(ed) about the organisation.

In this situation, the following might be good discovery questions:

- When you think back to when you decided to join, what was the thing that most attracted you?
- Tell me about a time when you were very enthusiastic about your work?
- What do you think is most important for success here?

- Tell me about the time you felt proudest of this organisation?
- What do you miss now that you no longer work here?
- What it is you really value(d) about this organisation?

Another way to solving this problem could be to look at the different approaches you use to retain top talent and work out what factors mean people want to stay. This would involve some in-depth investigation around the organisation in the form of focus groups. (For more about focus groups, see Chapter 10.)

When you've gathered enough raw information, you need to analyse the data to identify the factors that most contributed to the team or organisation's past and current success in this particular area. That way, you can find out

- What is most valued?
- What employees find most motivating?
- What instills the greatest pride?

Step 3: Dream phase

In this phase, you and your team dream of 'what positively might be.' Think about how you can the factors you identify in the Discovery phase to reinforce them as you build a positive future. Here are some helpful questions:

- What's the best possible outcome?
- What would we be doing if we were best in class?
- What different and fantastic things could we see happening?
- How do we combine the best of what we know into the dream?

Once you have agreed upon your dream or vision, you can take it to the Design phase.

Step 4: Design phase

Building on the Dream, this phase looks at the practicalities needed to support the vision. Here you start to drill down the types of systems, processes, and strategies that will enable the dream to be realised. This is a classic brainstorming session.

Step 5: Deliver phase

This is sometimes called the Destiny phase and is the last of the Ds. This is all about implementation and therefore needs a great deal of planning and preparation. The key to successful delivery is ensuring that the Dream (vision) is the focal point.

While the various parts of the team will typically have their own processes to complete, the overall result is a raft of changes that occur simultaneously throughout the team or organisation, that all serve to support and sustain the Dream.

The strength of the technique

The power of Appreciative Inquiry comes from Steps 1 to 3. Steps 4 and 5 are just standard implementation steps. If you have your own preferred approach, you can, of course, use it instead.

Remember that Appreciative Inquiry isn't just a problem-solving technique. You can also use it as an organisational strategy tool or for something as simple as planning your personal development. Lots of people fall in love with it as a methodology. It isn't the answer to everything, but it is really useful when groups are stuck in a rut or demoralised.

Understanding Parallel Process

Lots of people who do group and interpersonal work have described parallel processes and why they happen. It doesn't matter why; the point is recognising what they are and knowing how to deal with them.

So what is a *parallel process?* It's when you pick up and mirror the internal processes of the group or people within that group.

You might be in one when

- The group or powerful individuals within it get stuck, feel helpless, frustrated, frightened or disempowered and so do you.
- There's a conflict within the group, and you suddenly find you are in conflict about what you're doing, too.

When it first happens, it can be disconcerting because you wonder what's going on. The point is to notice it because then you can do change or challenge what's happening.

The first thing to do is to understand that this might not be you, but it could be the group. Everyone's tendency is to think 'What have I done?' or 'How could this be happening?' But it may not be your stuff that's getting in the way.

Either way, here's what to try instead:

- **Stop** and give everyone a moment to reflect on where they and you are at a practical level. Reassess your agenda so far and get everyone to think through something positive so far.
- **Call a ten-minute break** and ask everyone to go outside rather than check their phones or emails. You want them to experience a new energy.
- **Lead an energiser** when they come back by getting people to move physically.
- **Ask everyone to swap seats.** Sometimes sitting in a new place gets everyone to see things differently.
- **Lead a paired exercise** to get everyone to think through what they are hopeful of in this situation. Everyone needs to articulate one thing to the group.

Doing all this should mean you have changed their energy and mind-set. Now you can challenge them to think about what they were saying and doing before if you feel it would be helpful. If they are a mature group, they will probably be able to have a reflective and interesting conversation. If they are immature, they won't – in which case, simply move on with your agenda.

When you have finished your session, think about what happened and write it down in your learning journal; the more often you are aware of a parallel process starting to happen, the less you will fall into one. And when you do, you'll recognise it for what it is.

Chapter 12

Running Remote or Virtual Meetings and Workshops

In This Chapter

- Getting ready for your remote or virtual meetings
- Managing a hybrid meeting
- Evaluating the tools and tech at your disposal
- Thinking about the challenges of remote and virtual workshops

There's one thing you can be sure of. You're going to be attending or running more remote meetings rather than fewer of them over the next five years. That means meetings when you can't necessarily see other participants because you are on a call together or using a platform to collaborate. And even if you can see your fellow participants, you're looking at a screen, so you've got much less information to guide you.

Online or blended workshops are exactly the same. Lots of workshops are moving to online, on-demand delivery because it's so much more cost-effective. When budgets are tight, remote and virtual get-togethers are a no-brainer.

And when remote meetings are run well, they are a super-effective way of pushing plans and projects forward. Unfortunately, remote meetings take more preparation than face-to-face ones because of the technological constraints and their implications. That means getting good at thinking everything through, so there are no nasty surprises. You want to walk on water because you did such a great job, rather than drown in embarrassment because you didn't.

This chapter helps you understand how to do things really well when you're meeting remotely or virtually. It gives you an overview of the technology available and insights into what you need to do to run successful remote or virtual workshops.

Managing Remote Meetings

It's simple. Everything that applies to face-to-face meetings remains really relevant for remote or virtual ones. You need to do all the usual planning and prepping, and then some.

Poor organisation ahead of the meeting make remote meetings much more chaotic; after all, no one can look around the room to see what others are doing. On top of that, everything is magnified by being taken in through fewer senses, so disorganisation or confusion feels much worse. And if you combine poor prep with weak meeting management, you are courting disaster.

To hold a productive remote meeting, you need to be rigorous about your process and management of it to make up for lack of visual input. With the best will in the world, if everyone shows up as disembodied voices or postage-stamp sized on your screen, you don't glean as much about their engagement as if they were in the room with you. Great preparation and tight management of the process lend structure and clarity to what you do.

This section takes you through how to plan and manage meetings whether you are using phones, tablets, web-based services on your PC or full-blown video conferencing.

Recognising when to have a remote meeting

If all you want to do is to share information or get general input, then send emails or share documents. Remote meetings should only be for discussion, deciding or sorting out confusing information. If you tell people things they already know, they won't thank you for it.

Inviting the right people

It's even more important when you are having a remote meeting to get the right people on the call. That's because the possibility of distraction is much greater when participants aren't in the room. It's better to have more frequent, shorter meetings than longer ones when half your participants are zoned out.

Collaboration happens most efficiently and effectively between two to three people, not more. The larger the group, the less productive it gets, so keep it small and keep it tight if you want to get stuff done.

That naturally implies a short agenda.

Limiting the agenda

It's better to cover a maximum of two to three agenda items if you want to ensure everyone's engagement and focus. Each topic you deal with needs to matter to everyone on the call, or you won't get the input you need.

So limit the agenda and limit the time you meet for: 30 to 60 minutes should be enough. Remember that no one ever says, 'I hated that meeting; it was so short.'

Finding a good time

Pick a good meeting time by consulting everyone; we all hate having meetings dumped in our calendars, so don't do it to others unless you absolutely have to. Instead, try to work with a shared calendar when you can, so you know who's available when. Some software and web-based calendars can select the most convenient times for everyone who needs to be there. Otherwise, to make your life easy, use a great app like Doodle. Everyone enters the dates that they are available, so planning a mutually convenient time is really easy if you are the coordinator.

When you work with people in different time zones, try to take everyone's working day into consideration. If it always works against the same people, they won't love you for it. In the same vein, take holidays and religious festivals into account when you can. And finally, for obvious reasons, avoid Monday mornings first thing and anything around close of play on a Friday.

Sending invitations and call details

Once you've found your time and date, make everyone's life easier by

- **Sending a meeting invitation** and adding a calendar reminder or alert, so they know what they have to do by when. The advantage with calendar invitations is that there's then no excuse for not being there; it's already in the diary.
- **Putting the agenda into the meeting invitation,** so participants don't have to look for it. Do the same for any ground rules you want to use.
- **Adding all the meeting details,** log in, software downloads necessary, and whatever Plan B is tech-wise. There's nothing worse than hundreds of emails flying about when you can't activate an online meeting, and it's a guaranteed way of losing people or making them cross.

Sharing materials

Attach small documents to your meeting invitation, so they don't get lost. Larger ones will need to be put somewhere everyone can access – for example, a cloud-based storage solution. For larger documents, you can also try using a tinyURL or bitly, both of which are web-based link-sharing platforms.

Just don't send a vast data-hungry document that may be rejected by other servers. Anyone accessing the document on a smart phone won't enjoy reading it and may not bother. And sending a monster document makes you look tech-unsavvy.

Managing your kit

If you're running the meeting, you need proper kit – like decent phones or microphones, a fast laptop and enough bandwidth so that people can clearly see and hear what you say.

You also need to know how to use it all properly. If you can't unmute a microphone, move forward in your presentation or manage chat, you look out of control. Make sure you practise beforehand and know what you're doing.

And if you're doing a videoconference, make sure you can move the camera so that whoever is speaking is visible. Get close-ups when possible, pan out if you can or ask someone else (your wingman) to manage the camera. A long shot of a boardroom table when you can't see the speakers is very dull – especially after an hour.

Getting going on time

We've all waited agonising minutes for everyone to attend a remote meeting and, in the awkward delay, had to endure waffling about someone's dog/cat/car repair/sports event/traffic jam.

Instead, ask the first person on the call a question about the agenda, a document or a relevant idea. As other people join the call, say hello and invite them to answer the same question when they are ready. This will encourage everyone to get sharing from the start; that should then continue as you switch into your main agenda.

Reaffirming the ground rules

It's worth running through the ground rules at the start of your meeting. You might feel you're being overdirective, but it's your meeting, and you can't shoot anyone a disapproving look when their behaviour is unacceptable.

Good ground rules include

- **State your name when you speak,** so everyone knows who's talking, especially if lots of people are on the call.

- **Turn your cell phone onto silent** if you're not calling on it, so it doesn't disturb everyone else.
- **Download everything you need before the meeting** and turn up prepared.
- **Use the mute button if you are somewhere noisy.** Ten people in different open-plan offices all on the same call is torture.
- **Don't answer emails** when you're attending your meeting. Typing is rude (and everyone can hear you unless you mute your line).
- **Use web software, IM or email to ask questions** when lots of participants are on the call. Then, of course, it's fine to type.

Stating your goal

Remind everyone at the start of the meeting why you are all getting together and what you want to do – even if it's just clarifying niggles in a project. Then once you've achieved your goal, draw it all to a conclusion.

Any Other Business becomes particularly painful on a call, so respect time and close the meeting. Your participants need to learn to be as planned and managed as you are, and they don't need to be if you're okay with AOB.

Using a wingman when working remotely

Wingmen are essential when it comes to remote meetings. That's because you can't manage the meeting and the tech issues at the same time. You do the former; your wingman does the latter. (See Chapter 5 for more about this topic.)

Wingmen can

- Manage any instant messaging (IM) group chat or activate any polls you want to do.
- Handle all troubleshooting like sound, refresh slides, bringing up video when you need it.

- Message participants who need to speak up because no-one can hear them
- Draw your attention to questions and challenges that come up through mails, chat or IM.

By the way, if you've got multiple presentations from different participants, your wingman will need deputies, too.

Keeping it relevant

As you share your screen, remember not to show everyone everything. They don't need to see your desktop; if there's nothing on it, they'll comment, and if there's lots on it, they'll comment, too. You can't win.

You also need to keep it relevant from a bandwidth perspective and recognise that in some countries or locations, bandwidth is dire. Those beautiful slides and videos just may not be visible or may load so slowly that you frustrate your meeting participants.

Handling PowerPoint

Slides can help or hinder you. If you've got graphs, charts and pictures to show, they help. Lots of words that result in a reading lesson will hinder you as they merely turn participants off. In fact, they are an open invitation to carry on with email.

Just jot a few ideas down of things you want to discuss instead, and you'll reduce your workload considerably.

Taking control when you can

It's unbelievably disruptive when someone who dials in puts your meeting call on hold for everyone else to listen to Greensleeves at best and corporate advertising at worst. It's also disruptive if someone listens in on a plane, train, automobile or office – anyplace with a noisy background.

If that happens to you, mute that participant; most platforms and apps allow you to do that. Some platforms also allow you to eject participants off a call if you need. That might seem harsh, but it's fair if your ground rules are clear about muting your phone when there's a lot of background noise – and at least everyone knows you mean business.

Being respectful of time

To maximise the effectiveness of each person and signal that you mean business, arrive early on the call and start on time – even if your most important participant is late.

And finally, finish promptly.

Signposting

Signposts are mini summaries of what you have talked about, are talking about or are going to talk about. They help your participants stay on track. (For more about them, see Chapter 6.)

When you run remote meetings, frankly signposts are a crucial tool, if not the crucial tool, in your kit. Without signposts, no one knows where you are going or what you are doing. You have to be even more overt about signposting because they form the foundations for structuring what you say.

Here are some examples of signposts you need in remote meetings:

- I'd like now to get ten minutes input from the delivery team. James, let's start with you.
- I want to turn now to issues we are facing over the next two weeks.
- Can we all now focus on what potential solutions might be?
- In summary, John, what you are saying is. . . .
- Just to re-iterate, developing the fix is the next 24 hours' primary task.
- I'm just going to stop you/interrupt to check that. . . .
- Let's move to the next topic on our agenda.

Using 'let's' to drive direction

'Let's' is a brilliant word to use on a remote call because it's a directive tool that sounds inclusive. When you say 'let's,' what you really mean is 'I want to. . . .' or 'We're now going to. . . . ,' which can sound way too uncollaborative and frankly bossy.

But 'let's' allows you to tell others what to do. For example when someone is being

- **A windbag,** try 'Let's stick to our ground rules of one minute's comment each.'
- **A waffler,** try 'Let's all pause for a few seconds and gather our thoughts, so we can be as concise and clear as possible on this subject.'
- **A hijacker,** try 'Let's get back on the agenda and hear more about. . . .'
- **A joker,** try 'Let's focus on what we're here to do.'

You get the picture for how you can use 'let's.'

Thinking about your voice

When you use a speakerphone, you are literally talking down to your participants as you lean towards the phone. That can affect your voice and make you sound bored and therefore patronising. And speakerphones often distort sound for the worse. You may feel daft, but headsets do help and mean you will talk to people rather than talk down to them.

Most importantly of all, when you are relying so much on your voice, you need to speak slowly and clearly. Muttering isn't great face-to-face, and it's much worse when you are a remote participant.

Another drawback with audio is that is flattens your voice, reducing *modulation* (the up and down range you have when you speak). That means you have to work harder to sound energised and interested. Using your hands as you talk will help with all of that, as does sitting up straight or standing, if you can. You'll also add more energy and interest to your voice if you make things personal, so think about what you are prepared to disclose about yourself on the call.

Remember to smile even if no one can see you. That way, you'll sound warm, interested and welcoming which will make your participants respond positively to you.

Asking questions for active participation

If you're working with a large group over different time zones and perhaps with some people who don't have English as their first language, you'll need to work hard to get everyone fully participating. This means asking frequent general questions to get a conversation rolling. Then you'll need to ask specific questions that mean you get the input you want from relevant individuals.

Make sure you pause a lot to allow everyone the chance to contribute. Some people need more silence before they jump in, so pay attention to who's talking and invite others to comment if they want to. That way, you are giving them the opportunity, and sooner or later they'll learn to take it.

Try to bear in mind that closed questions (see Chapter 4) don't work in the same way as they do in face-to-face meetings. If you ask, 'Do we all agree?' to a group of ten people on a conference call, you can't see possible disagreement. No answer is, in fact, a danger signal. You'll need to ask even more open questions to check who's onboard and invite everyone to put their concerns on the table. Using the chat function on a meeting platform can be really helpful in managing this.

If certain attendees don't actively participate and that's a surprise to you, ping them an email or private chat message and ask what's happening for them. They may not have told you they are somewhere noisy, distracted or simply thinking about what you are saying. But asking shows you are aware that they are behaving out of character. If you need to, contact them after the meeting to

- Find out what it meant that they didn't speak up as you expected.
- Explain how important their input is.
- Ask what they need to make sure that they contribute the next time.
- Check in to see if there's anything you could to do to support them.

Recording your meeting

Recording and capturing what happens makes following up and ownership of actions so much easier. Most web platforms and all conference call systems allow you to record your meetings for later viewing or reviewing. This helps your participants who can't attend and means that you don't need to update everyone on everything; they can update themselves.

There are also a whole bunch of other functions that make everyone's lives easier. In a traditional meeting, you often have to copy down what you wrote on a white board or transcribe flip charts and then send out the information. On many platforms, you can just save the white boards, chat logs and other visuals, all of which makes life so much simpler.

Saving all the information

Once your meeting is over, you need to make the recordings, materials and agreements clear and available to everyone as soon as possible. Let everyone on the call know how and when this will be, especially if you are running a kick-off meeting. Then if there are any questions, participants can refer back to what was covered by finding everything they need.

A shared network drive or a cloud-based storage service works well for keeping meetings materials available if, of course, you're not using a meeting platform. You can save your notes, presentations and recordings in one place so access is easy.

Reviewing your meetings

The beauty of web platforms is that you generally have a polling feature, so you can quickly review your meeting and get instant reactions to the work you just did.

We recommend asking one or two questions, so your participants don't get polling fatigue. Varying those questions after each meeting will give you great input and insights into the different aspects of what you do.

Managing Hybrid Meetings

Hybrid meetings are those where some participants are meeting in a room locally and others attend remotely. Hybrid meetings require even more planning because you need to think about your on-site audience, your remote audience and how you get both groups to work together. As you can imagine, it's really tricky to meet these three needs.

The biggest mistake that on-site participants make is simply to forget that remote participants are there, especially if there are only audio and no video links. Remote participants need active involvement at all times; they are not second-class citizens and will totally disengage if you treat them as such. So ask them first for their opinions. Don't just default to whoever's in the room with you. Check that they can hear comments or questions and repeat anything you think might be hard for your remote participants to hear.

Try to keep in mind that anyone outside the room can't see nodding around the table, observe raised eyebrows or hear side comments. They also may be less clued into the dynamic in the room. When you're not used to these kinds of meetings, it's easy to skip sharing this kind of important information – which, if you're outside the room, is excluding, frustrating and irritating.

Working with ten top best practises

Here are ten best practises for successfully managing a hybrid meeting:

- **Write everyone's names on a whiteboard or flip chart,** so everyone in the room knows who's there all the time and make sure that you send out a list or tell your remote participants who are physically present.
- **Describe what's happening**, so remote users understand what's going on. Get other people to emulate this by saying, for example, 'Aleksei is shaking his head at Peter.'

- **Check in, one person at a time,** on what participants think or how they react to important nitty-gritty comments, whether local or remote.
- **Gauge high-level reaction** by occasionally asking everyone for a 30-second review.
- **Ask remote participants** what has landed or not landed for them at regular points during the meeting.
- **Have a visual agenda** – for example, with a dashboard – so everyone can see what milestones you pass and when.
- **Keep meetings to a maximum of 75 minutes.** An hour may be too short, but 90 minutes is definitely too long.
- **Clarify any brainstorming process** before you do it. Remote participants hate having their ideas ignored and think that it's because they are remote that their stuff gets lost. You may have to work harder to help everyone feel equally included and valued.
- **Learn to use a whiteboard effectively** so that everyone can build ideas, see what's happening and contribute to work together. There are plenty of free apps suitable for remote sharing.
- **Get your wingman to help you co-manage** the bridge you make between your local and remote participants (in addition to the wingman's role with the tech stuff).
- **Take care with the mute button:** It's too easy to forget when it's on and off and then say something you really regret. And it's disrespectful to run a secondary meeting with those present in the room.

We'll end with one important tip: The hardest of hybrid meetings are those when you're leading it remotely while some of your participants are in a room together. You might be leader, but you may not know exactly what's happening, so it's tougher to gauge reaction. If this is the case, be upfront and check in regularly with your local participants about specifics. Or delegate running the meeting to someone else; it will be a great learning opportunity for them.

Quick informal virtual contact

If you want to connect informally with team members who are remote and get a quick question answered or check something out, take a look at Sqwiggle. It's a team app that shows constantly updated stills from everyone's webcams, so you can immediately see if your colleagues are at their desks. Should you want to chat, you just click on their picture. You can also share your screen and invite more than one person into a conversation, so it's brilliant for quick reminders, check-ins or questions. Used with the right intent, Sqwiggle is a great way of building social contact between everyone, regardless of where they are based.

Reviewing Available Technology

Finding the right technology can be hard because there's so much out there. So where do you start?

First and foremost, you want reliability and simplicity. If what you choose is slow or unreliable in your environment and participants can't use the kit because it's too complex, well, they just won't join you.

The easiest way to find the right solution is to make a list of everything you want your meeting platform to do and then prioritise that list. Then review the functionality of each solution and identify your top three to five favorite options.

You'll have to make some tradeoffs in your choices, so dig around on the Internet to check what's changed, what's been updated and what others say. Then get a demo and a free trial (if you go for a commercial option) for a proper period of time. That way, you get to see what it's really like before committing.

You don't want to trial everything that's out there, but you do want to know you're onto a likely winner before you give anyone the headache of learning to use it.

The following sections give you a mini synopsis of our favorites.

Adobe Connect

Adobe Connect has loads of features and can handle small to large meetings. Plus it supports remote and virtual learning.

Pros:

- Highly scalable to larger meetings
- Multiple simultaneous video streams
- Lots of extensions to add more functionality
- Mobile support is the best around
- Custom URLs

Cons:

- Premium pricing
- Not as easy as some to set up

Cisco WebEx

Market-leader WebEx has become synonymous with online meetings and for good reason: It works, and it works very well. But WebEx has found itself up against user-friendlier and cheaper competitors.

Pros:

- Recognised as a solid performer
- Supports sharing videos
- No need for anyone to install browser add-ons

Cons:

- More complex to learn
- Recordings come in a proprietary format

Citrix GoToMeeting

GoToMeeting is one of the most user-friendly and simplest options. Kicking off a meeting is as easy as clicking a button, or forwarding an email. But because of this, it has less functionality than its competitors.

Pros:

- One-click meeting start
- Mute individual people
- Includes free call-in phone number

Cons:

- Requires users to install browser add-on
- No whiteboard

Google+ Hangouts

Google Hangouts is a really useful tool that only requires a Gmail address to use. It works with other Google products that allow real-time document collaboration.

Pros:

- Free with additional paid features
- Loads of other tools and extensions
- Good mobile app

Cons:

- You need a Google+ account to get started

OmniJoin

OmniJoin lives up to its promise of 'HD webconferencing made easy.' It's simple to use, intuitive and not bandwidth-hungry, so it also works well on mobile. Being able to see a presentation and participants simultaneously is a great feature.

Pros:

- Brilliant audio and video quality
- Masses of functionality
- Simple and reliable mobile app

Cons:

- We can't find any!

Skype

Free is good, and if you usually do one-to-one meetings, Skype is simple and easy to use. A small subscription means you can do group video calls for up to ten people.

Pros:

- Intuitive to use
- Good audio and video quality when it works

Cons:

- Needs lots of bandwidth and soaks up RAM
- Not as reliable as some when video is on

Cisco Telepresence

Telepresence is a fabulous product with an equally fabulous price tag. In a class of its own, Telepresence involves kitting out a room with a special table, cameras and giant HD screens. When you sit down with remote participants, you really feel as if you are in the same room as you work together.

Pros:

- Uber cool
- Great for longer meetings

Cons:

- Not mobile
- Can only use it with other Telepresence users
- Very expensive

Understanding Remote and Virtual Workshops

Remote and virtual workshops fall into four basic categories:

- **Workshops run by phone conference call:** These tend to be more useful for transferring knowledge about simpler tasks or concepts. *Best use:* A group who knows each other; 90 per cent of the content is quick and simple to share or communicate.

- **Workshops run on any of the platforms (see earlier section in this chapter) that allow for more in-depth peer contact and sharing:** *Best use:* A group who knows each other or has strong common interest; at least 50 per cent of your content is quick and easy to communicate.
- **Workshops delivered via a Virtual Learning Environment (VLE):** These allow a group of people to work through a sophisticated and complex learning process together. They quite often involve a blend of face-to-face, group, individual and remote work. *Best use:* Multiple groups who may or may not know each other, are in different locations and often under time pressure. The content is more challenging and is best supported through individual and peer learning, online forums, offline work and social networks. In other words, it's not a one-off event for a single group of people because it needs time and investment due to the level of complexity.
- **Mobile learning on handheld devices:** The great advantage with m-learning is that it can reach a large number of people quickly and cheaply, offering bite-sized information and quick-fire interactivity. *Best use:* Just-in-time training to solve an immediate problem or get a quick update. It works really well when integrated with virtual and modular learning. One hundred percent of the content needs to be self-evident.

Embracing yet more technology

While the most sophisticated platforms look potentially scary to get your head round, they do offer huge benefits:

- **Greatly reduced overall costs** per person once you have gone through the development stage.
- **Easy access to content,** great use of subject-matter experts, peer support and permanently available material.
- **Fewer blocks of time** away from work so much less disruption, especially when delivering solutions for larger cohorts of people.

- **Continuous learning** supported by peers and experts is much more likely to result in application.
- **Immediate review** means it's easy to see what works, what could be better and then tweak content. Best of all updating content doesn't cost very much.

But, of course, there are challenges, too.

Recognising the challenges

There are lots of challenges you have to face when you start to think about delivering workshops in a virtual environment. It's especially tough to

- **Manage expectations:** You are not building a virtual world where participants are represented by avatars. You are putting the real world into a virtual space, which can be hard for some people to understand.
- **Keep people engaged at all times:** Your users need to want to join in and stay in, or they'll vote with their feet – or mice. You need more and shorter activities that are really well and clearly presented.
- **Develop reasonably priced content:** Great content can be costly to develop, but if your participants aren't wowed early on, they won't want to engage. You need a fabulous visual experience supported by compelling video and insightful experts.

Thinking about virtual learning

If you are considering virtual learning, you are thinking about introducing long-term strategic change into your organisation. Virtual learning is much more than a flat e-learning offering; e-learning pushes information from a source to an individual. But virtual environments support workshops in interactive events; that's because workshops always involve people and experts.

We know you know strategic change is tough. To make it easier, you'll need to be crystal clear about why you want to do this, the benefits it will deliver and how you might then go about it. This will help you sell in the need. To develop this clarity, work through these useful questions:

- Why are we doing this?
- What are our strategic aims?
- What's the business case?
- What are the outcomes we are looking to achieve?
- How will we know we are on our way to achieving them?
- Who do we want to support with this initiative?
- What are their needs?
- How can we test these needs and our ideas?
- Whose support do we need?
- What options do we have?
- What information and experience do we currently have?
- What additional information and experience do we need?
- Which providers could give us more information?
- Who else like us has successfully implemented a VLE?
- Where should we start?
- What's the cost of doing nothing?

To help you work everything out and to look like an expert, you need to use the right language. The basics are laid out in Table 12-1.

Table 12-1 Must-Know Acronyms

Acronym	*Meaning*
LMS	A Learning Management System (LMS) allows organisations to administer, document, track, report and deliver workshops or training programs.
VLE	A Virtual Learning Environment (VLE) is an integrated system that combines virtual classes and classrooms, libraries of online stored content, forums, tests and quizzes, homework, assessments, journals and social media. A VLE needs to integrate with any LMS.

Acronym	*Meaning*
CMS	A Content Management System (CMS) means you can upload and manage learning or workshop materials.
MOOC	Mass Open Online Courses (MOOCs) offer anyone with the Internet the opportunity to study at a top university for free but without a tutor. They are available to anyone, anywhere. While they are much talked about, they are also far less completed by learners; typically only 10 per cent actually finish any MOOC.

Vocab for VLEs

Assets: All the materials you use to support your workshops – for example, podcasts, videos, case studies, quizzes and tests, recorded webinars, quizzes and tests.

Gamification: Leverages everyone's natural competitiveness – for example, by providing leader boards so participants know who's done the most.

Flipped classroom: In a flipped classroom set up, trainers and facilitators get participants to understand and learn a concept by themselves. That frees up precious time to work directly with the group when they come together.

Learning journey: How you construct a group's start-to-finish experience to deliver a coherent, varied and logical pathway. It takes into account what will be learned, when, how and by whom.

Learning room: An area in the VLE that is dedicated to a particular subject and where participants can find a relevant materials (perhaps a forum to post on), and they can contact a subject matter expert in real-time (subject to availability) or by email.

Synchronous and asynchronous systems: Virtual learning can take place synchronously or asynchronously. In synchronous events, participants meet in real-time with live sessions in virtual meetings. Participants can communicate by talking, posting, IMing or writing on a message board. In asynchronous sessions, participants work at their own pace and in their own time.

Threaded discussion: Refers to online conversations about specific topics. You see the initial message, and all the subsequent posts are available, too. They are a fantastic way to share experience.

Virtual classroom: In virtual classrooms, participants take part in real-time activity together. The group and the facilitator are logged in and communicate generally through web-conferencing technologies. Message boards and chat help everyone connect.

You'll need to develop or use whatever virtual solution you are going to deploy.

Building your next steps

One thing is for sure: It takes time to get ready for, assess and develop a robust and rigorous virtual learning platform, and it's a build on everything you've done already.

To prepare well for introducing a VLE, you need to do the following:

- **Build your live workshops skills first.** Without being a fabulous practitioner face-to-face, you haven't a hope in a virtual space.
- **Get really good at using web-meeting technology** before you think about a VLE. You need to feel really comfortable with hitches and glitches as you will face some.
- **Attend lots of web learning.** Try Moodle, Coursera and ALLISON to see what you do and don't like.
- **Take one small step** before you start to develop the full banana. For example, consult to a pilot group and then build a module out on Moodle. That way, you can test the viability and appetite for something bigger.
- **Go to events** where there are lots of opportunities to see what's out there vendor-wise. Get some of them in for pre-sales calls to show you what you can do.
- **Make contact and get mentoring** from at least one person who's done it before.
- **Get other people involved in the project.** You need an executive sponsor who's really up for this to champion it and your IT guys to help you.
- **Start to think about what you do and don't want** right now, and what you might want your VLE to do in the future.

It's a given that when it comes to an IT project and a strategic implementation, you won't get things right the first time as you won't have a blueprint. That means you'll need to consult all the way and change what you're doing as you learn.

Part IV

The Part of Tens

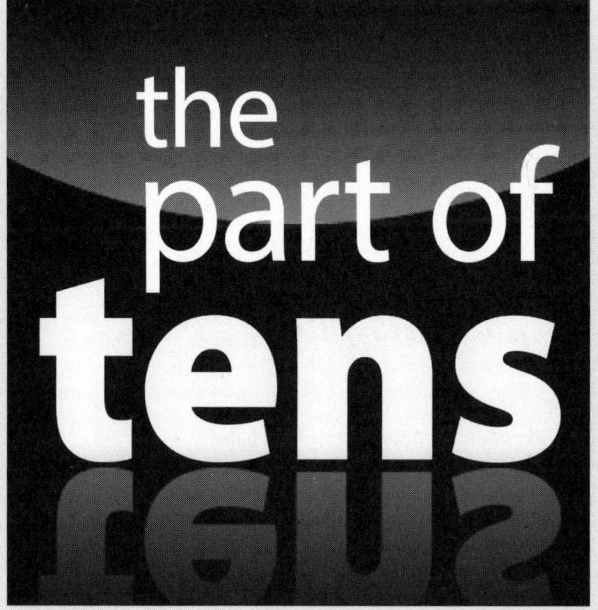

Enjoy an additional Part of Tens chapter online at www.dummies.com/extras/rungreatmeetingsworkshops.

In this part . . .

- Gain a reputation for excellent meetings and workshops.
- Avoid common mistakes on the big day.

Chapter 13

Ten Common Mistakes on the Day

In This Chapter

- Managing the group
- Dealing with individuals
- Controlling the process

It's all too easy to get group work slightly wrong – not disastrously wrong, but just enough that it doesn't quite work out. This chapter lists ten common mistakes that you just don't need to make. Go through the list and see which ones apply to you.

Failing to Set Up Group Work Properly

If you fail to set group work up well by forgetting to clarify expectations, timings and ground rules, you're facing a bunch of risks. When this happens, participants can

- Do lots of unexpected things because they don't have any boundaries
- Get aggressive because they don't know where they are going
- Provoke conflict with you as they feel unsecure
- Include random new suggestions to test you

- Give you poor feedforward because they don't know what success looks like
- Start turning up late and messing about generally as there are no clear guidelines for everything else

To avoid trouble like this, you have to go through a contracting process by setting ground rules and parameters with the group as you start; it's way too late to try and do it half way through and by then the group may well have lost confidence in you.

Talking Too Much

It's easy to talk too much, and it's a rookie mistake.

When you are leading a group, everyone else should be talking, not you. If you are doing all the talking, the group will be dying of boredom, and it's much more exhausting for you. And if you're doing all the talking, why didn't you send an email instead? Because what you doing isn't having a meeting. Instead, you are doing one or two of the following:

- **Updating everyone:** You couldn't be bothered to write a clear and concise email or document, preferring to ramble around an agenda-free zone dealing solely with your main interests.
- **Telling everyone how anxious you are:** Often, people who are nervous simply can't shut up. They gabble away in front of the group, circling around topics without saying what they want to say.
- **Illustrating your lack of preparation:** Yes, people who haven't prepared enough often talk a lot to cover up. It doesn't work.
- **Running a vanity session:** You are saying to your group, 'Hello, look at me. Aren't I the clever one?' You're not; you're just a windbag.

Nothing gets advanced by gathering people to witness any of the preceding scenarios. The point of getting everyone into a room is to benefit from their ideas and expertise.

That means not talking for more than 10 per cent of the time if there are nine others in the room, even if you are leading the session. If you are a teacher, well that's another matter. If you are the boss, then shut up and listen! What you say should provoke conversation, support or challenge others and, most importantly, get stuff done.

Ignoring Emotion

Sometimes conversations get out of hand as people struggle with fear, anger or embarrassment in a group. That's when individuals tend to get defensive. Of course, the easiest thing is to ignore what's going on because your own emotions get in the way. To help a group, what you need to do is

- Slow down and breathe so you don't get swamped by your own response.
- Ask the emotional individual(s) if they are willing to name their emotion (if they haven't done so already) and to explain where it comes from.
- Get them to use *I* statements rather than *you,* so they own their emotion. So a participant would say, 'I'm not comfortable with this' rather than 'When you experience this, it's not comfortable.'
- Help those with strong emotions describe what is happening for them.
- Ask the group what it wants to do about something everyone clearly feels strongly about.
- Use the others' reactions to open a conversation, if you need to.

That way, you'll stay in control of the situation, and you won't get swamped by it.

Failing to Join the Dots

If you don't signpost how subjects and themes link, your participants won't get how things link together. They can't experience what you are doing at a micro level and join it all together at a macro one. If you don't do this, your meeting or workshop will seem like a random series of discussions or activities, and everyone will leave dissatisfied. So make sure you

- Link forwards and backwards.
- Recognise themes that keep appearing in your session.
- Connect what you are doing with
  - Other parts of the organisation
  - The industry
  - Your competitors

Then what you are doing will feel connected and coherent.

Failing to Deal with a Difficult Person

When someone shows up as a difficult person, he or she quite often wants recognition from you or the group. If you try that and it doesn't work, then you need deal with this individual or the rest of the group gets disrupted, de-energised and derailed – and they won't thank you for it.

If someone doesn't want to be there let them go or take them to one side and invite them to leave. At least everyone else will get real work done.

Failing to Recognise an Expert in the Room

If someone is an expert in your subject during a meeting or workshop, don't be scared. Be grateful. If you acknowledge their expertise in front of the group, that person will feel recognised and, as a result, is much more likely to support and help you.

If you don't allow an expert to be part of what you are doing, you might just encourage difficult behaviour. So it is really wise to get your expert talking and sharing in front of the group, while you defer to the deep knowledge that's available. That way, you'll have a partner who can carry some of the weight for you – a win-win for everyone.

Failing to Change What You're Doing

It happens. From time to time, things just don't work as you imagined they would for a whole variety of reasons. Perhaps what you were doing didn't work, why you were doing it wasn't clear or how you were doing it didn't land. In short, your topic or activity didn't fly. That's okay. Just move on elegantly without beating yourself up in front of the group.

The same applies to energy. If you find the group has low energy, don't continue with another low energy activity. Get everyone up, get moving and, best of all, if you can, get outside.

Thinking about the Detail Rather Than the Big Picture

The mistake that novices make is to focus on what's happening minute by minute instead of the overall arc of the process and the people within that process. So beginners are really concerned about

- Am I doing okay?
- Am I on time?
- Is this going okay?
- Have I remembered what I needed to say here?
- What comes next?

None of these thoughts are helpful, and they mean that your focus will be way down in the weeds. Now we know it's difficult to wean yourself from thinking in a moment-to-moment manner. But it's essential that you do it. Instead, you need to focus on

- How is this overall process going?
- How's the group's energy, and how do I work with it?
- How am I connecting with everyone, they with each other and the topics we are dealing with?

This will mean you're thinking about the whole experience rather than the minutiae of it. And when you think about the whole, it will be greater than the sum of its parts.

Failing to Push a Group

Your role is to support and challenge a group as they go through what you planned for them. And it's key to remember that this is *support*, not sympathise, and *challenge,* not collude.

Groups often say they don't want to be pushed when, in fact, they do. When they kick back, what they are often doing is testing you. And when you challenge them in turn and they rise to it, that's when they dig deep to do better and more. They may have a bit of a moan at the time, but afterwards they will always turn round and thank you. After all, no one achieves their potential by doing anything easy or staying within their comfort zone.

Letting anyone off the hook isn't what they want deep down and they won't respect you for it either. (See Chapter 6 for more on challenging and working successfully with groups.)

Being Too Dogmatic

Life isn't black or white, and there are no silver bullets – which means that if you are too dogmatic, you will simply get participants challenging what you say. And that's not the reason why you get together. You spend time in a room to do work, and dogmatism will prevent that happening.

So, for example, if your participants don't like something you say, don't create a point of principle and insist. Instead,

1. **Ask them what would work better for them.**
2. **Amend your approach.**
3. **Check that they are okay with this.**
4. **Move on with your agenda.**

There's no point getting into an argument about what quite often is semantics. Someone doesn't want to make a promise? A commitment is fine. They don't like the term feedforward? Feedback is fine, too. The more pragmatic you are, the easier your job will be, and the more people will like you, too.

When you are new to an organisation or team it's really important not to be too inflexible. They will be evaluating you, deciding 'are you one of us?', and considering 'to what extent are you picking up on our culture?' Insisting at this time will mark you as an outsider, possibly forever.

Chapter 14

Ten Things You Have to Do When the Pressure Is On

In This Chapter

- Getting ready for your session
- Managing the group
- Managing yourself

The first time you kick off a project team meeting, run a workshop, deal with senior people or tackle a topic slightly out of your comfort zone, you need to plan more and be super-conscious of what you do on the day. That's because you've got much to lose when it goes wrong. This chapter helps you get it right.

Preparing Brilliantly

When the pressure is on, the first thing you need to do is prepare. That means

- **Planning well-presented and well-ordered documents and materials well in advance:** That way, you won't be working late to pull everything together at the last minute.
- **Sorting out the logistics and sending out clear invitations in advance of your session:** You don't want to be dealing with room issues or dial in numbers minutes before you start.
- **Knowing what you are going to say:** You want to look fluent and in control, so you need to say it, say it and say it. That means rehearsing out loud, so you have the words for any difficult bits on the tip of your tongue.

If you want to know how you come over, you should video yourself doing a tricky section and play it back with these questions in mind:

- What do I like about what I see?
- What do I want to do differently?
- How confident do I look and sound?

It's really important to remember that you may feel less confident than you actually look. But the benefit of watching yourself is that that will be abundantly clear.

There's a caveat here: if you are prone to beating yourself up because you are a perfectionist, get a close colleague or good friend to watch the video with you. That way, you'll get realistic input. What you are doing is difficult enough without outing yourself under extra pressure.

Having a Plan to Move Away from It

The point of all that preparation is that it will make you feel really grounded in what you are doing and when. So if a curved ball then comes your way, you'll be able to take it in your stride. In other words you have a plan to move away from it rather than to stick rigidly to it.

Now a natural reaction to being asked to flex or change what you do is discomfort, surprise or even shock, especially if you're inexperienced. But if it's what the group needs, then you need to take it in your stride: Bending won't break you, but it will build much more rapport and trust with everyone.

Creating Rapport

When working with a new group, what's important is that you help create rapport between you and the group as well as between everyone else. You build rapport by

- **Being friendly, warm, and approachable.** So smile, be interested in each person as they come in and greet them appropriately. Remember first impressions last, so put everyone at ease from the moment they arrive.
- **Remembering and using people's names.** Learn who they are the first time you meet them and use their names.
- **Finding things in common.** Chat before you start to find links with people.
- **Referring to what you know about them.** If you've met already, ask about their projects, families and interests.
- **Being attentive to everyone's needs.** Notice who has and hasn't had time to get refreshments, who needs support (and give it) and who needs to take time out (and make that easy).
- **Listening to develop relationships.** Don't interrupt them, but do acknowledge and paraphrase what others have said to show you understand.
- **Mirroring participants.** Notice how they are standing and talking and match what's positive.
- **Showing empathy.** See others' points of view and reflect back how you think they're feeling about things.
- **Disclosing something about you that is personal and important to you.** When you share something that matters to you, you are not only being authentic, you are building rapport.

Building Trust with the Group

You build trust when you set up a process and then stick to what you say you'll do. That way you meet everyone's expectations and show that you are reliable. You also build trust when you:

- Communicate clearly about what's happening
- Check in with the group regularly to see that everyone's okay with the process
- Recognise the talk openly about energy, problems, emotions and relationships within the group

- Are transparent about stakeholders and their impact
- Let the group give input and guidance to the work you do together
- Talk straightforwardly about issues without sweeping them under a carpet or ignoring elephants in the room
- Follow up on promised actions within a given time after the session and deliver on any other promises

Taking Breaks

Whatever time pressure you are under, you need to be able to schedule and manage proper breaks. Your participants cannot maintain focus or energy, let alone manage emails and calls without them. So don't cut breaks short; it's always tempting to and never worth it. Moreover, it's how you build trust. If you say that there will be a break and then you don't honour that, you aren't keeping your word. And if you aren't trustworthy for something small, what about the big things?

If timekeeping simply isn't your bag because you get so involved in what's going on, ask someone else to be your break supervisor. That way, she can give you a time check when you're ten minutes away from coffee, tea or lunch. Then you'll have enough time to get to a suitable stop.

Being Fair to Everyone

It's inevitable that when you work with groups that you will like some people more than others. That's normal. Regardless of how you feel, you need to be fair to everyone – even to someone you think is the original Mr or Ms Nasty-and-Difficult.

If you aren't fair in your work, what you'll find is that the group may turn on you instead of managing their recalcitrant team member. So check in with yourself to see that you are allocating your time, attention and energy equally across the group. That means neither ignoring your irritating participant nor allocating her all your attention. She is entitled to her fair share, and you can manage this if you set up clear ground rules and, with the group's help, enforce them.

Dealing with the Unacceptable

To use an old English expression, 'There's nowt so strange as folks.' Be prepared to be surprised a lot by what people say to you when you run groups. Over your career, you will come across comments that range from arrogant and insulting to anything – *ist,* including sexist, racist, religionist, ageist and alarmist.

The question is do you ignore or tackle off-beat comments? And the simple answer to that is that if you found something offensive, so will someone else. So deal with it on or off-line, whichever is most appropriate.

Now when you challenge people, some of them will tell you that they were 'only joking'. That's the line that a bully will always use. (For more on this topic, see Chapter 7.) Depending on how much you want to pull someone up, you can point that out with or without humour.

Using Humour

Humour is a great way of dealing with any difficult situation. Having a laugh bonds everyone and shows that although the work may be serious, you don't take yourself too seriously. Humour has the great effect of

- Creating rapport between you and the group.
- Increasing enjoyment of the work you are all doing.
- Raising energy for everyone in the room.
- Reducing any tension and stress associated with the work in hand.
- Putting the group at ease as you work together.
- Fostering creativity as it's impossible to problem solve when you are feeling blue.
- Building trust as the group gets to see the real and authentic you.

If you enjoy what you do and have a few laughs, the group will love being led by you. And this will make them want to attend your meetings and workshops. If humour isn't your thing, then don't try using it because it will simply fall flat and potentially embarrass you and the group. Most importantly, never make a joke at others' expense, or you'll find that the group will turn on you.

Noticing When the Group Is Going Off Track

The first thing to say is that it's fine to go off-track as long as you check with the group that this is useful. Sometimes it's the extra conversations that are the most insightful and productive, so if this appears to be the case, let the conversation run. Wait for a pause and then

1. **Point out that the conversation has off-tracked.**
2. **Say that it seems to you that the conversation is useful (if it is) or potentially not useful (if it isn't).**
3. **Ask whether everyone wants to continue off-track or get back on-track.**

   The way to frame this is by asking what would be most useful and getting everyone's buy-in for how to proceed.

Doing this means that once again, you'll be building trust with the group by recognising what's happening and helping everyone manage the process.

Holding It Together

You may be under pressure, but you mustn't let that show before, during or after your session. Tell your friends and family but don't, under any circumstances, let on to the group or any participants. All you do when you talk about your nerves is destabilise everyone, including you. The group wants to feel certain in your leadership, and they'll feel more certain if you behave like a swan. Be calm and serene on the surface, even if you're paddling like crazy beneath it.

By the way, the same goes for the bar afterwards. Holding it together isn't just for the performance; you've got the after show to deal with, too. When you're in the bar, please don't disclose your earlier worries. You are there doing a professional job, and that means from start to finish. And you never know who will use something against you, so don't give anyone any ammo.

Index

• A •

acronyms, virtual learning, 304–305
actionable, one-sentence objectives, 27
active listening, 87–88
active participation, 17, 294, 297
Activist learning style, 130, 131, 132
activities, workshop design, 68–69, 71
address conflict, 185, 187
Adobe Connect, 299
After The Meeting software, 195
agenda
  as barrier to success, 162
  gathering agenda items, 30
  lack of, meeting dislike, 12
  meetings, 11, 29–42, 287, 297
  order planning/structure, 34–36, 38–42
  outline in kick off, 115
  participation assessment, 34
  planning agenda items, 32–37
  recognising poor agenda, 37–38
  review, 38–42
  sponsors and stakeholders, 31–32
  writing, 29–30, 42
Agreedo software, 195
analysis, report, 205, 250
analytical social style, 129
AOB (Any Other Business), 41–42, 290
Appreciative Inquiry, 280–283
arrival of presenter, 111
ask for help, and conflict, 185, 187
asking participant to leave your session, 176–177
asking questions
  answering in remote meeting, 290–291
  debriefing for case studies, 215
  defining outcome questions, 54
  focus groups, 239–241
  one-sentence objectives, 28
  remote meetings, 294, 297
  testing yourself, 83–84
  types of, 78–84
assertiveness, Social Styles, 126–128
assess conflict, 185, 187
assets, VLE, 305
assumptions, book, 2–3
asynchronous systems, VLE, 305
atmosphere, kick off the session, 114–115
attend to needs, and conflict, 185, 187
attendees. *See* participants
attention and listening, 88–89
audio recording, focus groups, 244

• B •

barriers to success, 161–162
behaviour, difficult, 170–178, 312, 321
big picture, 136, 190, 313–314
body language, 89–91, 92
Bolton & Bolton Social/Behavioural Styles, 126–130
boring meetings, 12–13
brainstorming
  effective, 255–263
  for individuals, 266
  for large groups, 264–265
  problems with, 254–255
  skill building, 253–266
  for small groups, 265–266
  typical rules and reasons, 253–254
breaks, 69, 165, 320
business case
  meetings, 10–20
  workshops, 16–20

• C •

caffeine, 111
calm under pressure, 17, 322–323
CAQ-DAS analysis, 249
case studies in workshops, 210–217
cell phones, 290, 302
change what you are doing, 313
Cheat Sheets for book, online, 4
checking in, 136–137, 297
Cisco Telepresence, 301
Cisco WebEx, 299
Citrix GoToMeeting, 99–100
clarity, one-sentence objectives, 26
classroom, virtual, 305
closed questions, 79–80
clothing to present, 108–109
CMS (Content Management System), 305
code of conduct, 119–120
command, decision-making, 123
comments, dealing with, 149–151
communicating in a group, 98
complainers, 173–174
compulsory sessions, 165
computers. *See* technology
conclusions, report, 205, 250
conference calls, 301–302
conflict
  constructive or destructive, 181–182
  factions, 184–187
  four As to address, 185, 187
  group, 182–184
  healthy compared to unhealthy, 181–182
  ignoring, 181
  individuals, 184–187
  tough conversations, 186
  troubleshooting, 180–187
connections
  meetings/workshops, 139–140
  mistake handling, 311–312
consensus, decision-making, 122
constructive conflict, 181–182
consult, decision-making, 123
content
  meetings, 24–26
  workshop, 17
Content Management System (CMS), 305
context, one-sentence objectives, 26
Cooperrider, David (researcher), 280
cost analysis, ROI, 59–60
cost of poor meetings, 14–15
cover/title page, report, 205, 250
culture, workshops, 48
cynics, 175

• D •

data
  focus groups, 248–250
  performance, and ROI, 59–60
debriefing
  case studies, 215
  role play, 221, 226–227
decision trees for analysis, 267, 278–280
decision-making
  first session, 98–99
  starting sessions, 120–125
  weighted, 123–125
deep listening, 88–89
define, Appreciative Inquiry, 281
delivery
  Appreciative Inquiry, 281, 283
  of workshops, 16, 17
design
  Appreciative Inquiry, 281, 282
  of workshops, 60–76
destiny, Appreciative Inquiry, 281, 283
destructive conflict, 181–182
details
  emphasis on, mistake handling, 313–314
  reflecting, 190–191
difficult behaviour and persons, 170–178, 312, 321
discovery, Appreciative Inquiry, 281–282
discussions
  additional, 167
  facilitating group, 145–151
disruption of remote meetings, 291
distorted thinking, 170–171

distributing minutes, 194–195
dogmatism, handling, 314–315
draft workshop design, 69–70
dream, Appreciative Inquiry, 281, 282
drinking, prior to presenting, 110–111
driver social style, 129
Dummies.com online articles, 4

• E •

eating, prior to presenting, 110–111
elephant in the room, 148–149
emails, remote meetings, 290. *See also* technology
emotion, ignoring, 311
energy
  input, effort and energy matrix, 164
  managing, 155
  observing others, 93–94
  personal, for meetings, 43–45
enjoyment by workshop presenter, 17
evaluating meetings, 159, 197–198
Evernote software, 195
executive summary, report, 205, 250
expectations
  kick off, 116–118
  revisit and review, 158
experiential learning, 69
experts
  decision-making, 122
  delivery of workshops, 17
  recognising, mistake handling, 312–313
  workshops, 48
expressive social style, 129
external focus groups, 238–239

• F •

facial expression, 91–93
factions and conflict, 184–187
fairness, handling pressure, 320
fast-forward button, 120
feedback
  lack of, meeting, 13
  role play, 228–229
findings of focus groups, 251–252
fishbone group analysis, 267, 275–278
flip chart
  focus group, 244
  meetings/workshops, 141–142, 144
flipped classroom, VLE, 305
focus groups
  asking the right questions, 239–241
  characteristics of, 235
  data analysis and interpretation, 248–250
  disadvantages, 252
  goals for, 234–235
  implementing findings, 251–252
  kit preparation, 244–245
  observers, 245
  participants, 238–239
  pausing, 246
  preparing for, 234, 236–245
  purpose statements, 236–237, 247
  reasons for, 20
  recording information, 244
  reports, 234, 250–252
  running the session, 234, 245–246
  script writing, 241–243
  side effects of, 235
  for skill building, 233–252
  stages of, 234
  technology check, 246
  timeline for, 237
  when to use, 233–234
  writing up, 234, 247–252
focus on yourself to start the session, 108–113
follow-up
  feedback, 13, 228–229
  project closure, 201
  reflection, 190–191
  reports, 199–200, 205–206
  return on investment (ROI), 196–199
  review, 200–204
  writing meeting minutes, 191–196
food, prior to presenting, 110–111
force field analysis, 267, 273–275
force majeure, decision-making, 123
formal minutes, writing, 193–195
frame of mind, workshop design, 64

• G •

gamification, VLE, 305
gel factor, 101
Gnote software, 195
goals and outcomes
  clear articulation, 55–56
  defining, for workshops, 53–60
  defining questions, 54
  focus groups, 234–235
  meetings, 23–29
  for meetings, 15–16
  one-sentence objectives, 26–29
  remote meetings, 290
  return on investment (ROI), 57–60
  time spent on, 57
  workshops, 48, 53–60
Google Docs software, 195
Google+ Hangouts, 300
GoToMeeting, 99–100
greeting the group, 112–113
ground rules, 119–120, 222, 289–290
group analysis tools
  3Ws, 267–269
  decision trees, 267, 278–280
  fishbone analysis, 267, 275–278
  force field analysis, 267, 273–275
  Ishikawa analysis, 267, 275–278
  RACI analysis, 267, 272–273
  skill building, 267–280
  SWOT analysis, 267, 269–271
group norms, 97
groups. *See also* focus group; individuals
  brainstorming with, 264–266
  case studies, 215–217
  conflict, 182–184
  facilitating discussions, 145–151
  facilitating group discussions, 145–151
  input, effort and energy matrix, 164
  meeting and greeting, 112–113
  setting up work, mistake handling, 309–310
  support and challenge, mistake handling, 314
  understanding, 96–102
grumblers, 173–174
guests, managing, 155–157

• H •

healthy conflict, 181–182
hidden agendas, 179–180
Honey, Peter (researcher), 130
Honey & Mumford's Learning Styles, 130–133
housekeeping, kick off, 116
humour, 321–322
hybrid meetings, 296–297
hypothetical questions, 82

• I •

ice-breakers, 72
icons, book, 3
imagine yourself doing well, 108, 112
implementation stage, role play, 221, 225–226
implementing findings, focus groups, 251–252
individuals. *See also* groups; participants
  brainstorming for, 266
  conflict, 184–187
  difficult behaviour, 170–178, 312, 321
informal contact, virtual, 298
input, effort and energy matrix, 164
input to topic, for discussion, 146–147
instruction stage, role play, 221, 222–223
instructions, clear, 143–145
interests, workshops, 48
internal focus groups, 238–239
interrupters, 174
interruptions, 169–170
introducing discussion topics, 146
introduction, report, 205, 250
Ishikawa group analysis, 267, 275–278

• J •

joining, 75–76, 227–288
jokers, 176

• K •

key players, workshops, 51–53
kicking off the session, 113–120
kit preparation
  focus groups, 244–245
  remote meetings, 289

• L •

large groups, brainstorming with, 264–265
late arrivals, 113
laughter, 321–322
leading meetings/workshops. *See specific topics*
leading questions, 78
learning journey, VLE, 305
Learning Management System (LMS), 304
learning room, VLE, 305
length of meetings, 12
LessMeeting software, 195
lessons learned, 203
'let's' for remote meetings, 292–293
linkages
  meetings/workshops, 139–140
  mistake handling, 311–312
listening, 84–89
LMS (Learning Management System), 304
location, 40, 63
logistics, 40, 63

• M •

majority, decision-making, 122
managing process, meetings/ workshops, 136–145, 151–158, 163
Mass Open Online Course (MOOC), 305
materials, 40–41, 71, 75, 110
meeting the group, 112–113
meetings
  agenda, 11, 29–42, 287, 297
  business case, 10–16, 18–20
  compared to workshops, 18–20
  continuing session, 135–160
  dislike for, 10–16
  evaluating, 159, 197–198
  facilitating group discussions, 145–151
  follow-up, 189–206
  goals and objectives, 23–29
  managing process, 136–145, 151–158, 163
  need for, checklist, 22–23
  personal energy, 43–45
  planning, 21–45
  preparing for the first day, 77–104
  reflection, 190–191
  remote, 286–301
  reviewing, 158–160, 200
  starting the session, 107–133
  technology, 195–196
Meetin.gs software, 195–196
Microsoft OneNote software, 196
mistakes
  big picture, 313–314
  change what you are doing, 313
  common, 309–315
  details, emphasis on, 313–314
  difficult people, 171–177, 312
  dogmatism, 314–315
  expert, recognising, 312–313
  group support and challenge, 314
  ignoring emotion, 311
  linkages and connections, 311–312
  setting up group work, 309–310
  talking too much, 310–311
m-learning, 302
mobile devices, 290, 302
MOOC (Mass Open Online Course), 305
Mumford, Alan (researcher), 130
mute button, 290, 297

• N •

name yourself, remote meeting, 289
need for meeting, checklist, 22–23
needs, workshops, 48
negative comments, 150–151
neutral questions, 82–83

• O •

objectives. *See* goals and outcomes
observers, focus groups, 245
observing others
  body language, 89–91, 92
  energy, 93–94
  facial expression, 91–93
  first session, 89–96
  voice, 94–96
off-topic meetings, 11, 322
OmniJoin, 300
one-sentence objectives, 26–29, 33
online tools, 159–160
on-track meetings, 11, 166
open questions, 79, 80–81
open your session, atmosphere, 114–115
order
  agenda planning, 34–36, 38–42
  as barrier to success, 162
  sequencing in workshop design, 62
  writing detailed workshop, 73–74
outcomes. *See* goals and outcomes

• P •

parallel process, 283–284
paraphrasing, meetings/workshops, 141
parking lots, 153
participants. *See also* groups; individuals
  agenda assessment, 34
  asking to leave your session, 176–177
  focus groups, 238–239
  invitations, 75–76, 227–288, 287
  remote meetings, 287
  workshop design, 61, 75–76
  workshops, 48
pause button, 120
pausing, focus groups, 246
people. *See* participants
personal agendas, 178
personal frame of mind, 64
personal performance, video, 229–230
personal style questionnaire, 64–68
personality
  as barrier to success, 162
  conflict, 180–187
  difficult behaviour, 170–178, 312, 321
  in the room, 125–133
phones, 169, 302
planning
  agenda, 32–42
  meetings, 21–45
  project plan, 50
  the start, 62–63
  workshops, 47–76
poorly structured meetings, 11
positive comments, 150
PowerPoint slides, 12–13, 291
practising your presentation, 102–104
Pragmatist learning style, 130, 131, 132
preparing
  case studies, 214–215
  common mistakes, 309–315
  for the first day, 77–104
  focus groups, 234, 236–245
  handling pressure, handling, 317–318
  lack of, meeting dislike, 12
  remote meeting ground rules, 290
  role play, 221, 223–225
presentation practise, 102–104
pressure
  calm under pressure, 17, 322–323
  fairness, 320

going off-track, 322
handling, 317–323
humour and laughter, 321–322
offensive or unacceptable participation, 321
preparation, 317–318
rapport building, 318–319
trust building, 319–320, 321, 322
working from a plan, 318
probing questions, 81
procedures, report, 250
process management, meetings/workshops, 136–145, 151–158, 163
productivity of meetings, 13–14, 286
project closure, 201
project plan for workshops, 50
purpose
case studies, 212
focus group statements, 236–237, 247
of workshop, 212
workshops, 48
pushovers, 168

• Q •

qualitative analysis, 249
questions. *See* asking questions

• R •

rabbit holes, 152
RACI group analysis, 267, 272–273
random selection, focus group, 238
rapport building, 318–319
recommendations, hidden agenda, 180
recording, 244, 295
reflection as follow-up, 190–191
reflective questions, 81–82
Reflector learning style, 130, 131
rehearsing your session, 103
relationships, cost of poor meetings, 15
relevance, remote meetings, 291
remote meetings
active participation, 294, 297
agenda, limiting, 287
asking questions, 294, 297
controlling disruption, 291
goals, stating, 290
ground rules, 289–290
hybrid meetings, 296–297
informal contact, 298
kit preparation, 289
'let's,' 292–293
participant invitations, 287, 288
PowerPoint slides, 291
productive, 286
prompt start time, 289
recording, 295
relevance, 291
respect for time, 292, 297
reviewing, 295
saving all information, 295
sharing materials, 288
signposting, 292
smiling, 293
structure, 286
technology for, 298–301
time zone handling, 288
timing, 287–288
voice modulation, 293
when to use, 286
wingman, 290–291, 297
remote workshops
platforms for, 298–303
technology for, 298–301
understanding virtual learning, 301–306
reporting back, focus groups, 234, 250–252
reports. *See* writing
reputation, cost of poor meetings, 15
research, workshop design, 61–64
respect for time, remote meetings, 292, 297
responsiveness, Social Styles, 127, 128–130
results, report, 205, 250
return on investment (ROI), 57–60, 196–199

reviewing
- agenda, 38–42
- expectations, 158
- follow-up, 200–204
- meetings, 158–160
- project, 200–204
- remote meetings, 295
- video footage, 230–231
- workshops, 160

rewind button, 120
ROI (return on investment), 57–60, 196–199
role play
- considerations, 217–221
- debrief stage, 221, 226–227
- feedback, 228–229
- ground rules, 222
- implementation stage, 221, 225–226
- instruction stage, 221, 222–223
- preparation stage, 221, 223–225
- variations, 227–228
- workshop, 217–229

roles
- allocating, 118–119
- participants, and agenda, 41
- of presenter, kickoff, 115

room, workshop design, 63–64
rough workshop design, 69–70
running the session. *See also* specific topics
- described, 135–160
- focus groups, 234, 245–246
- order as barrier to success, 162
- troubleshooting, 162, 166–167

• S •

saving all information, remote meetings, 295
saving minutes, 194–195
scaling questions, 83
scribe for focus group, 244
script writing, focus groups, 241–243
seating, tactical, 177–178
self-awareness, building, 101–102
sequencing in workshop design, 62 *See also* order
sessions
- follow-up, 189–206
- running, 135–160
- starting, 107–133
- troubleshooting, 161–187

setting up group work, 309–310
sharing meetings/workshops, 48, 288
shutting up, 148
side conversationalists, 175–176
sideways conversation, 147
signposting, 138, 292
silent participants, 172
simulation (role play) in workshops, 217–229
skills and skill building
- Appreciative Inquiry, 280–283
- as barrier to success, 162
- brainstorming, 253–266
- developing, 78–96
- for experienced presenters, 253–284
- focus groups, 233–252
- group analysis tools, 267–280
- parallel process, 283–284
- participant knowledge and practise, 209–232
- remote/virtual meetings/ workshops, 285–306

Skype, 301
slide presentations, 12–13, 291
small groups, brainstorming with, 265–266
smartphones, 290, 302
smiling, remote meetings, 293
Social Styles, 126–130
software. *See* technology
specific, one-sentence objectives, 27
specific selection, focus group, 238–239
sponsors
- agenda, 31–32
- focus group, 235
- workshops, 53, 74

Sqwiggle team app, 298
Srivastva, Suresh (researcher), 280
stakeholders
- agenda, 31–32
- workshops, 50–53

start time for remote meetings, 289
starting the session
as barrier to success, 162
decision-making, 120–125
focus on yourself, 108–113
group, 107–133
kick off, 113–120
personalities in the room, 125–133
troubleshooting, 162, 163–166
sticky issues, 154–155
sticky notes to start meeting, 165–166
strategic change, virtual learning as, 303–304
structure
agenda, 34–36, 38–42
meetings, 11, 286
workshops, 17
style, personal, 64–68
summarising meetings/ workshops, 139
supportive social style, 129
surfacing issues and concerns, 99–100
SWOT group analysis, 267, 269–271
synchronous systems, VLE, 305

• T •

tables for tactical seating, 177–178
talking too much, 310–311
technology
choosing, 298
focus groups, 246
as interruption, 169–170
kit preparation, 244–245, 289
meetings, 195–196
platforms, 298–303
remote meetings, 286–301
remote workshops, 298–306
video, 231–232
TED talks, 72
Telepresence, 301
Theorist learning style, 130, 131, 132
threaded discussion, VLE, 305
3Ws group analysis tool, 267–269
time and timing
agenda items, 33
arrival of presenter, 111
design of workshops, 17
focus group, 235
goals and outcomes, 57
managing, 151–152
remote meetings, 287–288
start time for remote meetings, 289
troubleshooting, 167
when to conduct workshops, 49
workshop design, 61–62
workshops, 48
time zone handling, remote meetings, 288
timeline, focus groups, 237
tough conversations, conflict, 186
transcribe notes, focus group, 247–248
troubleshooting, 161–187
barriers to success, 161–162
conflict, 180–187
difficult behaviour and persons, 170–178, 312, 321
hidden agendas, 179–180
interruptions, 169–170
personal agendas, 178
running the session, 162, 166–167
starting the session, 162, 163–166
typical difficulties, 167–168
trust building, 319–320, 321, 322

• U •

unexpected situations, 157–158
unhealthy conflict, 181–182
urgent/important matrix, 154–155

• V •

video
focus groups, 244
personal performance, 229–230
reviewing footage, 230–231
technology, 231–232
for workshops, 229–232
virtual classroom, VLE, 305
virtual learning
acronyms, 304–305
preparing to introduce, 306

virtual learning *(continued)*
- as strategic change, 303–304
- understanding, 301–306

Virtual Learning Environment (VLE), 302, 304–306
visualising the session, 104
VLE (Virtual Learning Environment), 302, 304–306
voice
- modulation in remote meetings, 293
- observing others, 94–96

• W •

wasted time, cost of poor meetings, 14–15
WebEx, 299
websites. *See also specific topics*
- case study sources, 213
- online tools, 159–160

weighted decision-making, 123–125
when to use remote meetings, 286
whiteboard, hybrid meetings, 297
windbags, 172–173
wingman, 118–119, 290–291, 297
word cloud, focus group data, 249
wordle.com (website), 249
workshops
- building participant knowledge and practise, 209–232
- business case, 16–20
- case studies, 210–217
- checklist questions for running, 19
- compared to meetings, 18–20
- continuing session, 135–160
- deciding when to conduct, 49
- defining outcomes, 53–60
- delivery, 16, 17
- designing, 60–76
- elements of, 48–50
- evaluation levels, 197–198
- facilitating group discussions, 145–151
- follow-up, 189–206
- key players, 51–53
- managing process, 136–145, 151–158, 163
- planning, 47–76
- preparation needed for, 20
- preparing for the first day, 77–104
- productivity of, 16–17
- project plan, 50
- reflection, 190–191
- remote, 298–306
- reviewing, 160
- role play, 217–229
- sponsors, 53
- stakeholders, 50–53
- starting the session, 107–133
- video, 229–232

workshops, designing
- activities, 68–69, 71
- background research, 61–64
- business case, 16, 17
- ice-breakers, 72
- materials, 71, 75
- on- or off-site location, 63
- participant invitations, 75–76
- people stuff, 61
- personal frame of mind, 64
- personal style questionnaire, 64–68
- planning the start, 62–63
- process, 60
- room, 63–64
- rough design, 69–70
- sequencing, 62
- sponsor approval, 74
- time, 61–62
- writing detailed order, 73–74
- writing one-page design, 70–72, 73

writing
- agenda, 29–30, 42
- focus groups, 234, 247–252
- key information, meetings/workshops, 141–142
- meeting minutes, 191–196
- one-page design, 70–72, 73
- report for follow-up, 199–200, 205–206
- role play, 219–220
- workshop detailed order, 73–74

Notes

Notes

About the Authors

Jessica Pryce-Jones: Jessica is joint CEO of the iOpener Institute for People and Performance, an international consultancy headquartered in Oxford, UK. iOpener helps organisations achieve their strategic and commercial goals by maximising the performance, productivity and happiness of business-critical employees.

Over the past 10 years, iOpener has delivered 15,000 workshops, and Jessica has designed most of them. She knows that great meetings and workshops deliver focus, energy and results; changing them for the better makes an enormous difference to morale and output.

A frequent media commentator and keynote speaker, Jessica leads sessions for multinationals and world-leading business schools. Using her background in psychology and financial services, she is working on her next book about leadership in collaboration with Julia.

Julia Lindsay: Julia is joint CEO of the iOpener Institute for People and Performance. Her professional training as an accountant leads her to believe that the best measure of business success is delivering both numbers and objectives. This can only happen when everyone is totally engaged with their mission, their team and their tasks.

From her 15 years' experience at senior and executive level in the financial services industry, Julia knows the absolute importance of good meetings. When they are efficient and effective, everyone is aligned around their joint projects, and great work gets done. She has also experienced first-hand the extraordinary impact workshops can have in catalysing new initiatives that bring transformational results.

Dedication

This book is dedicated to our mothers, Clarissa and Tessa.

Authors' Acknowledgements

Here's a big shout out to everyone who helped with this book. We really appreciate your support and suggestions, whether past or present, direct or indirect:

Anna Armanno, Mike Baker, Anita Brick, Sarah Brammeier, Jo Bishop, Stephan Chambers, Intan Chen, Peter Cooke, Henk-Peter Dijkema, Katie Demain, Natalie Gough, Chris Gosden, Pippa Heath, Si Hood, Jane Kaye, Vik Kumar, Simon Lutterbie, Diane Lytollis, Kate Macintyre, Joe O'Connor, Wim Oolbekink, Susan Pratley, JoEllyn Prouty-McLaren, Janet Quek, Ibeth Ramos, Ruth Reiner, Diane Scott, Melita Samoilys, Ulrike Tack, Bridget Temple and Lorraine Vaun-Davis.

And, of course, special thanks goes to Chris Lindsay and David Shukman, who are our biggest cheerleaders.

Publisher's Acknowledgements

We're proud of this book; please send us your comments at `http://dummies.custhelp.com`. For other comments, please contact our Customer Care Department within the U.S. at 877-762-2974, outside the U.S. at (001) 317-572-3993, or fax 317-572-4002.

Some of the people who helped bring this book to market include the following:

Acquisitions, Editorial and Vertical Websites

Project Editor: Kelly Ewing

Commissioning Editor: Mike Baker

Assistant Editor: Ben Kemble

Development Editor: Kelly Ewing

Copy Editor: Kelly Ewing

Technical Editor: Michèle Down

Publisher: Miles Kendall

Cover Photos: © jsmith/iStockphoto.com

Project Coordinator: Melissa Cossell

FOR DUMMIES®
A Wiley Brand

SELF-HELP

978-0-470-66541-1

978-1-119-99264-6

978-0-470-66086-7

LANGUAGES

978-0-470-68815-1

978-1-119-97959-3

978-0-470-69477-0

HISTORY

978-0-470-68792-5

978-0-470-74783-4

978-0-470-97819-1

Laptops For Dummies 5th Edition
978-1-118-11533-6

Management For Dummies, 2nd Edition
978-0-470-97769-9

Nutrition For Dummies, 2nd Edition
978-0-470-97276-2

Office 2013 For Dummies
978-1-118-49715-9

Organic Gardening For Dummies
978-1-119-97706-3

Origami Kit For Dummies
978-0-470-75857-1

Overcoming Depression For Dummies
978-0-470-69430-5

Physics I For Dummies
978-0-470-90324-7

Project Management For Dummies
978-0-470-71119-4

Psychology Statistics For Dummies
978-1-119-95287-9

Renting Out Your Property For Dummies, 3rd Edition
978-1-119-97640-0

Rugby Union For Dummies, 3rd Edition
978-1-119-99092-5

Stargazing For Dummies
978-1-118-41156-8

Teaching English as a Foreign Language For Dummies
978-0-470-74576-2

Time Management For Dummies
978-0-470-77765-7

Training Your Brain For Dummies
978-0-470-97449-0

Voice and Speaking Skills For Dummies
978-1-119-94512-3

Wedding Planning For Dummies
978-1-118-69951-5

WordPress For Dummies, 5th Edition
978-1-118-38318-6